THE BOOK
OF LISTENING

10, 11, 12, 13 →

OTHER WORKS BY JEAN KLEIN

Be Who You Are

Who Am I?

Beyond Knowledge

Living Truth

I Am

Open to the Unknown

Transmission of the Flame

The Ease Of Being

In Spanish

Quien Soy Yo?

Translations also available in French, Italian, German and Chinese

The Book of
LISTENING

Jean Klein

NON-DUALITY PRESS

UNITED KINGDOM

First published November 2008 by Non-Duality Press

© Emma Edwards 2008
© Non-Duality Press 2008

Typeset in Palatino 11/14

Non-Duality Press, PO Box 2228
Salisbury, SP2 2GZ
United Kingdom

ISBN 978-0-9553999-4-7

www.non-dualitybooks.com

Acknowledgements

With deep gratitude to Mary Dresser for her invaluable contributions to the preparation of the original journals as well as her assistance in editing this compilation, and to Nancy Moshe who designed and oversaw the printing of the original issues. Thanks also to Philip Goldsmith for encouraging the publication of the journals in book form and for his useful comments, and to all those who have been of assistance along the way.

Introduction

This book is a compilation of Volumes 1 – 10 of Jean Klein's journal *Listening*, published on a limited basis between 1989-1995. The articles whose sources are not otherwise identified, are based on private conversations with Jean Klein usually around a single topic. I made notes as we talked, occasionally recording the conversations, and sometimes, as in the prose poem *On Love*, the "echo" of a conversation was later distilled into a few lines.

Each original volume was loosely arranged around a theme and included an original private discussion or a transcription of a public talk with Jean Klein, various favourite articles, one question answered in depth (*Your Question*) and a brief description from different angles of Jean's unique approach to the role of the body in his teaching.

Most of Jean Klein's teaching was simply through his presence and through question and answer dialogues where he "answered the questioner, not the question". Jean emphasised the direct approach to liberation, an approach free from emphasis on the attainment of progressively subtle psycho-somatic states. However, in this book there are ten short chapters dealing with Jean Klein's approach to the body. These will be clear to readers of the original journals who may have attended seminars, but a word of explanation is perhaps needed for the majority of readers.

In conjunction with dialogues Jean offered a unique form of what he called body-work or yoga. This was not taught as a requirement for understanding or realisation, but as a useful tool for getting to know one's conditioning. Our thought processes affect the body and mind and vice versa. The body-work was introduced to help clarify this relationship and bring an awareness that our real nature is neither the body nor the mind. The aim of this "yoga" was to bring about sensations of relaxation, expansion, light, space and energy which, when noted and welcomed, can deepen understanding of our real nature. This understanding in turn brings about a letting-go in our psycho-somatic structures. Insight and relaxation or letting go can bring about apperception as a total body-mind experience. While the understanding of our real nature is not dependent on anything, for many people Jean's philosophy came to life and light when experienced in this approach to the body.

The blend of mind and body had interested Jean since his early medical and musical studies. He was also an accomplished violinist and as a young adult was a voice coach and choral director. He combined a knowledge of music with his knowledge of the effects of muscle and mental tension on performance. Later he developed this psycho-somatic relationship when he added a Kashmiri style subtle energy yoga to his studies of traditional yoga learned in India with Krishnamacharya.

Jean experienced life free from memory, with an openness and freshness as if every event were new. He greeted old friends as if for the first time and welcomed those he had just met as if they were old friends. He took nothing and no one for granted. He might stop abruptly, taken by the shape of clouds or the play of light or the eyes of a baby or animal. What struck those in his company was how free from preconceptions he was and how he experienced everything as if for the first time and with a sense of exploration like a young child. He had a boundless energy for living and seeing things in a new way and it made his companionship a real joy, no matter the activity. Spending time with him always had the quality of a new experience.

This was all the more impressive considering Jean Klein's complex and often difficult life and his considerable intellect and many talents. He was widely educated and widely travelled and spoke four languages (Czech and German in his youth and French and English in adult life). After his return from a long sojourn in India he was invited to hold meetings in many countries including England, France, Germany, Greece, Israel,

Holland, Spain, Switzerland, Tunisia, and the United States. He was not a simple sadhu by any means and yet his presence conveyed utter simplicity.

Jean Klein had a great appreciation and knowledge of the Arts—painting, sculpture and poetry in particular. He enjoyed all expressions of beauty, both man-made and natural. Most of all he loved humankind and his adult life was devoted to helping in any way that he was asked and able.

I hope this compilation captures a little of the multi-cultural interests and tastes of this truly remarkable Renaissance man.

E.E.

Table of Contents

Introduction by Emma Edwards .... *VII*

Volume 1

The Disciple and the Guru 3
Jean Klein

Gitanjali 11
Rabindranath Tagore

Your Question: *How can I become more effective in
my enquiry?* 12
Jean Klein

Excerpts from *Transmission of the Flame* 13
Jean Klein

The Body Work: *Yoga and Advaita* 21
Jean Klein

Sayings of Atmananda Krishna Menon 23

Volume 2

Living With the Question 29
Jean Klein

Plato's Journey through Unknowing 37

Sin-Sin Ming 39
Seng-Ts'an

Excerpt from the Prologue to *Transmission of the Flame* 45
Jean Klein

Sayings of Old Man Tcheng 47

Your Question: *Is writing fiction compatible with
spiritual enquiry?* 62
Jean Klein

The Body Work: *You are what you absorb* 64
Jean Klein

Volume 3

The Great Forgetting 67
Jean Klein

The Grief of the Dead 76
Rumi

On Silence 77
Jean Klein

Sermon, *"Blessed are the Poor"* 78
Meister Eckhart

Excerpt from *Four Quartets* 85
T.S. Eliot

Dialogue in New York: April 27, 1990 86
Jean Klein

Your Question: *Follow the glimpse* 104
Jean Klein

To Know the Body: *The original body* 106
Jean Klein

Volume 4

The Glimpse 111
Jean Klein

"Whoso Knoweth Himself " 118
Ibn 'Arabi

Dialogue at the Day of Listening, May 1991 130
Jean Klein

Your Question: *How can I resolve my feelings of conflict about
the Persian Gulf War (1990-91)?* 142
Jean Klein

Excerpts from the *Tao Te Ching* 144

Body Approach: *Using the postures to dissolve ego* 147
Jean Klein

Volume 5

Gurvastakam 151
Sri Adi Sankaracarya
translated by Peter Harrison

Excellence of the Gift of Love 160
St. Paul

Devotion 161
Jean Klein

Sadhana: *On Desire* 171
Jean Klein

Adoration of Ra 172
from *The Egyptian Book of the Dead*

Dialogue in Santa Barbara: February 16, 1992 177
Jean Klein

Your Question: *How can my life have meaning
and fulfilment?* 182
Jean Klein

Body Approach: *A guided relaxation* 183
Jean Klein

Volume 6

Bringing the Perceived back to the Perceiving 189
Jean Klein

Tripura Rahasya 198
The Mystery Beyond the Trinity

Songs of Kabir: Number 20 207

On Welcoming 208
Jean Klein

Approach on the Body Level: *Sensing the brain* 210
Jean Klein

Your Question: *Is studying the mind beneficial?* 218
Jean Klein

Volume 7

On Love 223
Jean Klein

Love and Marriage 225
Jean Klein

Poem from *The Love Songs of Chandidas* 238

Sahaja 239
Ananda K. Coomaraswamy

Poem from *The Love Songs of Chandidas* 249

Living in Oneness 250
Jean Klein

Sadhana: *Love* 263
Jean Klein

Poem from *The Love Songs of Chandidas* 263

Your Question: *I find myself in moods that are beyond
my control* 264
Jean Klein

Approach on the Body Level: *The energetic body* 266
Jean Klein

Volume 8

Beyond Politics 271
Jean Klein

Sadhana: *Reference to the I-image* 285
Jean Klein

The King's Dohas
Translated by Herbert V. Guenther 286

Your Question 295
Jean Klein

Awareness Through Body Sensing: *Breath and meditation* 297
Jean Klein

Volume 9

The Day of Listening: July 2, 1994 303
Jean Klein

Sonnet 318
William Shakespeare

Your Question: *I find that I have come to an impasse* 319
Jean Klein

The Approach on the Body Level: *Listening to the body* 321
Jean Klein

Volume 10

Art and Artistic 327
Jean Klein

Sadhana: *From your silence comes creativity* 346
Jean Klein

The man that hath no music 347
William Shakespeare

Bhartrhari 348
Harold G. Coward

Wonder: Poems by William Wordsworth 350

The Theory of Beauty 351
Ananda K. Coomaraswamy

from Timaeus 366
Plato

Music and the Body 367
Jean Klein

Your Question: *Seeing from behind* 371
Jean Klein

Bibliography 373

LISTENING

Volume 1
1989

The Disciple and the Guru 3
Jean Klein

Gitanjali.. 11
Rabindranath Tagore

Your Question: *How can I become more
effective in my enquiry?*.................................... 12
Jean Klein

Excerpts from *Transmission of the Flame*.................. 13
Jean Klein

The Body Work: *Yoga and Advaita* 21
Jean Klein

Sayings of Atmananda Krishna Menon................. 23
Compiled by Wolter Keers

The Disciple and the Guru

Jean Klein: Ultimately speaking there is not a guru and not a disciple, no teacher or teaching, because what you are is not teachable. Have you anything to say?

Q. So in what sense can we understand the word "disciple"?

JK. To be a disciple means to prepare oneself to face the truth. It is a profound need to be one with truth. The preparation is the result of seeing that one's life is dispersed, that it is still meaningless, that one is lost in trying to escape from a meaningless life. When the question, "What is the meaning of life?" appears in all urgency, when one is ready to give all to this question, then one is a disciple, a disciple of truth, of life.

Q. So there is a clear moment when one is not a disciple and when one is?

JK. Absolutely. When you are a disciple of life all doings refer to the question, to truth. Life may not change outwardly, but there is a feeling of inner orientation, a conviction of the quest.

Q. How can actions refer to the truth when one is not yet established in truth?

JK. The threshold of truth is the absence of calculation, the not-knowing state. All that appears in you refers to this thoughtless ground, your silence. Every object appears and dies in this stillness.

Q. What are the signs for oneself that one is oriented, on the right scent?

JK. You have the inner conviction, from an insight, of the truth. You are free from day-dreaming, free from intention. You are free from compensations. You feel many moments without lack. You are more free from yourself!

Q. Is it necessary, when one is oriented, to have a teacher?

JK. You may need it because you are not yet established. The real disciple who refers all appearings to his openness, to his not-knowing, does not look for anything objective. He knows that truth cannot be found in an object. He lives only in openness, this waiting without waiting for anything. In this not-knowing, the desire may come up to meet one who is established in the openness. But a disciple will never go to see someone from curiosity or to look for a teacher, because he already knows that anything he finds is not the guru.

Q. So one lives in openness and in this openness the guru finds one?

JK. Yes, that is certain. It is only alert waiting without waiting for anything that brings you to the openness. The guru is the openness. So whoever goes looking for a guru can never find him because he is not objective and cannot be sought. As long as you look you are not open and unless you are completely open he cannot find you.

Q. So the guru is awake in the disciple before the disciple is found by the guru-as-human-being?

JK. Yes, only then can the guru in you find itself. The ego can only see an object, never the guru. It is only when you have the fore-feeling of truth, when you are a disciple of truth, that the guru can meet you.

Q. What then would you say is the role of this "human guru"?

JK. To help the passage of the self, which is looking for itself, to find itself. Only one who is established in openness can help with this passage because otherwise the personality blocks the passage. The guru is free from identification with what he is not. This presence in freedom stimulates the presence in the disciple.

Q. And this is the transmission?

JK. Yes, but you see there is nothing to transmit. Only to awaken what is already there.

Q. Because there is so much confusion over the transmission of this and that, energy, powers, states and so on.

JK. But all these belong to the phenomenal world. They have nothing to do with your real nature which is not phenomenal. They are experiences which, in the minds of the ignorant, are confused with the experience without an experiencer, the non-experience.

Q. Does one always know immediately when one has been found by the right teacher?

JK. The presence of the guru is instantaneous but if you are not ripe it may take time to penetrate.

Q. And by "ripe" you mean completely open, in innocence of all ideas, preconception, book-knowledge? Is it the same as when you are open to being surprised?

JK. Yes. When you find yourself in a state without reference you are open to the absence of yourself, the unexpected.

Q. So a real disciple already has a fore-feeling of the answer, he feels his autonomy and this autonomy is in a way confirmed by the presence of the teacher?

JK. Yes. When you feel more and more free from being something, free from need; when you feel at home in your total absence; when you are free from the teacher, you have found the right teacher.

Q. So if I have more than one teacher or I look for another teacher after my "guru" dies, I have not yet met the guru?

JK. No. There is only one guru. When you meet the guru it is forever. It is beyond your life, beyond your phenomenal appearance.

Until one has caught the scent all looking is in ignorance. People who go guru-shopping, looking for bargains, fall into the hands of merchants, so-called teachers who want students at any price, who need students for psychological survival. Guru-shopping is a lack of maturity, a lack of inquiry. The emphasis is on the person. Such people are not disciples. They are fundamentally lazy. A real disciple is never lazy.

In a mature student the quest is one-pointed, not dispersed. He or she gives all their love to the quest. A disciple already feels that the answer is only to be found in silent living with the question. There is no eccentric energy to go looking "outside."

Q. And by "silent living" you mean ...?

JK. Not to touch the quest, not to manipulate it with book-knowledge, comparison, interpretation, reference to the already known. As you said, to live in complete innocence with the quest.

Q. Can you talk a little more about those who are not yet oriented, who have not the fore-feeling of their real nature? What can they gain from being in the presence of one who is established in openness?

JK. When you look at the teacher as a person, as something objective, then you can never find yourself in this looking. You will find only the person over and over again and this will leave you dissatisfied, it keeps you in conflict. But a guru gives no hold to this projection and there may come a day when you feel the non-objective in yourself.

Everything must be submitted to what is non-objective. Surrender all that you are not. But before you can surrender this that you are not, you must know what it is that you are not. This calls for unbounded exploration. In knowing what you are not there is presence. Give all your love to this presence and you will discover it is not an object. Surrender is not a thought. You can only surrender to surrender itself.

Q. Are there any obstacles in that realm before one has a fore-feeling of truth?

JK. There may be the tendency to stay in old patterns, in ignorance hidden by a new vocabulary. Then there may come a lack of exploring where a lazy mind has taken over. This I call being in the garage.

Q. What about those who learn to articulate the words of the teaching and who may have had certain experiences? Often they think themselves ready to teach. Is this the case or are they in the garage?

JK. They are in the garage and look for compensation in teaching. The blind leading the blind. Real knowing comes from not knowing.

Q. Sometimes one feels a certain understanding and one has no more vital questions ...

JK. But one must have a question. When you don't have any more questions it is because you are lazy, tamasic, or the ego is in the way, wanting to be something or appear as something. When you are earnest in the quest you live in alertness and humility.

Q. What keeps the exploration aflame?

JK. Only listening, attention free from qualification and anticipation will keep you from falling into the old trap of projecting desires for this and that. Otherwise one lives in self-deception.

Q. Is it not normal to want to be in the company of the guru if he mirrors one's self? The lover with the beloved?

JK. When you have the right feeling of what you are, you are always with the guru. When you really feel what you are, there is not separation. It does not belong to space and time. You are still identified with an object. In your profound absence of ego, there is no need to be with or without. You are free from all objects.

Q. So if one feels the need for something when the guru "is away" or one feels lack ...

JK. Then you are not a disciple. You are still attached to the body-mind, to an object. As long as you take yourself to be a disciple you are not a disciple. When you take yourself for a disciple you will take the guru as a teacher and emphasize his person.

You must never look for a teacher as something perceived. To be the knowing is a fundamental, original feeling in yourself. So when you think of the guru, the thought is only a pointer to this original feeling which you have in common, where there are not two. There must be no fixation on the teacher. In other words, let his total absence remind you of what you are fundamentally. As I said, surrender all to the non-objective, the silence.

Q. What would you say to one who has a feeling for what you are talking about but has not yet consciously experienced it?

JK. He or she is potentially a disciple, and I would say the only thing to do is to live with all your attention, all your heart, give all your love to the sayings of the guru. It is only in living in deep intimacy with the sayings that there is an answer. Don't look for anything else. Everything else is rubbish. See how you jump constantly from one thing to another. When there is understanding, there is no more jumping. Then when there is an insight, when there is a moment of living understanding, transpose it into your daily life.

Q. And is this transposition a voluntary act?

JK. When you have understood something deeply the transposition is spontaneous to all areas of your life. It is only this transposition that assures you you have really understood. Otherwise the understanding remains abstract.

It is not a transposition of the words, nor looking for the equivalent in one's experience. The words are not the meaning. It is not a transposition in thinking but in action, in daily happenings.

Q. Surely a moment of fundamental insight or understanding strikes every corner of one's existence so that transposition is simply recognizing that the insight is on every level.

JK. Yes, that is precisely what it means. It is seeing all physical and psychological levels, all occurrences, from the ultimate view.

But first live with the sayings!

Q. As everything a guru says can be meditated upon, can you give us a few sayings which you regard as essential to live with?

JK. Certainly. I would say:

What you are looking for is already there, before all physical appearance. It is. So all looking can only lead to an object.

Don't try to find a cause for happiness or moments of fulfillment. There is no cause. As long as you look for, and give, a cause, you turn your back on the fullness, the message of the moment.

Come to understand clearly that there is no seen without seeing, no heard without hearing. Bring the seen back to the seeing, the heard back to the hearing.

You are the openness and it is only in waiting without waiting that you become open to the openness. In the end openness is what it is open to, waiting is what it is waiting for. This is all.

Live with these sayings. Let them become living understanding. This means, be aware how they act in you, how their perfume invades your body and your mind. Become one with this perfume. You can never remember this essence which is behind the words, you can only remember the sayings. But when you have once been attuned to the essence of the words they are no longer simply sayings but pregnant with their source. Then when you allow the words to be the Word, they have the power to transform. Live in identity with the silence in the sayings.

Gitanjali
Rabindranath Tagore

I had gone a-begging from door to door in the village path, when thy golden chariot appeared in the distance like a gorgeous dream and I wondered who was this king of all kings!

My hopes rose high and methought my evil days were at an end, and I stood waiting for alms to be given unasked and for wealth scattered on all sides in the dust.

The chariot stopped where I stood. Thy glance fell on me and thou camest down with a smile. I felt that the luck of my life had come at last. Then of a sudden thou didst hold thy right hand and say "What hast thou to give to me?"

Ah, what a kingly jest it was to open thy palm to a beggar to beg! I was confused and stood undecided, and then from my wallet I slowly took out the least little grain of corn and gave it to thee.

But how great was my surprise when at the day's end I emptied the bag on the floor to find the least little grain of gold among the poor heap. I bitterly wept and wished that I had had the heart to give thee my all.

Your Question

Q. I feel concerned with knowing my real nature but this concern does not seem to be deep or earnest enough to actually bring any real insights. How can I become more serious, more effective, in my inquiry?

Jean Klein: Being more concerned will not make you more concerned. To deepen your inquiry you must explore, adventure into uncharted territories. When you read books and live in compensation, escaping from your deepest desires and needs, you will become bored because you refer everything to the past, to what you already know.

Earnestness comes when you look closely at your body-mind. Inquire and question your motives for your actions. Ask yourself, "What am I really looking for in this act?" I don't mean go into an analysis of it, looking for compensatory motives. But discover the *ultimate motive* for what you do. You will see that the ultimate desire is to be desireless, the ultimate goal of all achieving is to be free from the need for striving, the ultimate motive for all becoming is to be free from all that you are not. So face the moment itself.

Explore how you waste energy in nervous and muscle compensations. See how you spend time in talking rubbish. Take note that perhaps the effort spent in working means more to you than the cheque at the end! Look how you function.

When you see your mechanism there will be discrimination in your life. You'll be less dispersed, an intelligence will come in. You will enjoy the quiet moment and look less for compensations.

It is only laziness which hinders a serious inquiry. Do not escape the ultimate moment. Face it and you will become concerned and earnest.

Excerpts from the book
Transmission of the Flame
by Jean Klein

Jean Klein: You cannot find your real nature. You cannot look for truth or enlightenment. All that you can find is objective. Our real nature is not an object and so it can never be perceived. When you realize that all you are looking for is an object, and that your real nature is not anything to be found or attained, you go away from looking. And you discover that the looker is what he is looking for. In this approach there is no system. There is nothing special established to do. It is an approach completely free from all volition, completely free from all intention.

You already know moments in daily life when you are completely free from all intention. You have taken these moments to be an absence, an absence of function. But these moments without function are not an absent state. Here there is reality, presence, with which you must become attuned, identical.

Q. So there is nothing to improve, one must simply be very peaceful and very quiet?

JK. This quietness you will find first in your body. Then you can transpose this quiet freedom from tension onto the level of the mind. But first you must become, as you said, quiet. To become quiet you must take your body as an object of your observation. First you will discover that you don't observe, that you come constantly to interpretation, to conclusion, to evaluation, comparison. I mean here a completely innocent observation, without any expectation, only taking note of any heaviness or tension of your body. And then you transpose this same quietness on the level of the mind.

Q. It sounds so easy and I find that when I'm by myself and I'm not doing anything, not organizing or cooking or rushing somewhere, there is a possibility of being quiet. But just the fact of having to do something puts me in a different state. I can't seem to keep that quietness and do things. And I'm sure a lot of people feel the same.

JK. But the quietness of the body, the quietness of the mind, is not this quietness of which we are speaking. This quietness, which is your real nature, is beyond mind. When you become more and more accustomed to listening to your body and listening to the movements in your mind, you will one day discover yourself in this listening, in this looking. You can never objectify this looking, this listening. It is totally in the absence of yourself.

Q. That's what you call attention?

JK. Yes. It is attention without tension. And attention without tension is when the attention is free from all striving and all anticipation, free from all end-gaining.

Q. Is there a feeling of sinking in, a kind of collapsing into the body like a very relaxed state?

JK. No, there is no identification with the body. You are not involved in the body. You feel the heaviness, feel the weight, the tension. But in this pure uninvolved looking, there's no longer an accomplice to the tension, to the heaviness. You will see then that there's a moment when the body becomes completely quiet, and you come to the different levels of your body, of energy. Because what you call body, physical body, is not your body. Your body has a much bigger extension than your idea of your physical body. You become aware of this extension of your energy when you are completely relaxed, expanded in space, when you are quiet.

Q. But I don't seem to have control of my quiet body. As I said before, when I'm in a busy situation, I can't control what's going on in me.

JK There's nothing to control. You must only listen. And then, when you really listen, the listening refers to itself. In this listening, there's not a listener, and nothing to listen to. There's only quietness. There's not systematic meditation, there's not systematic being quiet, because the moment you look for systematic meditation or quietness, then you create a state. Your real nature is not a state. Your home ground is not a state. It is a total presence when there is total absence, total absence of yourself as being somebody. It is only in this total absence of ourselves that we are the self.

Q. Do I understand you to say that you don't go through any process in order to detach yourself from identification with the person?

JK: The moment you look at your fear, anxiety, and all your striving force, your desire to change, you will find space between yourself and what you are looking at. You will find yourself outside the process. Then you are spontaneously detached, not identified. And when you are not identified with the body, you are also detached from the environment. Because your environment is only the five senses. So first become aware of your nearest surroundings, your body, senses and mind. When your observation is really free from all expectation, free from memory, then this observation refers to itself. Awareness refers to itself. What you are looking for can never be found in any object. It is objectless, like love, freedom, peace. You can never put these in the frame of a concept, in the frame of the mind.

Q: Does this awareness that you talk about, does this require effort on the person's part, or is it effortless?

JK: It is effortless because you are it fundamentally. To be still, you don't need to make any effort. It is only the giving up of effort. When you clearly see that you make an effort, then there is no longer an accomplice with the effort and it goes away. There is nobody who gives up. It is simply giving up.

Q: I find that when there is a giving up and I am without intention then I am also without interest in self-inquiry. It no longer interests me.

JK: What you observe must be interesting for you. It is the only way to sustain the observation. It is only in the giving up of all old patterns, memory, that your life can appear new and interesting to you. But you must come to the moment when what you observe dissolves in your observation, in your attention. In this moment there's no longer an observer and something observed, there's only stillness. What you observe is in space and time. But the observer is timeless. I don't speak of the relative observer; I speak of the ultimate observer: consciousness, awareness.

(long pause)

Q: In living the understanding but before being established in it, there is a going away from it into the object, becoming identified with it: you used a term, I can't remember your exact words, but you said there is a way in which you can find yourself back to it. I know you were not giving a technique. Perhaps you were again talking about organic memory finding you and bringing you back. Is there a subtlety here you can bring out?

JK. Every object is projected from you and has its homeground in you. Potentially, then, the object seen can bring you to pure seeing, an object heard can bring you to pure hearing. In this hearing and seeing there is nobody who sees or hears and no object seen or heard. There is only hearing, there is only seeing.

It is not in subject-object relationship. It is completely non-dual. This is the shortest way taught in the direct approach.

When you come to the understanding that you are not the psychosomatic body, in this moment you have a glimpse of what you are. But you can never have a glimpse of what you are when it is simply a question from the mind. The question "Who am I?" does not come from the mind. Asking "Who am I?" is accompanied by a tremendous energy, you are on fire. I think you can compare it to the condensed energy present when you are very angry or completely joyful. I would say this kind of energy must be there to ask the questions, "Who am I?", "What am I?", "What is life?". Then you have a glimpse of what you are. It is important that you have the glimpse for this is the understanding of the right perspective. Then you live with the right perspective. There is less and less dispersion. Your life becomes more and more oriented. You use all your energy in a completely different way. As your life becomes more oriented you see things differently. Before, you saw things only from the point of view of the I, the me. When you see things from the point of view of the I or the me, you live mechanically in choice, in selection. You may say, "I see it," but you don't really see it, because your seeing is coloured by selection, selection for security, for pleasure, to avoid and so on.

But when you have a glimpse of reality, it is already in a certain way in your background. You see things less and less personally. There comes the quality of global vision, where there is no choice, no selection. You see things more and more as they are, not as you wish them to be, but as they really are. You live in this perspective, you love it, it is a jewel you wear, maybe several times a day. Then there comes a moment in your life that even this geometrical representation, the perspective, dissolves in your real nature. And then there is no return. This switchover is absolutely sudden, instantaneous. You live now without anticipation, without end-gaining. You live absolutely in the now. Thinking is a practical, useful tool which you use when you need it, but you no longer think when there is no need to think. There is no more day-dreaming. You enjoy really freedom from thought. Oh! You will become a happy man! What more do you want?

Q. Is it possible to say, sir, what brings that about? That sudden change?

JK. You come to this point through inquiring. You undertake inquiring when there is discrimination, discernment. But the ego cannot discern: discerning comes from higher reason, from discernment itself, the insight that you are not the psychosomatic body. Inquiring about life calls for a serious character; it takes a profound seriousness. Be earnest! But I don't think it should be a problem for you to be earnest.

JK. (*addressing another questioner*) I see you here for the second time. I love you. Have you a question?

Q. I had a question yesterday.

JK. And today?

Q. It is the same question, the one I didn't ask yesterday. When I wake up sometimes the very thing I wake up with is fear.

JK. Be completely aware when you say there is fear. When you are alert the question naturally arises, "Who has fear? Who is afraid?" You have my guarantee that when you ask who has fear, the next day you will see, before the fear appears, that the I, the me, which you take yourself to be, is put in relation to certain circumstances in your daily life. The ego saw the circumstances and felt no security, so there is fear, there is anticipation. So first face the fear, face the sensation "fear." You will see that you, the knower of the fear, are not afraid, that only an object has fear. But don't push it away, face it completely, explore it in every corner. It is localized in your body somewhere. When you ask the question, "Who has fear?," you will see that the body wakes in the morning in freedom, but immediately you identify with the old representation of yourself. You put yourself in relation with some activity that you have projected. Remember that the personality who has fear is an object, and the situation which produced the fear is an object, too. So now there is a relation from object to object. The moment you see this you are out of the cage. Don't try to manipulate, touch or interfere because all this belongs to the cage and you remain in a vicious circle. You cannot reason your way out of the problem, only see that you are the knower of the problem and not the problem. When you are still, with your real self, there is no fear. Be careful also how you go to sleep. Don't take all your problems to sleep. There is a kind of hygiene in going to sleep and in waking up. Systematically lay your problems at the front door when you go to sleep.

Q. Sir, I assume that what you just described about investigating the fear is a good example of inquiry, and I am wondering if there are any other ways of inquiring you could tell us about or if we must come to inquire each in our own way?

JK. The first step is to face, become aware of, the mass of agitation, contraction, which you call fear. The name that you immediately give to the sensation you feel is not the actual fear. The word fear is memory, the word fear does not belong to the actual sensation, so free yourself from the concept fear and face only the perception. Then automatically you will know how to observe it, how to look at it with love and compassion. In this looking you don't give any food to the concept fear and an energy wakes up and integrates in your wholeness. So begin by asking, "Who has fear?", and then you will come more and more to know the mechanism. There are people who wake up every morning with fear, afraid of facing work, facing the boss, facing the news from the bank and so on. It is constant anticipation. But who has fear? It is absolutely indispensable, absolutely necessary to seriously ask this question. And live with the question.

Q. And that applies regardless of what the object is, even "Who has joy?", for example.

JK. Yes. Look again at the situation which apparently made you afraid, look again. But as long as we are an independent entity we are constantly vulnerable to fear.

Q. So the question brings a return to the silence.

JK. Absolutely.

(*long pause*)

JK. As long as there is any residue of a meditator and something meditated on, then you make meditation an activity of the mind. Every activity is a contraction. Meditation is not an activity of any kind.

Feel yourself vertical but don't try to make yourself vertical. When you feel that you are vertical you are in the timeless. All action is on the horizontal plane. Meditation is where time and timeless meet—in the heart.

Have the sensation of your whole body. Feel it in space. Go completely into the space that doesn't belong to time. Dissolve totally in this expansion.

Meditation is from moment to moment. The eyes see, the ears hear. The organs function. There is no interiorization, no concentration, no introversion, no withdrawing of the senses. Don't go into the old habits of withdrawal. Go in the directionless expansion, the spaceless space. This is not nirvikalpa samadhi (which is still in a very subtle subject-object relation). It is not savikalpa samadhi (direct perception). It is sahaja. Savikalpa is perceiving and nirvikalpa is conceiving. Sahaja is the natural non-state where function takes place in beingness.

The Body Work

Q. How does your teaching of yoga and pranayama fit in with the no-teaching of advaita?

Jean Klein: Yoga is an exploration of the body-mind. Pranayama is a purification. This exploration takes place in an awareness that is completely innocent of any reference, not looking for a result or a goal. So the exploration brings you back to objectless awareness.

Q. But sweeping the floor or looking at the flowers can do the same if all objects refer to awareness, so why the asanas in particular?

JK. The body-mind has been conditioned by the I-concept and in exploring specifically the body in choiceless awareness, it is given the opportunity to integrate into its original state. But this exploration can only be done on the energy level.

Q. And why is it important that the body comes to its original state?

JK. Because it is rare that one has a glimpse of reality with a conditioned, tamasic body.

Q. If reality is not the body, what difference does it make what condition the body is in?

JK. A tamasic body is not apt to conceive the subtleness that belongs to the insight. The insight does not belong to the body-mind but the body-mind feels the impact of the insight.

Q. You mean that the insight is, in a certain way, expressed or fulfilled in the body-mind?

JK. Absolutely. But when the body is conditioned this is difficult. Then the insight must be exceptionally strong to cross all the conditioning. A subtle, sattvic, sensitive body is much more open to the insight, to all the subtle solicitations of being, of grace.

Q. So you strongly advocate looking after the body?

JK. Yes, taking into account right movement, right eating, right thinking, right feeling and so on. This has nothing to do with yamas and niyamas (observance and abstinence). It comes as a result of looking at the body completely objectively, how it feels and functions in certain moments of the day. Right thinking and feeling comes when one transposes the understanding that there is no personal entity and, therefore, no intentional doing and thinking.

Q. What would you say to all those who are too old or too ill or simply too stiff to do yoga?

JK. To work earnestly on their understanding. When the insight is strong it overcomes all obstacles. Even a robber or murderer can come to the profound understanding of their real nature, despite all their conditioning, because nothing can refuse the instantaneous apperception of being! And as the body is only energy, there is no need, as we said before, to actually do any asanas with the physical body. One can work purely with the energy body.

Sayings of Atmananda
Krishna Menon

Q. Is there any difference between the spoken and written word of the Guru?

Krishna Menon: When the Guru talks to you about the Truth you certainly hear the words, but the words disappear at once. Nothing remains for you to refer to or to depend upon, except the Guru himself. So if you are in doubt you approach the Guru again any number of times; and each time he explains it in different words. Each time, you understand the same sense more and more deeply. Therefore, it is evident that it is not from words or their meaning that you understand the sense, because the words used each time are different. From this it is clear that something else follows the words which comes from the Guru. It is this something that penetrates into the innermost core of the disciple and works the miraculous transformation called experience. [1]

When you read the written word before listening to the Truth from the lips of the Guru, that something, which follows the spoken word of the Guru, is entirely absent; and you have to depend upon the dead word which is still before you and the meaning as your ego is inclined to interpret it in the dark light of its own phenomenal experiences. Naturally, therefore, you miss that divine experience when you only read the written word; though it is so easily and effortlessly obtained in the presence of the Guru, or after even once listening to the Truth from him.

When you listen to the spoken word of the Guru, even on the first occasion, your ego takes leave of you and you visualize [2] the Truth at once, being left alone in your real nature. But when you read the same words by yourself, your ego lingers on in the form of the word, its meaning, etc. and you fail to transcend them. To visualize the Truth, the only condition needed is the elimination of the ego. This is never possible by mere reading, before meeting the Guru. Therefore, listen, listen, listen and never be satisfied with anything else. After listening to the Truth direct from the Guru and after visualizing the Truth in his presence, you may well take to thinking deeply over what the Guru has told you. This is also another form of listening and takes you, without fail, to the same experience you have already had in his presence.

Q. How should I look at objects?

KM. An object is innocent in itself and serves you in accordance with the perspective through which you view it. If you view it as dead, inert and as distinct and separate from you, it takes you from the centre of your being to the world outside. But if you look upon it as something appearing in consciousness and if you emphasize that consciousness aspect of it, immediately it points to you—the source of that appearance—consciousness being your real nature.

Q. How can I love my relatives?

KM. You have been shown that you are that permanent changeless principle beyond your body, senses and mind. Consider your relative also as that principle. You cannot love a changing thing, you love only love or consciousness. So it is the permanent principle in you that loves the same permanent principle in the other. Love is the real nature of both. For this you have only to recognize deeply that love is your own real nature. No more effort is needed for its application. It follows automatically and does not stop till the whole world is absorbed into that love.

Recorded by Wolter Keers, 1954

NOTES

1. Experience here means the ultimate experience without an experiencer, what Jean Klein calls the non-experience.
2. Krishna Menon's use of the word visualization has nothing to do with the usual sense of the word. It is an instantaneous apperception.

LISTENING

Volume 2
1990

Living With the Question.............................29
Jean Klein

Plato's Journey through Unknowing......................37

Sin-Sin Ming...39
Seng-Ts'an

Excerpt from the Prologue to
Transmission of the Flame.............................45
Jean Klein

Sayings of Old Man Tcheng.............................47

Your Question: *Is writing fiction compatible
with spiritual enquiry?*................................62
Jean Klein

The Body Work: *You are what you absorb*.............64
Jean Klein

Living With the Question

Q. I would like to ask you what you mean exactly by "the question"?

Jean Klein: The question is the answer. Before the question was formulated, the answer was already there. The answer was there before you were conceived.

Q. So when you say, "Live with the question," you're talking only about the ultimate question, not just any question?

JK. Yes, the ultimate question to which all questions, in the end, refer. You come to the ultimate question when you have explored all the relative questions. By relative questions, I mean those questions which do not fully express what you are really looking for. Any question which has a residue of book-knowledge is relative. Any question which comes from memory, from past conditioning, is relative. Any question founded on emotional desire is relative. So question your questions and you will see their limits. This seeing brings you nearer to the nearest: the ultimate question.

Q. You said that when you first met your teacher, you asked him many questions, and he gave you gracious and suitable answers. But when he left and you did not see him for several weeks, there was a growing feeling that you had not asked the question, that you had not formulated the real question. You said that you felt, at that time, that if you could ask more profoundly, you would receive more profoundly. Was this the moment when you saw the limits of your mind, when you saw the difference between relative and absolute questions?

JK. Exactly. Every human being lives with questions, but these are often not formulated. People live in a blind fog of becoming, unaware of their motives for thinking and acting. They follow money-making and don't even know what to do with the money when they have it! So the first step is to become aware of one's motives, to formulate the questions, to ask, "Why am I doing this? What am I looking for? Where am I going?" In asking these relative questions, it will become clear that all your striving is for the survival of the I-concept. You discover there is a "person" involved. And the ultimate question begins when you question the entity who is asking the questions.

You become liberated from relative questions only when you one day ask yourself, "What is this person, this 'I' called 'myself'?"

Q. So one begins by questioning. Then one questions the questions and, finally, one is brought to question the questioner. But this questioner is still an object, so all of this belongs to the realm of relative questioning. How can one come to the ultimate question?

JK. You must profoundly explore the questioner. Ask what is his nature. Then you will see that it has no existence in itself. It is an image built up by education, hearsay, beliefs, experiences, in short, by society.

Q. So, as long as there is any residue at all of a belief in an "I", I cannot ask the ultimate question?

JK. When the person is eliminated, the self asks the self. The ultimate question is an inner state which comes from the answer itself. This inner state is beyond formulation. But you must go through formulation to become absolutely clear about this inner state.

Q. If it is a state beyond formulation, in which way can you still call it a question? It seems that you are now using the word question in a new way? Is it the same as contemplation?

JK. All questions proceed from an "I don't know"; otherwise, you would not ask a question. All questions come from the possibility of knowing; otherwise, you would not ask a question. In other words, a question has its seed in the knowing, in the answer. This is also true on the most profound level: all questions arise in the answer.

Q. So that inner state, without formulation, which arises when the "I" is seen for what it is, does this inner state still have the basic nature of a question? It proceeds from "I don't know" and has its seed in the answer?

JK. Yes, but the difference is that in relative questioning, there is still an "I" who projects something to be known. The "I don't know" is temporary. Whereas, in the absence of the "I," there is no projection of a known and there is a spontaneous dwelling in the not-knowing. In the absence of a questioner, the question becomes questioning, questioning without a questioner.

Q. If there is no personal entity to project or know anything, then the answer cannot be made an object of knowledge, and one is left with it as experience. Is this what you mean by "the question is the answer"?

JK. Yes, absolutely. The question is the openness present when there is no one present. The answer is nothing other than this openness. Openness is your real nature. It is all you are. The openness, the answer, refers to itself. There is nothing eventually knowable. There is a complete absence of visualization, representation, wishful thinking. There is no impulse to try to understand, to frame the answer with thought. It is ultimately negative in that it cannot be experienced as an object. Openness refers to our totality.

Q. Can we return to "living" with the question? By this do you mean, then, living in openness, in not-knowing, and how can we come to this living in openness?

JK. By living in non-concluding from moment to moment. See how your mind races backwards and forwards like a worried dog. See how you don't live in not-knowing, how afraid you are to live in not-concluding. Living in non-concluding, in openness, is, as you said, contemplation without a contemplator. This inner state is the answer and the question.

Q. It always seems that if I give up concluding my life will fall apart, or worse, come to a complete standstill!

JK. Living in non-concluding does not mean being passive. Let us be clear about this. Non-concluding means you don't conclude through personal interference. Things, situations, conclude by themselves when you leave them alone. Is there a choice for the girl on the tightrope? You can be sure she does not think of left or right, but is established unthinkingly in the centre. She is spontaneously in non-conclusion. When you are established in globality, it is normal to live in choiceless awareness like the ballerina in the circus.

So, you see that action and non-action both belong to the mind. In our fullness, our globality, which is only present in the absence of all counterparts, there is spontaneous, pure action.

Q. And, as there is no one choosing to act in this or that way, the action is spontaneously correct?

JK. Yes, the facts bring the conclusion which may not always be according to the ego's preference, but is always right, an appropriate solution. When you are beyond choosing, like the dancer on the rope, when the mind does not plot, the conclusion comes instantaneously when the facts are "ripe." Live open to all perceived, open to the openness.

Q. When you say live open to all perceived and do not interfere with comparison and judgement, it reminds me of the beautiful text the "Sin Sin Ming," which begins, "The great way knows no difficulties/Since it is beyond all choosing." What struck me about this translation over others I have read, is that it is the *way* which is emphasized, which is beyond choosing, not that one must not choose. Very often I think people interpret your teaching as being about a state without flavour, without difference, where every object is alike in some way to every other. In fact, it is not that there are no differences, but that we are beyond differences.

JK. You are the sun which creates all objects. In openness there is difference but not distinction, difference but not preference. Living without preference is not a correct vision. It is still putting emphasis on the object. The emphasis should be on the subject. It is not that all objects are the same, but that there is no longer an "object." When you live in openness, the emphasis falls in the right place. Each "object" has, then, its own significance, its real meaning. In non-conclusion the world is rich and intelligent.

One must come to the state where there is a complete shift in energy from living in the known, to living in the unknown. This is not the result of attitude, but the natural reorchestration of energy which comes as the result of understanding, specifically the understanding that only in your absence is there ultimate presence.

Q. So all one's sadhana, all one's spiritual aspiration, must be in the direction of this understanding which results in the shift of energy?

JK. Absolutely.

Q. Does this understanding, this sudden insight, first take place on the level of the brain?

JK. Yes, but not in the mind which functions in complementarity, duality. What you are fundamentally is beyond the brain, but the brain makes it perceptible. The moment of insight is taken by the brain and transferred to our totality. And then it expands; it is felt immediately on every other level of the psychosomatic structure. Only when it has become global, affecting every cell, can one say "it has become understanding."

One is aware of a physiological change immediately. The insight resonates on every level. But to come to its full actualization, to penetrate the core of every cell, takes time.

Q. Can the body be prepared for this impregnation so that it is receptive more quickly?

JK. Yes, because it is, in a certain way, waiting for its perfect state, its perfect health.

Q. You said that living with the question is exactly the same as living in openness, in not-knowing, and you also said that this capacity, the willingness to live in not-knowing, to welcome it, is the result of having had a glimpse of truth, of reality without someone to experience it. What meaning, then, can "live with the question" have for all those who do not have this understanding and the spontaneous shift it brings from living in the known to living in the unknown? It seems that you are speaking to a very few mature souls, but how can those less blessed hear you and benefit?

JK. I have given the real meaning of living with the question, but living in not-knowing on many levels will bring you to a question. Inherent in the human being is "I want to know." That has nothing to do with maturity. It is an innate urge.

I would say that one should begin by taking note how, the moment you wake up in the morning, you anticipate. The whole day is spent in anticipation, in striving, in end-gaining. See how you live in taking, in grasping, in constant knowing. So I would say, begin by spending half a day in seeing all the moments when you are not living in not-knowing. And then what happens? How can this help? When you see that you are always doing, you will find moments of discontinuity in you, because it is you, John Smith, who is forcing the continuity. In these spaces, these moments of discontinuity, you feel yourself in non-objective presence. It is not an experience because there is nobody there to experience it, but it is a moment when there is a "feeling" of eternity.

Q. So these moments open my eyes to knowing myself without relating to anything?

JK. Yes, for a moment you are taken by an open window, a window on eternity. Once you have had a glimpse of your objectless self, you will be solicited more often by it. Then one day you will find yourself living in the not-knowing.

Q. Is this a sudden switch-over?

JK. Yes, at a certain point you are pushed.

Q. Or pulled?

JK. Pulled, yes. And these moments of absence, of objectless presence, leave an echo. This echo is the shadow which brings you to its source.

Q. You would not, of course, regard this half morning of taking note of all the anticipation, as a practice ...!

JK. It is a practice without an entity practising, so how can it be called a practice? Many of you want something to do, and when I give you practical advice, you don't heed it!

Q. You have given dire warnings about the results of a progressive approach so we don't want to fall into the trap!

JK. When one hears the truth from the lips of the teacher, there can be no progression because it is a seed that is transmitted directly.

Q. Can one be on a progressive path and have found the guru?

JK. No, because the starting point is false. On the progressive path you are living in becoming, believing there is something to attain. But at the moment of transmission you find yourself in the now, free from the future, free from intention.

Plato's Journey
through Unknowing

He who has been led by his teacher in the matters of love to this point, correctly observing step by step the objects of beauty, when approaching his final goal will, of a sudden, catch sight of a nature of amazing beauty, and this, Socrates, is indeed the cause of all his former efforts. This nature is, in the first place, for all time, neither coming into being nor passing into dissolution, neither growing nor decaying; secondly, it is not beautiful in one part or at one time, but ugly in another part or at another time, nor beautiful towards one thing, but ugly towards another, nor beautiful here and ugly there, as if beautiful to some, but ugly to others; again, this beauty will not appear to him as partaking of the level of beauty of the human face or hands or any other part of the body, neither of any kind of reason nor any branch of science, nor existing in any other being, such as in a living creature, or in earth, or in heaven or in anything else, but only in the ever present unity of Beauty Itself, in Itself, with Itself, from which all other beautiful things are derived, but in such a manner that these others come into being and pass into dissolution, but it experiences no expansion nor contraction nor suffers any change.

Whenever a man, ascending on the return journey from these mortal things, by a right feeling of love for youths, begins to catch sight of that beauty, he is not far from his goal. This is the correct way of approaching or being led by another to the realm of love, beginning with beautiful things in this world and using them as steps, returning ever on and upwards for the sake of that absolute beauty, from one to two and from two to all beautiful embodiments, then from beautiful embodiment to beautiful practices, and from practices to the beauty of knowledge of many things, and from these branches of knowledge one comes finally to the absolute knowledge, which is none other than knowledge of that absolute beauty and rests finally in the realization of what the absolute beauty is.

Symposium 211
Translated by *S.H.*

Sin-Sin Ming
Seng-Ts'an

(Sin-Sin Ming is one of the first known treatises of Ch'an. Seng-Ts'an, the author, was the third patriarch of Ch'an after Boddhi-Dharma. He died at the beginning of the 7th century.)

The Great Way knows no difficulties
Since it is beyond all choosing.
Be free from hate and love;
Then it appears in perfect clarity.

If one strays from it by a hair's breadth
Heaven and earth are born.
If you wish to find it
Be neither for nor against anything.

The conflict between for and against
Is the sickness of the mind.
If you do not understand the deep meaning of the Way
You waste your time pacifying the mind.

As perfect as vast space,
Nothing is lacking to the Way; nothing is beyond it.
It is due to making choices
That we lose sight of its nature.

Neither pursue the world of causality,
Nor dwell in inner vacuity.
When the mind rests serene in the One
Dualism vanishes of itself.

When the unity is not lived
We lose sight of the Way:
Denying the world can lead to its total negation,
And maintaining the void is a contradiction in itself.

The more we speak, the more we intellectualize,
The further astray from the Way.
Away then with wordiness and intellection
And all ways freely open to us.

Returning to the root we regain the meaning,
Chasing after appearances, we lose the origin.
The moment our attention turns inward,
We go beyond the void of worldly things.

The play of manifestation appears real
All because of ignorance.
No need to search for truth,
Just put an end to points of view.

Do not linger in duality,
Attentively avoid remaining there.
If the least trace of right and wrong appear,
Confusion ensues, clarity of mind is lost.

Duality exists because of the one,
But be not attached to this one.
Once the mind is undisturbed
We give no hold to the ten thousand things.

If things do not attract or offend us, they are as if non-existent;
When the mind is undisturbed, where is the mind?
When the subject is desireless, where is the object?
Non-existent object, non-existent mind.

The object exists for a subject
And the subject exists for an object.
Know that this relativity has its root
In the oneness of the void.

In the oneness of the void, the two are one,
And each contains in itself the ten thousand things.
Making no distinction between this and that
How could a prejudiced or fragmentary view arise?

The Great Way is vast and serene.
In it nothing is easy, nothing is difficult.
Particular points of view are wavering and irresolute.
Conceived in haste, they only detain us.

Attachments know no bounds.
We are sure to go astray.
Let go and things follow their own nature,
Their essence remains unaffected.

Intervene not in the nature of things and you are in accord
with the Way,
Serene, at ease, free from all conflict.
But if our thoughts are restrained we turn away from the truth,
They grow dull and heavy, and are subject to error.

When they are in error, the mind is disturbed.
Then, what is the use of avoiding this and desiring that?
If you want to follow the path of the One Vehicle
Harbour no aversions to objects of the six senses.

With neither complicity nor aversion for objects of the six
senses
You dwell in Enlightenment.
The wise are not willful
While the ignorant forge their own chains.

Although the Dharma knows no distinctions,
We blindly stay attached to particular things.
It is our own minds that create illusion,
Is this not the greatest of contradictions?

Ignorance begets the duality of rest and unrest.
Illumination annihilates attachment and aversion.
All forms of duality
Are traps contrived by the ignorant mind.

Visions in dreams, flowers in the air:
Why should we bother to grasp hold of them?
Gain and loss, true and false,
Let them go once and for all!

For an eye which never sleeps
All dreams vanish of themselves.
If the mind does not lose itself in differences
The ten thousand things are of one single identity.

Once we understand the mystery of things in their single
identity—
Suddenly, all attachment leaves us.
When the ten thousand things are seen in their oneness
We return to the source and remain what we are.

Seek not the wherefore of things
And you attain a state beyond comparison.
Arrested movement is no movement,
And rest set in motion is no rest.

The frontiers of the Ultimate
Are not guarded by rules or measures.
The mind integrated in the essence of unity,
All activity has its source in silence.

When doubts are swept away,
All hesitation disappears, right faith is restored to its natural straightness.
Nothing to retain,
Nothing to remember.
All is void, lucid and self-illuminating.
No strain, no effort, no wastage of energy.

The Absolute is not a place measurable by thought,
Knowledge is unable to fathom it.
In the supreme realm of true identity
There is neither "other" nor "self."

In not being two, all is the same.
There is nothing not contained therein.
The wise in every locality
All enter into the primary origin.

The origin is beyond time and space.
One instant is like unto ten thousand years.
Neither present nor absent despite all conditioning,
It is manifest everywhere before you.

The infinitely small is infinitely large
When one is not lost in the manifestation.
The infinitely large is infinitely small
When the eye no longer splits things apart.

What is is the same as what is not,
What is not is the same as what is.
There where this state is not evident
One must not sojourn.

The one is in the multiple—
The multiple is in the one.

If this truth is realized
Of what use to attain to perfection?

The vacant mind is non-dual,
And the non-dual is the vacuity.
Here the paths of language fail,
For this is not of the past nor present nor future.

Excerpt from the Prologue to the book
Transmission of the Flame
by Jean Klein

Q. How, then, did you meet your "unknown teacher"?

Jean Klein: Some of the friends I met and with whom I spoke of peace, freedom and joy, had a spiritual guide. One day I met their teacher and on this and several other meetings, I asked him many questions, questions that expressed all my earnestness to find my real centre.

Q. It seems that you trusted him at once.

JK. I was open to him. I was struck by his lack of striving, his humility. He never tried to impress or convince. There was simply no personality. All his answers came from nowhere, no one, and yet his gentle openness was apparent. I was struck, too, by his argument that potentially you are, it only needs actualizing. He never saw anyone as not knowing. He gave no hold to my personality.

He gave me many answers, but during the several weeks that I didn't see him, I became aware that all my questions had been an escape, an evasion of the real question. The existential crisis I had always lived in became acute. I lived with this feeling that I had missed the real question, a question I was not able to formulate.

Then I had the opportunity to visit him where he lived in a little room in the Sanskrit College at Bangalore where he was a teacher. Two other young Indians were present, and they were talking about the Karikas of Gaudapada and the Mandukya Upanishad. The talk was of the four states, waking, sleeping, dreaming and turiya. He said that turiya is not properly speaking a state which one enters and leaves. It becomes a non-state when you are awake in it. It is the absence of ourself which is our total presence.

Then there was a silence, the other students left, and he suddenly looked at me and asked, "Do you know yourself?" I was a bit disturbed by this question because I didn't really know what he meant. I couldn't find a way to look at it. I said hesitatingly, "Yes," because I was thinking I knew my body, senses and mind very well. He said to me, "You are the knower of your body, senses and mind, but the knower can never be known because you are it, and there's nobody to know it. It can never become an object of observation because it is your totality." This saying had a very strong impact on me. I had a glimpse of reality in this moment because it stopped all intellectual faculties. We were silent and I left.

Q. And did this impact remain with you when you got home?

JK. It left a very strong echo in me of freedom from old beliefs. I went home and lived with it free from all conceptualization and felt myself awake in this not-knowing. It was completely new, there was no absence of knowing.

Q. Did life change or go on as usual?

JK. Life went on, eating, meeting people. But there was now a feeling that I was behind all daily activities. I saw Pandiji many times afterwards and realized that he was my guru because this profound impact could only come from a guru. So, you see, he found me when I was not looking for him!

The Sayings of Old Man Tcheng

Foreword

The sayings of old man Tcheng convey a Sense which is dependent neither on time nor place, nor on the words and he who uttered them, nor on signs or letters and those who have transcribed them.

Since old man Tcheng looks on himself as but a block of resounding wood, it would be vain to seek to know who he is or to give oneself to commenting, comparing or speculating concerning his sayings and, thus, remain at the level of historicism and intellectualism, as well as proving that nothing had been understood of his sayings and that one's heart was closed to the Sense they bear.

It is therefore important to keep these sayings in their unspoiled freshness so as to preserve the fullness of their power and ensure that their Sense will ever remain untainted.

* * *

Old man Tcheng, he said:

I, old Tcheng, do not intervene to maintain, modify or change the course of things by following the desires of the individual mind. Let there be neither distrust nor revolt but only the necessary act. If I behave in a different way with you, it is so that you might, at last, by yourselves, directly see original spirit instead of always seeking it through the mediation of dead fellows or by running after scatterbrains like me.

My own manner, indeed, is to shake you like saplings in the mountain wind. Thus, I break up all your struts and props and, there you are, all undone, with nothing more to hold on to. But since I sap up all that you rely upon and, thus, you are filled with fear, you say, to reassure yourselves, that I sin against the law and convention and am but a vile blasphemer. So you go on desperately clinging to appearances and accessories instead of letting them depart from you by themselves, without striving to hold onto them.

My words find no echo in you, so I play a trick on you and tell you they come from a great and famous fellow who has been dead for centuries. But you still do not understand that they are your direct and immediate concern. On the contrary, you seize on them as something precious, good for keeping and to cultivate. Bald-heads, by holding onto futilities, you simply waste your life away and the evidence of original spirit slips through your fingers. What a shipwreck for you!

*

Nitwits, original spirit does not appear when sleep leaves you and does not disappear when sleep comes to you. Original spirit is nothing and is totally independent of that which changes and dies.

If original spirit were truly your sole occupation, you would see all that alters and dies in the same way that you perceive the movements that dancers give to their streamers, and would resolve to constantly seek that which in you neither varies nor dies and, once you find it, then not one of the thousand worlds could divert you in your thoughts for the instant of a flash or in the slightest degree make you stray from it in your actions.

You believe you aspire to original spirit but you only actually seek the satisfaction of a condition, or learning, and of merit. Because of this, nincompoops, you are entirely under the fascination of all that in you and outside of you is not steadfast and just dies.

That is why the sayings of old Tcheng simply go through you without making an impression, like the birds which leave no trace in the sky.

Bald pates, all that you think and say concerning original spirit is but the erring and wandering of your own puny little minds.

To that which nature spontaneously brings you, you respond only after interpreting it through all that you have placed on a pedestal above your heads.

Baldies, this being as artificial as the dragons made for festivals, how can you hope to see original spirit in its spontaneity?

*

In my youth, I went all round the land giving myself up to study and practices. I associated with those who had strayed and, imagining they had found the light, did nothing but cause others to stray. Then, I met him who enabled me to see all the useless mud I bore with me. The way of truth appeared to me and original spirit became my sole occupation. And, one day, everything suddenly collapsed into awareness.

I, old Tcheng, do not imitate so and so, or such and such a one. I hold to no belief, no school of thought do I follow, no one's disciple am I. In my true nature I know nothing, I own nothing, I am nothing... for there is no old Tcheng there! In the ordinary way, the things in which I take part, of themselves, just flow by, pass away on their own. Even original spirit is no longer my concern.

The words I speak to you come not from that which is learnt.

*

Shaved skulls, I have hidden nothing from you. What profit is there for you? Nothing but stuff and nonsense!

Exit old man Tcheng

Old man Tcheng said:
Original spirit has ever been present under your very eyes. You need acquire nothing to see it because you have never lacked anything for seeing it. If you are incapable of seeing it, it is because

of your unceasing chatter with yourselves and with others. You spend your time supposing, comparing, computing, developing, explaining, justifying and quoting what your puny minds have retained and thought they understood of the Scriptures and of the words of old jackasses like me, giving preference to sayings from those to whom, after their death, was given such authority as put them beyond all doubts. In these circumstances, how can you hope to see original spirit in its instantaneousness?

Dumbells, because you are as agitated as a wagonload of monkeys and spend your time in futilities, your existence passes by like murky, muddy water. No outlet for you.

*

To say that original spirit is not sheer void, without factual existence, that is just words. In thinking about original spirit lies your poison. Giving up this thought and thinking of the absence of this thought, there, again, lies your poison. Lamebrains, you are ever seeking with your thought, and you do nothing but fabricate thoughts. Thinking that original spirit can be seen by means of thought, that is where you perish.

Burning incense, reciting sutras, spending time bowing to the ground or concentrating on staying perfectly still, fixing or eliminating thought, this is where you stray. Numskulls, you are always intervening and you do nothing but keep acting thus and so. Hoping to see original spirit by means of actions, that is your illusion.

Venerating the Buddha, that is the evil (of attachment). Rejecting the Buddha, that is the evil (of impiety). Dolts, you are ever bent on expressing emotions and you do nothing but produce sentiment. Believing one can see original spirit by means of sentiment, there is your mistake.

Dimwits, you are convinced you will come to see original spirit in this manner. But it is you and you alone that you will catch... never, do you hear, never can original spirit be found that way.

You fail to hear my words because you wish to remain deaf and you do not see original spirit because you wish to remain blind. There is no hope for you.

*

When you consider the thoughts of others as something precious and sacred, and learn, recite and transcribe them with great care and veneration in order to transmit them as a great secret, that is what I call being chained up under the thoughts.

When you cultivate the thoughts of your puny mind, looking on them as something rare, worthy of being preserved, and giving vent to a whore's irritability if they are not respected or if in the restating of them the slightest mistake is made, that is what I call being chained up by thoughts.

When others' thoughts and your own appear to you as the waves of the sea which come and go, without any one of them being better or worse than the others and without a single one affecting you, yet you hold to the one thought of having attained a state of perfect calm, this is what I call erring above thoughts.

When no thought any longer holds your attention because evidence is born that, in regard to original spirit, there is nothing to keep and nothing to be obtained by thought, this is what I call being on the threshold of original spirit.

To be in non-time, non-place, non-form, non-movement and non-thought and to know what is perceived in the absence of any perception, this is what I call seeing original spirit.

When you have studied all the Scriptures and every treatise of every patriarch, when you have met all the awakened ones and mastered all the practices and mysterious forces, if you do not see original spirit, even if you have become summits of spirituality, of holiness and of science, your life, nincompoops, will never be other than a futile amusement.

*

Regarding the words traced on this scroll, which I have just read:

—if I tell you they are from the Buddha, you look upon them as sacred, and you are filled with veneration and fear

—if I tell you they are from Bodhidharma or from a great patriarch, you are filled with admiration and respect

—if I tell you they are by an unknown monk, you no longer know what to think, and you are filled with doubt

—if I tell you they come from the monk in the kitchens, you burst out laughing, thinking I have just played a trick on you.

Thus, what counts for you is not the truth that these words bear but only the importance to be granted them according to the fame of the one from whom they are said to have come. You are incapable of seeing for yourselves but only feel what you think should be felt, and think according to the opinion of those you have placed on a pedestal; you are forever adding to things, tainting them, falsifying them. That is why you are powerless to see original spirit without reference to who or whatever it might be. Nincompoops, you are nothing but fakes and tricksters. Your case is hopeless.

And old man Tcheng left the room

Old man Tcheng spoke:

You have heard it said that in order to see original spirit your puny mind must be empty. So, there you sit, rigid as a bamboo stick, looking at the wall, your tongue against your palate, striving to put a stop to your thoughts. You thus come to an absence of thoughts which you take for the vacuity or original spirit. The very next moment, the turmoil of your petty mind starts up again just as it does when you come out of sleep. In the absence of thought, what profit is there? And if a flash of light shakes you, there you go prancing like a young horse, bellowing that you have seen original spirit, that you have experienced something immense and that you were greatly privileged. What advantage is there in being struck as by thunder? All of that is a nice performance, just good enough for a circus.

Baldies, if you persist in your mania and your pretence at wanting to attain and possess whatever it might be, yours is a lost cause.

*

To see original spirit, is to see it whether thoughts are present or absent, whether one is motionless or active, whether one speaks as I am doing before you or whether one is silent, whether one is an emperor, a monk or a vagrant. What importance is there in that?

Between the Buddha and the uncouth, illiterate monk who can do nothing but chop wood but who sees original spirit, what difference is there? There is no original spirit special to Bodhidharma and another special to old Tcheng or to each one of you. Original spirit is original spirit. Nothing else can be said about it, and even that is saying too much.

What others have said concerning original spirit and what I say of it can be of no other use to you than to incite you to directly seek it yourselves, without resorting to any authority and without artfulness. All the rest just blurs your vision and turns you away from the only question which should entirely possess you wherever you might be and whatever you might be doing: meditating, sweeping the yard or attending to the private requirements of nature. But when I see what you do with the sayings of the patriarchs and with mine, it would have been better if the patriarchs had been drowned at birth and me along with them.

Dolts, you have caught a deadly disease.

*

Shaved heads, the world and you are nothing other than thoughts of the individual mind since both disappear when sleep overtakes you. This is equally true of all the old tattery notions of your puny mind regarding the Buddha, the Way, and original spirit.

Once and for always, understand the uselessness of all your efforts to penetrate the impenetrable by thought and action: you might as well try to capture the wind. But if you are unencumbered, entirely available to original spirit, then will you be directly seized by it.

Having heard speak of the void as being the supreme accomplishment, you seek to attain it. Thus, you fall into the torpor and insensitivity which you take for the vacuity of original spirit.

Having heard speak of the absolute as being the ultimate state, you imagine that all things are equal and that none is worthy of respect. Thus, you fall into the rakishness and anarchy which you take for the oneness of original spirit.

Having heard speak of purity as being complete happiness, you strive to attain it. Thus, you fall into a diehard attitude of rigidity which you take for the transparency of original spirit.

Having heard of detachment as being the only freedom, you try to become separate from the world and from yourselves. Thus, you fall into indifference which you take for the independence of original spirit.

Baldies, it is original spirit which is said to be vacuity, oneness, transparency and independence, and the element of the wheel of existence that you are will never be able to possess any of these faculties. But if you saw original spirit, then you would know that it is your true nature without any possible qualification and that, in reality, no name can be given it. You would then also know that what we call void, absolute, purity, detachment, and even original spirit, are nothing but words which exist from your point of view alone, only because of your blindness and your ignorance.

Simpletons, your wanting to simulate original spirit spells the end of you.

*

Because you have become monks, followers of the law of

the Buddha and disciples of a famed Master, you think you are different from the laymen on whom you look with condescension. You are as ignorant of original spirit as only the grass of the field can be.

*

You are much engrossed in getting to know who I am, from what parental stock I am issued, who were my Masters, where I have come from, what I believe, and many other things equally devoid of interest. Some think that if the Master of this abode has asked me to speak to you, I can only be an enlightened one, and others, on the contrary, that they have before them but a scandalous and insolent old fool who should be thrown outside because he has no respect for the sayings and men of the past as revered by tradition, neither has he any respect for the sayings and men of the present exalted by their fame and renown. Thus, you hold merely to the envelope and to the appearance of things, and, because of this, you fail to perceive in you, the true man.

Fools, you put mud in your eyes and then complain of being blind.

And old man Tcheng went off with much gesticulating...

Old man Tcheng returned the next day and spoke thus:

Shaven ones, by completely abandoning yourselves to the will and whims of another whom you have exalted to the point of relying on him for all things, you imagine your attitude to be just and, thus, yourselves to be without concern and without desires. In reality, you merely behave as do very young monkeys which do not leave their mother for a single moment, desperately clinging to her, so full of fear are they. And, in course of time, you become like those dried-up trees which look like the other trees in winter but which, when spring and summer come, have no leaves and bear no fruit. In such passivity, how can you hope to see original spirit?

Smooth pates, you are already dead.

*

Every man is enlightened by original spirit. Some see it, others ignore it, that is the only difference between them. As for you, shavenheads, you are as a drunken man, who, on the outside of an enclosure clings to the bamboo sticks, shouting that he has been shut in, that he is innocent, and implores to be set free.

Dunces, no one but you is holding each of you a prisoner. What a disaster for you!

*

Powerless to see original spirit and, thereby, to live of yourselves, you conceal your insignificance by wearing the clothing others have cast off, be they dead or alive. You accumulate viewpoints and cultivate shades of meaning, differences and convergences. Thus, you strut about. Because you dazzle fools with your tricks, you take yourselves to be enlightened men.

Nitwits, you are but chatterboxes and cheap jugglers. You have led yourselves astray. Your ill is incurable.

You need no one to see the light of the sun. All that others can say on this subject is useless to you. You are in the light. It warms your body, and, yet, you cannot seize it and put it into a box. All attempts to possess it are doomed beforehand to failure. You can neither catch it nor get rid of it. That has already been said by this old chatterbox and by others before him.

Likewise, original spirit. It is ever present, as bright as the light of the sun. You cannot increase it nor diminish it. Dolts, if you cannot see it, this is due to the rubbish you have cluttered up in your heads. You cannot see it because you are taken over by your efforts to trap it in your thoughts, your adorations and your practices. You imagine it to be afar, and it is here. You want to grab it, and it escapes from you.

If you were entirely simple, you would only need to open your eyes to see it, just as you see the light of the sun. No need to intervene for that.

He who has seen a grain of sand has seen every grain of sand on every shore and the bed of every sea in the world. If you see original spirit, then you see all of original spirit and you are a Buddha.

I am before you as a resounding piece of wood. There is nothing deserving or important in this for there has never been a lack of, nor, till the end of men, will there ever be a lack of beings like old Tcheng to resound in the same way.

But, nincompoops, it is to your misfortune that you are ever preoccupied with mere appearances and see here only the block of resounding wood. Because of this, original spirit finds not in you the echo which would suddenly make you realize that you are not, and have never been, other than it.

And old man Tcheng retired

The following evening old man Tcheng entered and said:
Shorn skulls, look upon all the patriarchs and all the chatterboxes like me as impostors, since they speak to you of what they can neither show you nor give you. The only usefulness one may, perhaps, grant them is that they inform us that every being has the nature of the Buddha. But it is for each one of you to seek this by himself, without being led astray by whatever else, so that you may see it in a great flash of reality. Baldies, if you let the words and magic tricks of the patriarchs affect you, then you are lost.

Nitwits, in the hope of seeing original spirit, you have accumulated much knowledge inside your little minds, just as rice is heaped up and stored. Acting thus, you have done nothing but disguise your ignorance with learned words to discuss the true and the untrue, good and evil, the eternal and the ephemeral, heaven and earth, all the subtle and gross elements that compose man, the merits of the various ways and practices, the extent of so and so's Enlightenment, and a great many useless things, all of which shows your incapacity to find the rightful attitude.

Numskulls, your vice dwells in your arrogant pretense to want to measure the incommensurable.

If there be any among you who, while listening to me, are struck by something greater and deeper than my words and which is not the sort of sanctimonious torpor in which so many take delight, thus imagining they are at one with original spirit, but see it as a simple, clear and active light, then to these I can but indicate the true direction and show them the way. Their own muddy contour will one day break up, all at once drop off, and they will see the radiant beauty of the jewel of original spirit.

In this matter, I do not personally intervene. I am but a mode of transit for original spirit whose presence some may feel through me, old Tcheng, who am also for others as caked mud round a precious stone.

So long as I am asked about original spirit I can but remain speechless or answer: no.

As for he who sees original spirit, he has no need of old Tcheng.

*

If you were true men, your thoughts and acts would be just, and each moment appropriate to their end or object. But as you are incapable of seeing your Buddha nature, you fill up your ignorance by copying the thoughts, behaviour and acts of those you have put on a pedestal. Your preoccupation in mimicking like monkeys what others think and do, that is the cloud that stops you seeing original spirit. Dolts, you are naught but thieves and robbers. No hope for you.

Baldies, your fundamental nature in no way differs from that of the Buddha. You only lack the unambiguous knowing of it and that alone. That is what you lack and that is what impels you to seek to become what you have never stopped being. To be clearly in original spirit is the sole meaning of your existence. If you so much as slightly stray from it, you immediately fall into error and the unending swirl of causes and effects. This, alone, is what old Tcheng teaches.

And old man Tcheng left the room

Old man Tcheng declared:

Bare skulls, the thought of original spirit is but the reflection of that spirit in a particular mind, as the image of the moon seen in the water of a pond is but a reflection of the moon. Original spirit remains present, unchanged and unaffected by the tumult of your thoughts and acts, as the moon remains unchanged and unaffected whether the water in the pond be clear or muddy, calm or agitated or whether the pond be full or empty. It is only the image of the moon which is changed or absent in such case. There is no moon in the pond.

Bald heads, you should understand that with all your inventions of purity to be attained, of detachment and freedom to be obtained, of stopping your thoughts every three hours and all the other practices you perform with a view to seizing upon original spirit, you are scooped up by your own mind like a fish in a net, you act as stupidly as if, in order to directly see the moon, you cleaned the water in the pond, took away the plants that cover it, built a bamboo fence so that the wind would not disturb the surface of the water, or as if you emptied the pond.

Dumbos, just see that you merely allow yourselves to be fettered by your own thoughts and by your pitiable actions.

*

Dunces, it is because of your blindness that old Tcheng speaks to you of original spirit and of the individual mind as if he were referring to different things. For old Tcheng, original spirit and individual mind, the eternal and the ephemeral, wisdom and ignorance, enlightenment and blindness, nirvana, the sutras, the system of law, all the bodies of transformation and the Buddha himself are nothing but the whirlwind of thoughts, similar to a lot of dead leaves which give the impression of being alive when the winter wind lifts them but the next moment are dead again. Dolts, the true nature of beings and of things is not great for he who sees it, neither is it small for he who ignores it. It remains unaffected by being known or being unknown and by all that you thrust upon it.

You are free, shaved ones, to go on straying to perdition by way of distinctions, shades of meaning and subtleties. There, I have told all.

*

Bald heads, the Buddha first sought original spirit through the individual mind. He found this to be vanity. The Buddha then sought original spirit through disciplines and practices. There again, he saw this to be vanity. Under the Bodhi tree he still had not found original spirit, but he knew that the individual mind and action were incapable of giving him the vision of his true nature. Then, did the Buddha give up using the individual mind and action, he accepted his ignorance and recognized his powerlessness to put a stop to it.

The Buddha was then nothing more than unknowing and waiting, affected by nothing, as still as a piece of dead wood, when, at the sight of the morning star, original spirit flooded him with light.

Such is the experience of the Buddha. Such is the example and such is the primal teaching that he has left.

But all of you, disciples of the Buddha, what have you done? You have taken possession of the Buddha to make of his life a legend over which to marvel, and to make of his person an idol for your adoration; you have seized upon the sayings of the Buddha to make of them a sacred thing worthy of being unendingly learnt, recited and transcribed. Concerning the life and the words of the Buddha, you have founded a great number of different schools, written treatises without number and never stopped chattering and blabbing. You have built temples and put up statues. You have lighted the incense and made the camphor burn. You have snuffed out beliefs and established dogmas, rules, disciplines and practices.

Nitwits, you have fallen into the trap and seduction of all that the Buddha had recognized as being error which can only lead astray. In this manner, you built a wall as high as heaven blocking yourself from the original spirit you long to see.

Shaved skulls, if you persist in the error of your ways, what a total failure your life will be!

*

Now, baldies, listen to me with greatest attention. I will reveal to you the great secret of original spirit. This is the most important thing ever said in its regard...

Here it is: **There is no secret about original spirit.**

With a graceful pirouette, old man Tcheng disappeared and since then no one has heard speak of him.

Your Question

Q. I am a writer of fiction, novels, actually. Recently, I discovered your books and have been immensely struck by what you say. I see how all my life I have taken myself for somebody and have let this somebody dictate my life. The problem I have now concerns my writing.

As you know, novels are created through the interplay of characters and the thought and action of these characters. I indulge in a terrific amount of imagination, day-dreaming and wandering through the corridors of the mind. I live a thousand situations through my characters. Fiction writing involves mental jugglery, an expression you used in your book *Who Am I?* I love language and shaping it gives me pleasure. But language is thought and thought comes from ego. It seems, then, that by writing I am reinforcing the ego and the ego of the reader, even if a novel can uncover the way we live and self-deceit in our lives and social structures. But maybe so many hours spent in illusion will further increase the illusion.

I know that a good novel can point to the hollowness of what we habitually call fulfilment. It can show how beauty is lost. But all fiction writing involves states, plays with its own states. The question is whether it is possible for fiction writing to be open to a global insight and to communicate it. It seems that there must be a way to make fiction writing and spiritual inquiry compatible.

Jean Klein: Writing, like music or any of the arts, is a way to encounter the reader. It is where author and reader meet. The work is not created by "the writer." It is only created the moment the reader participates in it. In other words, when you write, it is not a piece of ego-expression, but an offering for the reader, an offer to share in the creative process. The reader encounters his own creativity and feels stimulated and delightfully surprised by this encounter.

In creative writing, the reader is compelled to complete the image, to complete what you, the author, have "ignored." What you do not say is vital to creative participation. Like any relation. When you are free from being "the author," you naturally do not say too much. When you have no bone to grind, there is a spontaneous economy of language. The only thing that hinders really creative writing is memory. I don't mean functional memory, but psychological memory. Psychological memory and "the writer" are one and the same, so in writing "the writer" must be forgotten.

When you are free from the person, you are free from personal memory, and then you are open to universal memory. And you will be surprised in which directions you are pushed. Your hand will not be able to keep up with it! When you are free from being "a writer," "an author," "an intelligent, creative person," you will create drama in which the "me's" come and go from moment to moment. In the end, all these "me's" will become free from the "I." In other words, when you know your own freedom, and you have a talent for writing, you will be able to write showing how the "me's" function and how one can live free from the "I." But it is important that reason, memory, does not interfere, that you go with the flow.

The Body Work

Q. You have said that a subtle, expanded body is more receptive to global insight, and that the insight can be more readily established when the body is receptive. I know the exercises you teach help relax and decondition the body, and I wondered what else we can do on the physical level to maintain the sattvic state?

Jean Klein: Our body/mind is composed of the five elements, so that the air we breathe and how we breathe it, the water we drink and how we drink it, the food we absorb and how we absorb it, and so on, all maintain our body. We must become aware of how all the elements act on us.

The assimilation of food should bring us to lightness rather than to heaviness. Very often what is called food is not food at all. Real food has not gone through any transformation. It is eaten as it comes from the ground. Any product which has been chemically altered is not food. This includes sugar, coffee, tea, meat, alcohol and other invented foodstuffs.

The incorrect combination of food requires a tremendous supplement of energy to be disgested. This energy is taken away from other sources of energy in our body. We may feel mentally or physically lethargic or over-excited, depressed or nervous. We may laugh, talk or act impulsively. There may be physical discomfort.

One cannot feel or be aware of the subtler energies involved in spiritual inquiry when the body is polluted by wrong absorbtion. When we live with right eating, we become sattvic, light, receptive—in complete availability. A serious truth-seeker must be open at all times and on all levels.

Q. Is this because one never knows when the moment of grace will come?

JK. Yes. You must keep your temple of the Lord in availability.

LISTENING

Volume 3
1991

The Great Forgetting...67
Jean Klein

The Grief of the Dead...76
Rumi

On Silence...77
Jean Klein

Sermon, *"Blessed are the Poor"* 78
Meister Eckhart

Excerpt from *Four Quartets* 85
T.S. Eliot

Dialogue in New York: April 27, 1990.....................86
Jean Klein

Your Question: *Follow the glimpse* 104
Jean Klein

To Know the Body: *The original body*.....................106
Jean Klein

The Great Forgetting

Jean Klein: The whole problem of dying is based on the premise that we are born and that this born something or someone dies. So the first step is to question: Who or what is born and who or what dies?

The idea of being born is just that, an idea. It is second-hand information. It is what our mothers told us. If we ask ourselves, "Do I know that I am born?" and we look closely, we will see that, yes, a perception is born and dies, but we cannot say, "I am born."

It is vital in all genuine exploration to become free from second-hand information, free from common sense. If we begin by questioning the questions, we will find that we are led to question the questioner. This is the beginning of self-inquiry.

When we let go of second-hand information, we are face to face with bare facts, percepts rather than concepts. When we leave aside day-dreaming, hypothesis and the taken-for-granted, we are left with the core of the problem, which I would say in this case is: Why speak of death before knowing what life is? Because if we don't know what life is, how can we even begin to talk of death? So let us first talk about life.

The expressions of life appear and disappear in our awareness. We know what time is, we know what space is, we know what an experience is. How could we know these things if we did not, in some way, also know what timeless, spaceless, experienceless means? Can we know white without reference to black? Can we know dark without reference to light? We know impermanence because in some way we "know" permanence. This permanence is not an experience in time and space. It is not a condition. It does not belong to existence because existence is in time and space. It is essentially nothing, yet in some way we refer to this nothingness very often. It is the background from which we function. It has nothing to do with succession, with past and future. It is causeless and cannot be born.

When we discover this background, the problem of death becomes completely meaningless. When this timeless awareness from which we function unconsciously becomes aware—aware of itself—then we know that what we are is timeless and spaceless. We know what life is, and it does not enter our mind to even think of death because we live knowingly in this timeless background, in the now, and succession is only an expression of this now.

The real question then is: how can I come to know life so that death is meaningless? I would say that we can never know, in an objective way, what life is. We can only be life, be the knowing. This knowing is an instantaneous apperception, free from space and time, in which there is not a knower and something known. It is the awakening of life in its fullness.

This awakening is our real birth. The phenomenal birth is only an accident and it remains an accident as long as our real nature, our real birth, is not explored. Once we are awake in life, we are profoundly aware that we are not a conceptual object. The object and the reflex to objectify oneself does not arise. It is a state of profound openness, a total absence of being anything, where there is simply life, "isness." It is timeless and dimensionless, and cannot be objectified, that is, experienced. It is not born and what is not born cannot die. In this original non-state, the idea of death does not even occur.

The fear of dying comes from mis-taking oneself to be the body-mind. This mistake is a thought only. So really the fear of dying comes from the capacity to think. When there is no thought, there is no space and time. Space, time, coming, going, past, future, exist only in thought. They have no autonomous reality. All the fear created by society and religions around so-called dying is mind-fabrication. But it is only an object which can be afraid and you are not an object.

Dying on the biological level does not create fear. Fear is in the mind, not the body. The fear of dying is only anticipation that "I" will disappear. The idea of a final disappearing destroys all security for the I-image. But this "you," "me," this self-image is also a thought construct built up from memory. The powerful instinct for what is wrongly called self-preservation (the term shows how we have identified with the body-mind) is merely biological survival. Life is desireless but the body-mind is an expression of life, so one could say that the desire to stay alive comes from life itself. As an expression of life, the body accomplishes the course inherent to its nature.

The real meaning of death and dying is completely different from that usually understood by these words. When one knows the continuum that is life, all perceptions (of which our body is but one) are felt as appearing and disappearing in awareness or consciousness. This appearing and disappearing is the real meaning of birth and death. We are born every moment a thought or sensation appears and we die every moment the concept or percept disappears. We die every evening before going to sleep, and we are born every morning. So we need to become acquainted with this dying, this letting-go of the objective world.

We should ask ourselves in our most profound intimacy: What is there before the thought appears? What is there when the thought disappears? What is there before the body goes to sleep and before it wakes up? When we observe closely, we will find, not the absence we took for granted, but a presence, a presence that cannot, however, be objectified. It is too near, it is our nearest.

If we really know how to go to sleep we will know how to die. We will be already familiar with dying, already familiar with the dissolution of the born. To do this, one must, before going to sleep, lay aside all qualifications. We must become as naked psychologically as we are physically. This means that we put aside all opinions, thoughts, worries, ideas before we sleep. It is an offering of all that we are not. In letting go there is an expansion of mind and body and in all expansion is the fore-feeling of reality, our globality. This should be done each time we sleep until we find that, before the body wakes up in the morning, we are. Presence is already there.

It is better not to postpone this letting-go of the personal entity and all its qualifications until the actual moment of death. Otherwise, it is necessary to have someone who knows life to assist in the final letting-go. This is supposedly the priest's role in the last rites. The function of the priest, shaman, lama or other, is to help one go knowingly through the threshold from the object world to the objectless world. It is to help the dying one forget all the residues of the person and so be open to a new dimension of life. It is an offering back to life of all the expressions that life gave us temporarily. Then what remains is original consciousness.

But whoever is assisting someone over the threshold must be qualified to do so. This simply means that the personality must be absent. In assisting someone to die, one must die with them. The moment you die with the dying one, he or she is stimulated by your dying, by your giving up of all qualifications. Timeless presence, love, has the power to free the dying person from the residues of identification with the phenomenal world. There is no place at all in this assistance for feelings of sadness, pity, fear, nor is there room for talking. All this keeps the dying one grasping onto the objective world.

Ideally, the best way to die is in silence. But when one is steeped in the rituals of a religious tradition, these may help one, in the absence of a qualified priest or real friend, to let go of specific attachments. But the rites must be impersonal, give no hold to the person as, for example, certain sounds draw one beyond the world of sentiment and emotivity.

The way to come to this letting-go is, as I said, the same as before going to sleep. Everything that appears in the moment is seen as a fact. One takes note of the fact without analysis or interference and feels the welcoming in this unconditional taking-note. When we face, in this way, everything that appears, then the openness, attention, in which the perception was welcomed, comes back to us. We find ourselves in the light. This is a natural giving up without intention. So, whether we are dying (and we must!) or assisting someone to die, it is the same procedure. We take a knowing stand in consciousness.

It is crucial to come to know death while still alive. The quality of life is completely different for one who knows letting-go in the waking state. This is the real meaning of the word death. It is the real significance of the word sacrifice. As Meister Eckhart said, "God is when I am not." We are only born after the death of all that is personal. Only when we are awake in nothingness can we speak of fullness.

But there is another reason for not leaving the real dying until the last moment. There is the real danger that one will remain stuck to the expressions of life and, at the moment of death, emphasize the object, so that one is taken passively to what is beyond. Passively here means "not knowingly."

The question may arise: What difference does it make how I die? Consciousness is not affected by birth or death. There is not one moment without consciousness, so after the death of the body, consciousness is always there. But how one dies does make a difference, because after the death of the person, although consciousness is, it can be awake—conscious of itself—or not. Generally, after the death of the body-mind, this being consciousness is passive, it is not consciousness conscious of itself. What is of utmost importance, therefore, is to be knowingly consciousness and this can only come about before the body dies. Since most of us only know ourselves as objects and do not know ourselves as consciousness, few, after death, dissolve in consciousness which knows itself.

Consciousness which knows itself is fulfilled and does not look for further expression. As the residues of the body disperse in global energy, consciousness dissolves in its own light. There is nobody to go anywhere and nowhere to go.

All ideas about different states and stages of the dissolution of energy are, therefore, meaningless to the awakened one and a hindrance to the one who is in the process of letting go of all qualifications and attachments. Such concepts cause confusion. They are mind-constructs since there is no one left to know such things. As long as there are such ideas, there is still a somebody to know. And as long as there is still a somebody to know, there has been no real dying.

It is possible that in one who is still fixed on the objective world, identified with the personality, children, spouse, money, vocation and so on, it may be difficult for the energy to dissolve. It remains concentrated. That is why there are rituals of various kinds which help dissolve the energy and aid the giving up of all hold on the phenomenal plane. And it is why sometimes, though the body is not visible, there may still be residues of the personality. One should accept these and take several sessions to systematically empty oneself of all ideas, memories and feelings for the dead person. It is a process of elimination. Then one sees that there is much more to the relationship than one could remember. Memory belongs to our minds, but the real relationship is not limited by memory.

The problem of physical suffering during dying needs to be addressed because the question naturally arises as to how one can come to a real letting-go in the face of acute pain. The first thing to clarify is that pain must be seen as an object like any other, from the perspective that what we are fundamentally is not an object and cannot be afraid or feel pain. So we must be absolutely clear about our profound non-involvement in the events surrounding the sensation we call pain or illness.

We cannot say, "I am afraid, I am in pain, I am dying," because the "I" is unchanged and unchanging. It is the body which feels sensation and the mind that creates fear. Once there is clarity about what one is not—the body and its sensations, the mind and its thoughts—the suffering is dramatically reduced. Then the sensation, the illness can be faced squarely without psychological interference.

Pain, like every object, is a pointer to our real nature. It must be seen objectively, in front of us as if the body belonged to another. In objectifying it, we are extricated from it, no longer drowned in the illness, the sensation. And in the psychological space thus created, there will be a glimpse of real freedom from the burden. It is not enough to vaguely note this brief feeling of detachment. We must become truly interested in this feeling of freedom, that is, make it, in turn, an object of attention, sustain and live in this free feeling. With it comes the conviction that one is neither the healthy nor the unhealthy body.

Illness and death are an opportunity, par excellence, to clarify the fundamental error of our existence: that we have identified awareness, consciousness, life, with its object and it is through this mis-take that all conflict and suffering arise. Illness then is a gift, a gift to help us realize more quickly what we are not. It gives us an opportunity that should not be refused: to be what we are.

Our living in wholeness stimulates our surroundings, our family and friends. I would say it stimulates the life in them. Knowingly or unknowingly, they share life with us and, at death, neither we nor they will feel isolated. This feeling of life will remain and continue to stimulate them because life is eternal and in it all are oneness.

But generally family and friends do not have an honest relation with the dying one. They continue, in some way, to hold onto, to try to save, the person. They do not let him or her meet the light. This is because relationships in the family are of object to object, person to person. So it is better not to have the family present at the moment of dying if they cannot perform the last rites, be priests, so to speak, that is, die with you.

It is important that the dying one offer up the expressions of life consciously. However, in certain circumstances, clarity may be impaired by the intensity of the pain or the use of medications to relieve it. At the very moment of the final release, nature usually takes itself in charge and pain does not cloud awareness, so when assisting a dying person, a doctor has a great responsibility. First and foremost, he or she must represent health, life and, like the priest, prepare the patient for the final release. The doctor must also die with the patient. All his talent is needed to first help the patient distance himself from identifying with the object, and then to see precisely how much medication is necessary to make this distancing possible. The patient must retain a profound awareness of what is happening.

Either prolonging life artificially or taking one's life prematurely is a deep lack of respect for all life has given us. It is a lack of gratitude, a profound ignorance. Life gives us the opportunity for a real birth and all interfering is a refusal of this opportunity. When one awakes in the real "I," the destiny of all that we are not no longer has any meaning. Pain, an accident, death, is on the film, but we are the light which illuminates the film. So, thinking about the fate of the body and trying to interfere is a mark of ego-centredness and a lack of love.

Only an ego can have concepts and intentions, and as long as we live as the contracted ego we will have a false view of what life is. What we generally call "my life" belongs only to the mind and thus appears to take place in succession. The illusion of life as time gives us the impression that we can interfere. This wrong seeing is sometimes corrected before dying when there is a panoramic memory of one's whole life. This is because there is a sudden letting-go of the mind's control, of the channelling of one's being into strict succession in time and space. In this sudden letting-go we are ejected into the timeless and facts appear to us without all the intervening thoughts that generally qualify every fact. This panorama usually occurs at a crisis when there is a very dramatic letting-go. In a natural death one is gently dissolved in being.

Real death is, then, the death of conceptual living. Life is presence, always in the here and now, the moment itself. In the absence of the "person" there is simply living, non-volitional acting. Non-volitional living is living in happiness. It is only in non-intentional living that there is acceptance, and it is only in accepting, in welcoming, that all the elements of a situation can be clearly seen. When we live in accepting, illness has no hold, no substance, and we have the greatest possibility of getting better.

All the changes the body undergoes are hypothetical and transitional, but there is nothing hypothetical about what we really are—consciousness. It is prior to body. It is prior to thought. It is between two concepts or percepts. It is silent awareness, nameless, without attribute. It is the total giving up of all qualifications, freedom from all identifications. It is the eternal presence we take for absence. When one lives knowingly in this presence, there is no death.

Then when you see the moment to go has come, and you have learned how, I would even say learned the technique of giving up, it is extremely beautiful. Dying then is thanking, a thanking for having had the opportunity to know life, to be the knowing, to be thanking itself. In the great forgetting of all that we are not, dying is the total release into openness, openness to the light.

The Grief of the Dead
Rumi

The Prince of mankind (Mohammed) said truly that no one
  who has passed away from this world
Feels sorrow and regret for having died; nay, but he feels a
  hundred regrets for having missed the opportunity,
Saying to himself, "Why did I not make death my object—
  death which is the store-house of all fortunes and riches,
And why, through seeing double, did I fasten my life-long gaze
  upon those phantoms that vanished at the fated hour?"
The grief of the dead is not on account of death; it is because
  they dwelt on the phenomenal forms of existence
And never perceived that all this foam is moved and fed by the
  Sea.
When the Sea has cast the foam-flakes on the shore, go to the
  graveyard and behold them!
Say to them, "Where is your swirling onrush now?" and hear
  them answer mutely, "Ask this question of the Sea, not of
  us."
How should the foam fly without the wave? How should the
  dust rise to the zenith without the wind?
Since you have seen the dust, see the Wind; since you
  have seen the foam, see the Ocean of Creative Energy.
Come, see it, for insight is the only thing in you that avails: the
  rest of you is a piece of fat and flesh, a woof and warp (of
  bones and sinews).
Dissolve your whole body into Vision: become seeing, seeing,
  seeing!
One sight discerns but a yard or two of the road; another
  surveys the temporal and spiritual worlds and beholds the
  Face of their King.

Translated by R.A. Nicholson

On Silence

Jean Klein: Silence is our real nature. What we are fundamentally is only silence. Silence is free from beginning and end. It was before the beginning of all things. It is causeless. Its greatness lies in the fact that it simply is.

In silence all objects have their home ground. It is the light that gives objects their shape and form. All movement, all activity is harmonized by silence.

Silence has no opposite in noise. It is beyond positive and negative. Silence dissolves all objects. It is not related to any counterpart which belongs to the mind. Silence has nothing to do with mind. It cannot be defined but it can be felt directly because it is our nearness. Silence is freedom without restriction or centre. It is our wholeness, neither inside nor outside the body. Silence is joyful, not pleasurable. It is not psychological. It is feeling without a feeler. Silence needs no intermediary.

Silence is holy. It is healing. There is no fear in silence. Silence is autonomous like love and beauty. It is untouched by time. Silence is meditation, free from any intention, free from anyone who meditates. Silence is the absence of oneself. Or rather, silence is the absence of absence.

Sound which comes from silence is music. All activity is creative when it comes from silence. It is constantly a new beginning. Silence precedes speech and poetry and music and all art. Silence is the home ground of all creative activity. What is truly creative is the word, is Truth. Silence is the word. Silence is Truth.

The one established in silence lives in constant offering, in prayer without asking, in thankfulness, in continual love.

Sermon,
"Blessed are the Poor"

(Beati Pauperes Spiritu, Quoniam
Ipsorum est Regnum Caelorum, Matt. 5:3)

Meister Eckhart

Blessedness opened its mouth of wisdom and spoke: "Blessed are the poor in spirit, for theirs is the kingdom of heaven."

All angels and all saints and all that were ever born must be silent when the wisdom of the Father speaks, for all the wisdom of the angels and of all creatures is pure foolishness before the groundless wisdom of God. And this wisdom has said that the poor are blessed.

Now there are two kinds of poverty: an external poverty, which is good and is to be much praised in a man who willingly accomplishes it through the love of our Lord, Jesus Christ, because he was himself poor on earth. Of this poverty I do not want to speak any further. Yet, there is still another kind of poverty, an inner poverty by which our Lord's word is to be understood when he says: "Blessed are the poor in spirit."

Now I beseech you to be just so poor, so as to understand this speech. For I say to you by the eternal truth: So long as you do not equal this truth of which we now want to speak, you cannot understand me.

Various people have asked me what poverty is in itself and what a poor man is. That is what we want to answer.

Bishop Albrecht says that a poor man is he who finds no satisfaction in any of the things that God ever created—and that is well said. But we say it better still and take poverty in a yet higher understanding: a poor man is he who wills nothing, knows nothing and has nothing. Of these three points we are going to speak, and I beseech you for the love of God that you understand this truth if you can. But should you not understand it, do not worry yourselves because of it, for the truth I want to speak of is of such a kind that only a few good people will understand it.

First we say that he is a poor man who wills nothing. What this means many people do not correctly understand. It is those people who in penitential exercise and external practice, of which they make a great deal, hold fast to their selfish I. The Lord have pity upon such people who know so little of the divine truth. Such people are called holy on account of their external appearance, but internally they are asses, for they do not grasp the actual meaning of divine truth. Indeed, these individuals, too, say that he is a poor man who wills nothing. However, they fancy this to mean that one should never fulfill one's own will in any way, but rather strive to fulfill the ever beloved will of God. These people are right in their way, for they mean well and for that let us commend them. May God in his mercy grant them entry into heaven. But in all divine truth I say that these people are not poor people nor do they resemble poor people. They are highly considered only in the eyes of those who know no better. I, however, say that they are asses, understanding nothing of divine truth. Because of their good intention may they receive the kingdom of heaven. But of that poverty of which we now want to speak, they know nothing.

If someone asks me now what a poor man is who wills nothing, I answer and say: So long as a man has this particular wish to fulfil the ever beloved will of God—if that is still a matter of his will, then this man does not yet possess the poverty of which we want to speak. Indeed, this man then still has a will with which he wants to satisfy God's will, and that is not the right poverty. For a human being to possess true poverty he must be bereft of his created will as he was when he was not yet. Thus I say to you in the name of divine truth: as long as you have the will to fulfil God's will, and as long as you have the desire for eternity and God, you are not poor; for he alone is a poor man who wills nothing and desires nothing.

When I still stood in my first cause, I had no God, I was cause of myself. There I willed nothing and desired nothing, for I was a pure being and a knower of myself in full enjoyment of the truth. There I willed myself and willed nothing else. What I willed, I was, and what I was, that I willed.

There I stood, clear of God and of all things. But when by free will I went out and received my created being, then I had a God. Indeed, before there were creatures, God was not yet God, but he was what he was. But when creatures came to be and received their created being, then God was no longer God in himself, rather he was God in the creatures. Now we say that God, so far as he is God, is not a perfect goal for creatures. Indeed, even the lowliest creature possesses that high a rank within God. And were it that a fly possessed a reason and could intelligently seek the eternal abyss of divine being out of which it has come, then we would say that God, with all he is as God, would still be incapable of fulfilling and satisfying this fly. Therefore we beg God to rid us of God so that we may grasp and eternally enjoy the truth where the highest angel and the fly and the mind are equal. There I stood and willed what I was, and was what I willed. So then we say: If man is to be poor in will, he must will and desire as little as he willed and desired when he was not yet. And in this way a man is poor who wills nothing.

Furthermore, a poor man is one who knows nothing. We have said on occasion that man's life should be such that he lives neither for himself, nor for the truth, nor for God. This time, however, we say it differently. We want to go further and say: whoever is to be so poor (as I am describing it) must live so that he not even know himself to live, neither for himself, nor for truth, nor for God. He must be bereft of all knowledge to the point of neither knowing nor recognizing nor perceiving that God lives in him; even more: he should be devoid of all knowledge that lives in him. For, when man still stood in God's eternal being, nothing else lived in him (than that being). All that was alive, there, was he (that man) himself. Hence we say that man should be so devoid of his own knowledge as he was when he was not yet. He should let God accomplish whatever God wills, and man should stand void.

All that ever came out of God is set to unmixed activity. The activity proper to man, now, is to love and to know. It is a point of controversy, though, in which of these happiness consists primarily. Some masters have said that it lies in knowing, some say it lies in loving, still others say that it lies in knowing and in loving; these are closer to the mark. We say, however, that it lies neither in knowing nor in loving. Rather, there is a oneness in the mind whence flow knowing and loving. It itself does not know and love, as do the forces of the mind. Whoever comes to know this (oneness) knows what happiness consists in. This (oneness) has neither before nor after, and it is in want of nothing additional, for it can neither gain nor lose. That is also why it is deprived of understanding that God is acting within it. Even more: it is itself that identical self which is its own fruition, quite as God. Thus we say that man shall keep himself rid and void so that he neither understand nor know that God works in him. Only so can man possess poverty. The masters say that God is a being, an intelligent being, and that he knows all things. We say, however: God is neither being nor intelligent nor does he know this or that. Thus God is free of all things, and therefore he is all things. Whoever is to be poor in spirit, then, must be poor of all his own understanding so that he understand nothing either of God or of creatures or of himself. That is why it is necessary for man to desire that he become unable to understand or know anything at all of the works of God. That is the way to be poor of one's own understanding.

Thirdly, he is a poor man who has nothing. Many people have said that this is perfection that man possess none of the material things of the earth. And, indeed, that is certainly true in one sense: when one holds to it with resolve. But this is not the sense that I mean.

I have said before that he is poor who does not even will to fulfil God's will, that is, who lives in such a way that he is devoid both of his own will and of God's will, quite as he was when he was not yet. Of this poverty we say that it is the highest poverty. Secondly, we have said he is a poor man who himself understands nothing of God's activity in him. Whoever stands as devoid of understanding and knowing as God stands void of all things, then that is the purest poverty. Thirdly, the poverty of which we are now going to speak is the strictest: that man have nothing

Now pay close and serious attention. I have often said, and great masters say so too: Man must be so clear of all things and all works, be they inward or outward, that he can become a proper abode for God, wherein God may operate. But this time we say it differently. If man comes to actually keep himself free of all creatures, of God and of himself, but if it is still the case that God can find in him a site for acting, then we say: So long as that is so, that man is not poor in the strictest poverty. For in his doings God does not strive for a site that man leave him to work in. Rather, only that is poverty of spirit when one keeps oneself so clear of God and of all one's works that if God wants to act in the mind, he (God) is himself the place wherein he wants to act—and this he likes to do. For if God finds man so poor, God operates his own work and man suffers God in him, and God is himself the site of his operation, since God is an agent who acts within himself. Henceforth, in this poverty, man recovers the eternal being that he was, now is and will eternally remain.

There is a saying of Saint Paul which reads: "But by the grace of God I am what I am" (I Cor. 15:10). My own saying, on the contrary, seems to hold itself above grace and above being and above knowing and above willing and above desiring—how then can Saint Paul's word be true? To this one must answer that Saint Paul's words are true. God's grace was necessarily in him: for the grace of God effected in him the completion of accidental into essential being. When grace finished and had completed its work, Paul remained what he was (that is, what he had been from eternity).

Thus we say that man must be so poor that he is not and has no place wherein God could act. Where man still preserves some place in himself, he preserves distinction. This is why I pray God to rid me of God, for my essential being is above God insofar as we comprehend God as the principle of creatures. Indeed, in God's own being, where God is raised above all being and all distinctions, I was myself, I willed myself, and I knew myself to create this man (that I am). Therefore, I am cause of myself according to my being which is eternal, but not according to my becoming which is temporal. Therefore also I am unborn, and according to my unborn being I can never die. According to my unborn being I have always been, I am now, and shall eternally remain. What I am by my (temporal) birth is to die and be annihilated, for it is mortal; therefore with time it must pass away. In my (eternal) birth all things were born, and I was cause of myself as well as of all things. If I had willed it, neither I nor any things would be. And if I myself were not, God would not be either: that God is God, of this I am a cause. If I were not, God would not be God. There is, however, no need to understand this.

A great master says that his breakthrough is nobler than his emanation, and this is true. When I emanated from God, all things spoke: God is; but this cannot make me happy, for it makes me understand that I am a creature. In the breakthrough, on the other hand, where I stand devoid of my own will and of the will of God and of all his works and of God himself, there I am above all created kind and am neither God nor creature. Rather, I am what I was and what I shall remain now and forever. Then I receive an impulse which shall bring me above all the angels. In this impulse I receive wealth so vast that God cannot be enough for me in all that makes him God, and with all this divine works. For in this breakthrough it is bestowed upon me that I and God are one. There I am what I was, and I neither diminish nor grow, for there I am an immovable cause that moves all things. Now God no longer finds a place in man, for man gains with this poverty what he has been eternally and evermore will remain. Now God is one with the spirit, and that is the strictest poverty one can find.

Those who cannot understand this speech should not trouble their hearts about it. For, as long as man does not equal this truth, he will not understand this speech. For this is unhidden truth that has come immediately from the heart of God.

That we may so live as to experience it eternally, so help us God. Amen.

Excerpt from *Four Quartets*
T.S. Eliot

I said to my soul, be still, and wait without hope
For hope would be hope for the wrong thing;
  wait without love
For love would be love of the wrong thing; there is yet faith
But the faith and love and the hope are all in the waiting.
Wait without thought, for you are not ready for thought:
So the darkness shall be the light, and the stillness the dancing.
Whisper of running streams, and winter lightning.
The wild thyme unseen and the wild strawberry,
The laughter in the garden, echoed ecstasy
Not lost, but requiring, pointing to the agony
Of death and birth

  You say I am repeating
Something I have said before. I shall say it again.
Shall I say it again? In order to arrive there,
To arrive where you are, to get from where you are not,
  You must go by a way wherein there is no ecstasy.
In order to arrive at what you do not know
  You must go by a way which is the way of ignorance.
In order to possess what you do not possess
  You must go by the way of dispossession.
In order to arrive at what you are not
  You must go through the way in which you are not.
And what you do not know is the only thing you know
And what you own is what you do not own
And where you are is where you are not.

Dialogue in New York:

April 27 1990

Jean Klein: When we grow to a certain state of maturity, naturally we are open to another state of inquiry. Our coming here is to inquire and explore together what life is and what are its expressions, or, more precisely, "Who am I?" To explore really, you must be free from the explorer, free from the inquirer, because as long as there is an explorer there is anticipation and the explorer lives in end-gaining. So one must be acquainted with a way of listening free from any directions—simply listening. It is a state of inquiring where you are completely open, totally free from anticipation. Then the inquiring refers to itself. Real inquiring can never be an object.

When you ask yourself, "Who am I?" you cannot have an answer, because any answer can only refer to the already known. So you live in "I don't know," free from knowledge. You live for the time being in not-knowing. This not-knowing has its own taste, its own flavour; the mind is not furnished; you feel yourself completely in space. You are really free when you live in questioning, in the "I don't know."

Then you will discover that the questioning is the answer. You will discover that the questioning, the asking, cannot be localized—it is not an object, you cannot think it, objectify it. In that moment the questioning refers to itself. You will find yourself in this stillness, this not-knowing, where there is a total absence of yourself. In this total absence of yourself there is presence. It is a presence beyond space and time. It is presence in presence and absence. It is not in subject-object relationship.

The mind functions in subject-object relationship, but when you once find a moment when you are in your absence, you will find yourself in your totality, in your globality. You are no longer living as a fraction. As long as you take yourself for a person and are identified with your personality, you live as a fraction. When you identify yourself with your personality, it is no longer a function. It cannot function efficiently. A real personality is free from the personality, so in your absence of the idea to be somebody you live really in spontaneity, in globality, in fullness. But we are so accustomed to living in subject-object relationship...

We should first discover ourself in the asking, in living with the question. We must let the question live its own freedom and not manipulate it with the already known. In the end you will see that the answer is in the question. Any other answer is an object, but what you are fundamentally can never be an object. What you are is the ultimate subject, the subject of all objects. The objects in your life constantly change, but the subject never changes. It is the eternal background which you must live knowingly.

You certainly have something to say. Our dialogue is open.

Q. When I ask myself the question "Who am I?" there are many answers and it takes years to get through all those answers. I understand the "I don't know" in theory, but it is very difficult in practice.

JK. But when you say many questions and answers appear, it is memory, the already known.

Q. Does that make it not true?

JK. All that comes up is an object. But there will be a moment when there is a stopping, not a stop of anticipation where you begin again to think, but where the question refers to itself and does not look beyond itself for an answer. The question then refers to your absence as a personality, a somebody. When you wake up in the not-knowing you will face all your life, all your situations from this not-knowing, this freedom in globality. Then you will live with facts and face only facts, and only then can there be spontaneous action. Otherwise you live only in reaction, in memory, because the personality is memory.

Q. Why ask the question "Who am I?" in the first place?

JK. Before you ask the question, you are free from the answer. But when you ask the question you are also free from the answer, are you not? You live in the question.

Q. No.

JK. Then where are you living?

Q. In the moment.

JK. When you live in the now, the eternal moment, then you cannot ask the question. In the now there is no question, there is only the living answer.

Q. But is it worth asking the question?

JK. You don't need to ask the question when you are living in the answer. But live really knowingly in the answer. One day you will see that the answer is in the asking. All other answers belong to memory.

Q. How can I observe myself in that moment in order to know the moment?

JK. There is not an observer. In this moment you don't live in the subject-object relationship of a knower and something known. You are one, one with the moment. You live your totality.

When you observe beauty you are, in that moment, completely one with the beauty. Only later do you say, "I was very moved seeing the beauty." Then you make a state of it. But in the moment you live in the beauty you are one with it.

Q. Is it possible to know that you lived it when you are no longer there?

JK. You know it without knowing it. You know it, not as you see this flower, but you know it. It is your nearest.

Q. Is there not a danger that people may think they are already realized and that this pride may lead to a lack of spiritual evolution?

JK. But when one comes to deep relaxation one does not say, "I am relaxed." One simply is relaxed. One is too relaxed to say, "I am relaxed"!

Q. Then I am talking about pseudo-enlightened people and there are more of those than the really enlightened.

JK. I think that here we are all earnest people and someone earnest would not think, "I am this or that." All the rest are perceptions where there is a perceiver and something perceived.

Q. How can I attain enlightenment?

JK. You *are* the oneness.

Q. I am?

JK. Yes! But as soon as you think, "I am Joseph Smith," you are no longer in the oneness.

Q. But I do not know that I am the oneness.

JK. You can never know it as you know things. There is not a knower to know it. If there were it would not be oneness.

Q. Thank you.

JK. There's nobody to thank. (*laughter*)

Q. In the moment, is "he" and "I" the same energy?

JK. In the moment of action there is only action, there is not an actor; there is only doing, not a doer. That you are the doer comes only afterwards to your mind.

Q. In the question, "Who am I?" is the "who" and the "I" one and the same?

JK. Put away the "who." Say only "I". You will see when you say "I" that you cannot think it, you cannot represent or formulate it. This pronoun is the only word you cannot think, so it brings you immediately back to your verticality.

Q. Then in just "I" there's no question.

JK. Yes.

Q. Please elaborate on what you said earlier: that the object changes, but the subject never changes.

JK. The subject is the eternal subject. It was before your father gave semen to your mother. It was before. It will be forever.

Q. I was wondering what your background and training are to come to these teachings.

JK. When we speak of a background I would say you must free yourself from the teaching, because there is nothing to teach. What you are fundamentally, you are it; it is your nearest, it is before the idea, the thought, of being somebody appears. So what is important is that you must accept that what you are looking for, you already are. There is nothing to become, nothing to achieve, nothing to gain or take. All this takes you away from what you are.

Q. In my opinion, since we are not yet consciously realized, some teaching helps.

JK. The moment you find the opportunity in your life to ask the question "Who am I?" you will take note that all you can find is memory—you already know it. All that you know is an experience, a state, but what you are can never be known or experienced as an object or a state. When this really hits you, you must take note how it reacts on you. That is very important, not just seeing it, but feeling how the seeing acts on you. Then there is a stop and you are freed from all striving, all end-gaining. This moment is not a moment according to your watch; it is timeless. You can never go to it, it comes to you, it is looking for you. So you must come to the moment of allowing it, of permitting it to come to you.

Q. But when you say, "come to you," who is the you that it comes to?

JK. It's a way of speaking. One could say He is looking for Himself.

Q. Can an awareness of relativity co-exist with oneness?

JK. Of course. You know moments when awareness refers to an object, when you are aware of something. But there are also moments in daily life when there is no reference to anything. Then there is "I am." But in this "I am" there is not a knower; it is knowing. When you walk in the forest in the morning and see the rising sun, is there a knower at this moment? You can make an object of it, but there are moments when there is simply walking, simply admiring.

Q. Where does action or doing emanate from?

JK. It is a robbery for the personality, the "me" to appropriate an action to itself, because in the moment of acting there is no doer. A doer is a concept. It doesn't exist. When you see things from your globality, your totality, there is no choice, there is no selection. You completely face facts. Real action comes from the situation, and every situation has its own solution. But the action that comes from the facts of the situation does not go through the choosing, selecting mind. It is direct, instantaneous. You know perfectly well these spontaneous moments in daily life, and you know also when the "I", the "me," puts them in question, which you should never do.

Q. If there is only action, what about right and wrong?

JK. The problem of right and wrong has no more role to play. When there is spontaneous action there is no question of right or wrong. You do it spontaneously.

Q. But you do distinguish between spontaneous and impulsive action, don't you?

JK. Yes. Impulses are reactions, habits, based on the person, on memory and conditioning.

Q. Many of us are conditioned by these impulses, and there are techniques for de-conditioning ourselves…

JK. The first thing is to be more and more acquainted with your body. Inquire what happens in your body. For some moments in your life let the body become an object of your earnest observation. You must get to know your mechanism so that you are not bound to it. The body is mainly feeling. I would say it is only feeling sensation. So as soon as you inquire into this sensation you will discover reactions, defences, fear, anxiety, aggression, all on the level of the body, in the muscles and bones and tissue. Become acquainted with all this. Don't escape it, don't try to change it, only take deep note of it. This is loving it. When you take deep note of it you will no longer be an accomplice to it, and there will be a liberation of the fixed energy. The energy will integrate. This is the first thing, if we can speak of doing something.

Q. You said that right acting comes from seeing only the facts of the situation. Does this mean there is no creating situations?

JK. Exactly.

Q. So then one just sits and waits for situations?

JK. Yes.

Q. So...

JK. Things may appear to your imagination. You may become creative, but you are waiting.

Q. So I will have no role to play in creating situations? But that conjures up an image of total passivity.

JK. Oh, no. You are passive-active. Passive in that you don't interfere as a "me", an "I". But you are eminently creative and active in looking at it free from memory. It is memory which hinders you from being creative. Memory is the basket in which we have put things for thousands and thousands of years.

Q. But will I not be the author of creating situations?

JK. No, you are a channel, but not an author. It is the divine play which plays through you.

Q. But what about all the situations I want to create?

JK. It is only the "me," the personality, who wants to create those situations, for its security. When you are on stage as an actor you must be free from being an actor in order to be creative. You cannot create creativity. Creativity is a gift which comes to you when you are free from yourself, free from the idea of being an independent entity.

Q. This active-passivity is difficult to maintain when there are people who depend upon you and act towards you as if you are supposed to be making decisions for them. This pulls me back into the personality, and that makes me very frustrated.

JK. The teacher must be free from his teaching. When the teacher is free from the teaching he or she is no longer a teacher and no longer projects anything onto the disciple. When there is no longer a disciple who is qualified as "ignorant" and a teacher who has a "teaching", then there is a coming together. There is togetherness. What is important is that the teacher, if we can still call him or her a teacher, helps the disciple be free from being a disciple, be free from so-called unknowing. When you have to do with someone who teaches you, it is important that already at the beginning you experience a certain freedom from yourself. Otherwise you must put the teaching in question. What brings you to a teacher is that you feel yourself bound, you feel yourself in bondage. And the only important thing is that the teacher frees you from bondage. Otherwise it's not a teacher.

Q. Would you say something about the role of meditation in being in the present moment?

JK. The word meditation is very often taken in many directions. In meditation there is not a meditator and nothing to meditate on. There is only meditation. When there is something to meditate on, this object of meditation belongs to the mind. When you see this, that you always come back to what you know already, then there is a disappearing of a meditator and an object of meditation, and what is left is a current of love.

Meditation is what is behind all activities. You will first discover it in the silence between two thoughts or two perceptions. You will discover it before going to sleep and before the body wakes up. These are moments of oneness. But this oneness has nothing to do with the presence or absence of activity. It is here, from moment to moment. It is beyond the three states of waking, dreaming and sleeping. It is. These three states are superimpositions on this current of being which we all have in common. There is nothing special in it.

If you do not approach meditation in this way you create a new state. You make yourself silent and try perhaps to stop thoughts. You fix yourself inevitably somewhere, usually in the head, but that is not meditation. If you really want to sit in a meditation laboratory I would say first let your body become an object of observation. Then you will discover all that happens in your body—tensions, resistance and so on. There will come a moment when you will find in your body a current of energy, a kind of being silent everywhere, no more contours or borders, only emptiness. But you can only come to this emptiness when there is no more intention. In this observation there must not be intention, and then you will see that what remains as an object-body dissolves in your non-intention and there is only beingness. That is meditation.

Q. I meditate regularly and it seems to have brought me a sense of presence which is much stronger than all the data that used to go on. My question is that I am attached to this presence, this sense of expansion and quiet and clarity. It seems that I am on a progressive path and I'm drawn to self-inquiry, but I don't want to give up those feelings of expansion and pleasure.

JK. Be more acquainted with observation. You will see that in daily life you don't observe. Take note that you don't observe. Don't try to observe because observing is your natural state. Observation is a certain function of your brain, but it will change quality and become alertness, awareness, consciousness. It expands. So the only way is to become more this observing in daily life, an observing which comes to no conclusions. Try for some time to see things without conclusion. What happens when you see things without conclusion? You are completely open.

Q. Without likes or dislikes?

JK. Yes.

Q. In the presence I was talking about, likes and dislikes did not matter...

JK. Apparently I have not answered your question. But when you look more deeply, it is the answer. Be completely open without conclusion. But feel yourself in this non-conclusion. Don't emphasize the object, but emphasize the inner state of non-conclusion. There must be no training. In training you are fixed in a subject-object relationship. When you listen to your surroundings without any conclusion you will see that you find yourself in a non-state where you will not go in and out. Your way of doing meditation can bring you to understand what it is not. You can never understand what it is, only what it is not.

Q. Can we speak about the process of art? I am an artist.

JK. What is the inner need to produce art? You must ask yourself this question. When you go deeply you will see it is a form of offering. There is nobody to offer and nobody to offer to, there is only offering. And when you look deeper still, you will see it is a thanking, a thanking for being allowed to be.

Q. How is that different from creating circumstances, as I was asking you earlier?

JK. Question your surroundings without concluding. In the state of non-conclusion you become intelligent and creative because there is no more memory. Free from psychological memory you are open to universal or cosmic memory, and then creativity comes to you. But we must remain in a state of inquiring, because in inquiring there is no room for a person. It is very important that we come to the point where Mr. Smith doesn't exist. Mr. Smith is a concept, hearsay; it comes from society, education, experiences and so on. There will be a moment when you will see that you have lived so long with Mr. Smith, and when you awaken to this fact he will go away forever. I would say, you will no longer have even the reflex to take yourself for Mr. Smith.

Q. So if Mr. Smith writes a play and struggles to write it and along the way he becomes realized, will he then lose interest in writing the play?

JK. Creativity comes when there is no Mr. Smith. It comes from inquiry. I will not say there is no use for the faculty of memory, but there is no longer psychological memory. You have an insight and it must then be realized in space and time. This means you need a certain knowledge, how to mix colours or how to work with proportion and so on. This realization calls for memory. But the first insight comes without memory, often while waking up in the morning when you say: "That's it!"

Q. I want to ask you about social action. If I have an idea that something needs changing, this idea comes from the person. I can't fit this in with the freedom from the person you are talking about.

JK. You must really live with your creation. Don't be in a hurry to finish, to conclude. When you see the work of great painters—I am thinking of Braque—when one went to Braque's studio all his paintings which were half-finished were already hanging on the wall. He was living with them, just looking, and perhaps he saw them differently a month later. So it is important to live with the creation, especially on the level of what we call finishing a work, a poem. It is the "I" which pushes you to finish, because the "I' finds temporary security in conclusions. So don't let yourself be pushed!

Q. Is there any value in following an archetypal role, like the warrior, for example?

JK. You must be sure it is the archetype, the real archetype. You can only live it when there is a total absence of yourself, an absence of the idea to be somebody. It is free from all representation; otherwise it is not the archetype.

Q, What if a man says, "I am a provider. I am going to take care of my family." Is he acting in presence?

JK. The presence of which we are speaking is beyond past, present and future. You can never think of this presence, because the moment you think it, it is already the past.

I propose a few minutes break...

JK. It must be clear for you that the answer is before the question. You could never formulate the question if there was not the forefeeling of the answer. So, in reality, the question is the answer. When there is a question in daily life, live with the question without trying to manipulate it with the already known. Be free from the known, live with the question in openness. Then you will feel space in your living. What you need is space, outside and inside, because, in the end, it is this space which is neither inside nor outside which is the answer.

You will never find an answer to the question "Who am I?" You can only be the answer. And being the answer is not in duality. There is not an observer and something observed. There is no subject nor object. You may say that you don't know moments free from subject-object relationship, but that is not true. For example, when you are in wonder or in astonishment, there is no one who admires or is astonished in that moment. There is only astonishment. When you really say, "I don't know," and are free from any eventual knowing, there is a giving up of all the so-called known. In this state of not-knowing there is no thinking, no feeling, no representation, but you are completely attuned to this not-knowing.

Real understanding is when you see that you can never perceive yourself, because you are the perceiving. It is a global feeling. So you can never find yourself through techniques or systems or therapy. Because what you are looking for, you already are. When you really come to the understanding that you are not body, senses and mind, and that these have no reality in themselves, that they need consciousness to be known, then there is a natural giving up and you will find yourself attuned to stillness, to silence. Silence is the background of all knowledge. Speaking again about art, all real art points to the silence. Art becomes sacred when it points to silence—many Chinese paintings, beautiful architecture, certain music, point to silence.

Q. What is the difference, from the psychological point of view, between the merging together of two personalities—what psychology calls symbiosis—and oneness, as you talk about it?

JK. As long as there are two people, there is no togetherness. Generally, relationship is from object to object, personality to personality, and when you see really the nature of the person-ality, you will see it is only looking for security and approval, to be loved and so on. The personality is a very important tool in daily life, but it has nothing to do with my primal being. When this distinction is clear in you, you will feel free from the personality, the "I-image," and there is a natural giving up. Then you will live in love. When you live in love you will see only love. Then there cannot be two people, only one. There is really togetherness; otherwise there is only looking for security and approval. In the absence of yourself there is humility. Otherwise, it is only demanding, asking for something. When you live knowingly in your background there is nothing to demand. There is completeness, fullness, giving. But in our society, relation is only from object to object.

Q. Is there a distinction between life and death?

JK. There is no one who lives and no one who dies. If you consider yourself to be born, it is only to have the opportunity for the real birth, to be born in your real nature. The physical birth is more or less an accident, an accident between two people.

Q. There are some spiritual teachers, especially in the West, who have taught that there is an individuality, a uniqueness in us that has to be fulfilled. I'm thinking especially of Swedenborg and Steiner. Can you comment?

JK. But teachers who emphasize the personality...

Q. It's not the personality, but rather a higher ego.

JK. It's still an ego, but just a better ego than another. Of course, you are unique on the phenomenal level of multiplicity. But in our essential nature, our "I am," we are one. What is important is not to fulfil the multiplicity in itself, but the oneness.

Q. You look as if you are in a very good mood. Why are you so happy?

JK. Because it is my real nature and yours, too. Why do you think you are unhappy?

Q. Because a lot of the time I feel unhappy.

JK. Think that you are happy.

Q. Is it that simple?

JK. Yes. Think that you are happy!

Q. Earlier you said that no system or technique or psychology can help you discover yourself. So often teachers of the direct path say that, yet they themselves have many different teachers and experiences before they discover the direct path; then they disavow their experiences.

JK. Dear friend, the progressive way is in the mind. The mind functions in subject-object relationship. When you go the progressive way you reinforce the subject-object habit, and when you come to the last object—and there is always a last object—then you are stuck, stuck in the subject-object relationship. This is a terrible state to be in. It calls for the most powerful guru to bring you to freedom from the subject-object relationship at this point. On the progressive path you live in states, beautiful states to be sure, but still states. Then when you have a problem with your girlfriend or paying the rent, where is your beautiful state? What you are fundamentally is beyond any states. The mind is a useful tool, but you are not the mind. The mind functions in positive-negative, complementarity. It is split.

Q. Although you don't like to give techniques because people become fixed on the technique, I would ask you: What are the techniques that you would recommend?

JK. The only technique, if we can call it that, is to know what you are not. And to know what you are not, you must know what it is that you are not. How can you say, "I am not my body, senses, and mind," if you don't know what your body is? So explore your body. Only when you have explored the body can you say, "I am not the body." So the first thing is to be free from what you are not. It is inquiring, it is listening, it is looking. Listen without a listener, look without a looker. When there is looking without a looker, all that is looked at comes back to you, to your looking. And looking or listening is not an object.

Q. All that belongs to the body draws us to it. How can one be free from the physical side of being?

JK. There's a switch-over, so that you no longer live in the body, but the body lives in you. It is very important that you see that the perceived is in you, but you are not in the body. Otherwise, how can you speak of the body? You must be out of the process; otherwise, there is no knowing possible. The ultimate subject is out of the process. It is looking, listening without conclusion. Be the ultimate subject. When you are without conclusion you no longer emphasize the object, but the non-conclusion. What does it mean to emphasize the non-conclusion? It means you are in openness. When there's really openness there will be a day when you are open to the openness.

What is important is that the understanding is transposed into daily life. Otherwise, the understanding has no meaning and remains a collection of objects you look at on Sunday morning. You must be able to transpose the understanding.

Q. What do you mean by transpose?

JK. That your looking and listening is on every level of daily life and is free from anticipation, comparison, judgment, interpretation and so on. See that you don't act according to the understanding and that you cannot try to act according to the understanding because there is no observer in it. If there were an observer it would not be globality. So there is only observing. Observing is not a concept; it is awareness, consciousness. A listener, an observer is a concept. In listening itself there is no place for a concept. Be very clear about this; otherwise you are in confusion. Don't create an observer and somebody who comes to conclusions.

Q. What does one do when one finds oneself in anger, for example?

JK. You are the knower of the anger; otherwise you could not speak of anger. Anger is not the word "anger." "Anger" is a concept. Real anger is a perception, a sensation in the body, somewhere in your chest, shoulders, abdominal region, lumbar region, somewhere. This state of resistance you call anger. So what is important is to free yourself from the concept anger and face the perception creatively. Be aware in which part of the body it is localized, then give me news. When you observe it you are no longer an accomplice with it.

Q. And observing has its own action?

JK. Absolutely. It is the only transformer, the *only* transformer. Thank you.

Your Question

Q. I agree with every word you utter and my whole being seems to absorb it with great eagerness. Why, then, the resistance? Why do I find myself battling with an ego I don't have any use for, and doing things I despise and letting words come out of me that I feel are not mine? Only at intervals am I wholly one and stateless. I try to be "beyond" emotion but am dismally vulnerable.

Jean Klein: You must live with the truth until you are completely impregnated by it. You have had a glimpse of understanding, the understanding that you are not the body-mind. Follow this glimpse as you would follow a shadow to find its substance.

This glimpse is a feeling, a feeling of freedom. It is like when you stand on a cliff and look at a very wide horizon. You feel yourself expanded in the space. Let yourself be taken by this feeling of freedom. Don't let it remain an idea, but feel how it actually acts in your body. See how it acts on you inside. It is only when you feel how it acts in you that there can be an impact, otherwise it remains in the intellect and you will lose it.

Real understanding is in not-knowing. All knowing dissolves in not-knowing, and it is in this not-knowing state that there is transformation. The mind can never change what is not in the field of the mental. When you see this, you are out of the cage of the mind, and all that belongs to the mind dissolves in not-knowing, in no mind. In your not-knowing there is still some knowing hiding in your pockets and behind your knees. Let go of all desire to know. But keep your terrible eagerness.

When you have let go of all residues of the desire to know, you will no longer be directed. This living in the directionless is living in not-knowing. Keep the flame alive, but do not channel it. Let it burn freely. In the non-directed fire all residues will burn. When you are free from direction, you have no reference to anything. You have no desire for anything.

It is important to live this directionlessness, this not-knowing, this waiting without waiting for anything. It acts on your cells, on your psychosomatic body, bringing them to dilation and harmony. All that remains is your directionless awareness. Live in this absolute absence of yourself. It is the threshold. You are in complete openness, open to nothing, free from all ideas, free from all hope. And when you are completely transparent, open, open to openness, you are taken by Truth, by Grace. That is certain.

To Know The Body

Jean Klein: The body is memory. It is not your body which wakes up in the morning but your memory. The body is the past. It is a crystallized pattern of reactions, resistances, fears and so on. For example, when you were a child perhaps you did not follow your lessons in school and, walking home with your school report, you were afraid of your parents' anger or disappointment. After several repetitions this feeling of fear becomes chronic and manifests as a permanent contraction of muscles and joints in your body.

There are hundreds of situations in our life which, repeated a few times, bring us to a chronic state of contraction. This contraction paralyzes the real energy feeling of the body, our tactile sensation, which is our birthright. But, having forgotten what a relaxed, completely expanded, light body feels like, we call the contracted—and often heavy and stiff—matter, our "body." We often don't love this body since it no longer feels lovable, and we abuse it with wrong so-called food, too much alcohol or other drugs. Or we punish it with fierce exercise. But we can never become free of the body until we know it, and we cannot know it by abusing it. We cannot, in other words, change one reaction by another reaction.

How, then, can we come to love our body and so to know it, and, knowing it, know that we are not it?

We must look at our body completely objectively, as we look at a tree or a table or any object which does not have a strong psychological impact on us. We will then feel, without comment, the weight, contraction, agitation, and so on. We accept the facts without psychological: interference.

In accepting the sensation of the body—accepting, not tolerating—the various sensations can come fully into our acceptance, our awareness. You feel the agitation of the body. You are all sensation. There is no psychological commentary. There is not a feeler, nothing felt. There is only feeling. The sensation, the weight, the agitation, etc., then become really articulated.

It is very important that this articulation occur, otherwise all the sensations are lumped together in one mass and remain unconscious, i.e., residues. Once a sensation has fully blossomed in your awareness, you can let it go, and what remains is only the acceptance, the awareness, the light. This lightness, acceptance, is not localized in the head. It is not localized anywhere.

Once the perception has unfolded in awareness, energy is liberated and dissolves in light. This light, energy, is spontaneously felt on all levels of our phenomenal being. We spontaneously become aware of a new body-feeling, a feeling of energy, light, space, emptiness, expansion. This body is the real body, the organic body. This is the body which carries the qualities of its source and is the true expression of its source: light. This body is eminently lovable and can only act in love.

When you have once felt the organic light body, its feeling will return to you often, because it is older than any conditioned body. It is your original body. The cells have an ancient organic memory of their perfect state. So it is important, when you have once felt it, not to return to the old patterns. Sustain it. Remember it in all situations in daily life.

For one who is fully established in truth there is no going back. But to be established means that the insight is fully transposed on all levels of existence. Someone who has not fully explored the transposition on the body-mind level, even though the insight is real, may well be taken again by the body-mind. For the fully established one, the body-mind is truth because it is a perfect expression of truth. Only such a one knows what the "temple of God" means. Take care of your temple!

LISTENING

Volume 4
1991

The Glimpse.. 111
Jean Klein

"Whoso Knoweth Himself " 118
Ibn 'Arabi

Dialogue at the Day of Listening, May 1991......... 130
Jean Klein

Your Question: *How can I resolve my feelings of
conflict about the Persian Gulf War (1990-91)?* 142
Jean Klein

Excerpts from the *Tao Te Ching*.................................. 144

Body Approach: *Using the postures to
dissolve ego* 147
Jean Klein

The Glimpse

Q. You speak very often of an insight or a glimpse. What is the nature of it, and how does it manifest?

Jean Klein: Imagine that you live in a dark room and are more or less accustomed to the dark, then one day you suddenly see a crack through which light comes. This light represents the insight; it is a glimpse of reality in the context of being understanding. It is truth.

In the same way when you understand clearly that an object can only be explained by referring to another object, but that all objects find their meaning in the light of consciousness, you will no longer be bound to the object world. In the moment you see the crack of light, light which comes from beyond the object world, in this moment you are liberated from bondage to objects.

Q. Can we do anything to bring about this insight?

JK. An insight is produced spontaneously by life, or a teacher can bring you to the threshold by informing you of your true state: that you are objectless. Through higher reasoning on the ultimate subject, the teacher brings the mind to its limits. The point where the mind is exhausted and says, "I don't know," is the threshold where the insight occurs.

We must become free from being stuck in ignorance, taking the dark room for granted. The crack of light is always there, it must only be seen.

Q. So the one and only condition for the insight is an exhausted mind?

JK. Yes. When we are free from projecting, constructing situations, strategizing, in short, thinking, then we are in a state of openness. In openness nothing is expected, nothing is lost or gained. In openness we are open to the present. There is no memory in openness, no anticipation. It is a state of waiting without waiting for anything.

The teacher brings you to this waiting for nothing state through reason. He or she informs you of the real state, the facts of life. Life itself can bring you to the state of openness through the unexpected, a crisis of some kind. In this case, as the mind is not informed and therefore not exhausted, very often people live again in the object, make the insight an object, an experience, an accumulated piece of knowledge. It is vital to live in identity, in oneness with the moment where thought dissolves in silence and there's being understanding. What is important is not to fall into the trap of objectifying the insight. We leave it; it never leaves us; it is always.

Q. It seems that it takes an effort not to fall into the trap.

JK. You cannot try to objectify moments of oneness. Take note only that you do objectify. This being aware of it is not effort. It is alertness.

Q. We are so conditioned to function through the ego, the individual entity, how can we begin to function from a non-individual perspective without an insight first?

JK. We must face what is actual from moment to moment, see that we function and face our daily life through striving, selection and anticipation. We should take note that we function from the split or divided mind. In other words, we must be completely aware of it, an awareness free from trying to control and justify. In this simply being aware we are out of the whole process and transformation is free to take place.

From the whole, there is neither positive nor negative existence. It is in the abeyance of both that the truth is discovered. You must begin with what is actually present here and now and the insight will come in your openness to it. It is like the sudden cry of a bird in stillness. You may have been in stillness but not knowingly, but the sudden cry in the stillness makes you aware of the stillness. So be aware of your stillness before and after all mental activity.

Q. Once we have a glimpse of living from the non-individual stance, how can we sustain this new position?

JK. The glimpse brings a very deep impression in you. It leaves a deep echo in you and will find you again. But don't remember it or you will make a mind construct of it. Let it reappear in you as completely objectless and all your surroundings will be touched by it, by freshness, sacredness and holiness.

Q. Our body, that is our sense organs, is conditioned by the idea of a person who is the sole author of his actions. When we have the insight that we are not the author, how exactly is our body affected?

JK. No matter what you may do or not do, it is "I" who will do it or not do it, for there is no "you." Be aware that doership is superimposed on doing. During the doing there is no place for a doer or the concept of a doer. Two thoughts cannot occur simultaneously. To interrupt doing in order to introduce a doer would hinder the doing. Our spontaneous body movement would be interrupted.

When we have the insight that we are not the individual, the body takes itself in charge. It is no longer interrupted in its action.

Q. What exactly is *direct* perception? Is it, for you, the same as pure perception? What is the mechanism in direct perception that is different from simply perception? After explaining what direct perception is, would you tell us why it is so important and how to come to it and then sustain it?

JK. Perception as it is generally understood is a qualified seeing, hearing, and so on. This has no place here. Pure perception is the only kind of perception we are interested in. It is pure because it is free from all conceptualization, thinking. There is no intermediary between subject and object, perceiver and perceived. In the act of perceiving there is not a perceiver and nothing is perceived. There is pure objectless seeing, hearing, touching, smelling, tasting. Every object has the power to bring you back to seeing, to hearing, that is, to awareness, but the object must be free to do that. The heard is its hearing, the seen is its seeing and so on. Direct perception is when you are in identity, in oneness, with your timeless nature.

Q. Using your earlier example of the bird cry in the stillness, could we say that pure perception is the state you are in when you hear the bird, free from all thinking, etc.? And direct perception is when this sound brings you back to your silence?

JK. Exactly.

Q. And being knowingly in the silence is apperception.

JK. Precisely.

Q. You say we must "begin from silence." How can we begin from what we know not? How can a blind man begin from sight?

JK. Just taking note that there is something before thinking and acting take place makes you open to this "something," even though you don't know what it is. You are available to it without qualifying it. In this availability you are taken by stillness.

You may explore what never changes in you. It is a feeling free from all objects, from all thought constructs.

Q. As a blind person must be led to understand objects of sight by reference to the other senses, is there a pedagogical form to help us understand the ultimate through reference to the relative?

JK. There is no reference but there can be analogy. For example, we have moments of our total absence as an "I" when we are in wonderment or astonishment where there is no "me" present, only the feeling. These moments, which we call absence, are analogous to our total presence, because they are free from objects and duality. Analogy is employable on the level of objective phenomena but we can never find an analogy for what is beyond the mind. The less cannot find the more. The unknown something between thoughts is a reference, a pointer.

Q. And so is the space you teach in the bodywork, is it not?

JK. When the body is experienced as space there is no more periphery. We are completely awake in space, completely unfurnished, where even the walls disappear. We are this space. Our real being is space.

Q. The insight that we are not who we think we are brings us to a deep alertness—the threshold of being. But when one does not have this insight and is living the sayings of the guru, or trying to, how can one be alert? To let go of volition and be open to no-thing makes me passive. What do you suggest to those of us who are earnest but have had no real insight? How can we stay out of the garage?

JK. Living with the sayings of the teacher that you are not the person you think you are, frees you from all the stuff that society, education, parents, beliefs, second-hand information have made you. Our wholeness is not a kind of knowledge. All kinds of knowledge are conceptual and in space and time. Consciousness cannot make its own wholeness an object. There is no "thing" here to cognize. Any kind of attempt to understand, comprehend, cognize wholeness is an obstacle and prevents the apperception of what we are.

The seed must be there. The seed is the sayings of the guru which grow in you. The seed appeals to your real nature, wakes in you the desire to be. When you love something you are effortlessly alert; if you do not love the sayings then live in the garage! The seed comes from life or a teacher. It is feeling that makes the seed grow.

Q. "In your absence there is His presence." Is God only present when we are not? In what way present? Because you and certain Buddhists teach that consciousness is anyway always, whether or not we know or are ignorant.

JK. In our total absence as an "I," our total presence appears. This presence is completely objectless. The "I"-concept is merely a deep-rooted reflex. Take note of it in daily life. Be aware of it. This is the only way to ignore it and then forget it.

Consciousness is always, but you are not knowingly consciousness. Without being consciousness knowingly you are a useless being, a parasite on our society! You are not a real human being until you are knowingly consciousness, because your real nature is consciousness, and if you don't know your real nature, you don't know yourself. When you don't know yourself, you are like a particle of dust blown in any direction. You live in objects blindly. To know yourself is the only real energy belonging to life. When this energy is related to objects it is blind.

Q. Where does the desire to be absent come from?

JK. Our original desire is to be free from objects. The desire for a car or a gold watch or to be a successful businessman or for liberation is the same desire. The desire to be successful or to be liberated is exactly the same, the same energy. When desire is related to an object it causes obscurity. So at the moment of desiring the gold watch or success, let go of the object, the watch, car, money, fame, and remain only with the feeling of desire. Live the energy of this desire and you will find yourself in a certain stop. Only in the ignorant one does this create frustration. But in the sincere truth-seeker it brings inquiry. We question the nature of desire and feel the impact of the stopping moment. This stopping is where the energy that was eccentric (towards the object) is dissolved. It is then, in a certain way, available in all directions. Energy is no longer channeled, it is directionless.

A different pedagogy is to take note of the precise moment a desire is attained. In this moment of desirelessness the original object is absent. This desireless state is the goal of all desire. But our conditioning quickly propels us towards a new desire. So don't let this objectless, desireless moment pass you by. Be aware of it and how it is the Desire of all desires.

Desire for an object binds us, limits us. Our profound nature is complete freedom. Freedom can only appear in desirelessness. Welcoming is desireless. In welcoming all that is, we live our freedom, openness, directionlessness, desirelessness.

"Whoso Knoweth Himself..."
from
Treatise on Being
Ibn'Arabi

A Word from Jean Klein…

This text did not emerge from thinking. It was a total experience, it was felt. In Sanskrit one would call it pure sruti. *What is important when reading the text is to be aware of the impact it causes in you. Otherwise it remains intellectual, just words and concepts. You cannot read this text. It reads to you. You must be completely open to it, because its real power and meaning will not appear to your customary understanding and conditioned language. To welcome the impact of this text, its actuality and freshness, one must be free from conditioned representation.*

The sayings in parenthesis after every reference to the Ultimate (whose name be exalted) and the Prophet (upon whom be peace) oblige us to stop and live in silence, in unfurnished silence. We must remain open, abide in waiting, because it takes the human being a certain period of time to have the deep insight that all that is perceived has its only reality in perceiving—the seen is in the seeing—that there are not two. We cannot bring this insight about by intellectual argument because it is more than intellectual understanding. It is a sudden being understanding on every level of our existence. Our stance can only be one of welcoming, availability, a surrender of the thought process, a being open to openness itself because there is only the Ultimate and the Ultimate looks for itself.

So we must keep the feeling that permeates us when reading this text and not try to remember the text but live in the echo it leaves in us. When this feeling remains unconditioned by intellectual representation, it grows in us, in our oneness.

In the name of God, the Merciful, the Compassionate, and Him we ask for aid: Praise be to God before whose oneness there was not a before, unless the Before were He, and after whose singleness there is not an after, except the After be He. He is, and there is with Him no after nor before, nor above nor below, nor far nor near, nor union nor division, nor how nor where nor when, nor times nor moment nor age, nor being nor place. And He is now as He was. He is the One without oneness, and the Single without singleness. He is not composed of name and named, for His name is He and His named is He. So there is no name other than He, nor named. And so He is the Name and the Named. He is the First without firstness, and the Last without lastness. He is the Outward without outwardness, and the Inward without inwardness. I mean that He is the very existence of the First and the very existence of the Last, and the very existence of the Outward and the very existence of the Inward. So that there is no first nor last, nor outward nor inward, except Him, without these becoming Him or His becoming them.

Understand, therefore, in order that thou mayest not fall into the error of the Hululis.[1] He is not in a thing nor a thing in Him, whether entering in or proceeding forth. It is necessary that thou know Him after this fashion, not by knowledge (*'ilm*), nor by intellect, nor understanding, nor by imagination, nor by sense, nor by the outward eye, nor by the inward eye, nor by perception. There does not see Him, save Himself; nor perceive Him, save Himself. By Himself He sees Himself, and by Himself He knows Himself. None sees Him other than He, and none perceives Him other than He. His Veil[2] is His oneness; nothing veils other than He. His veil is the concealment of His existence in His oneness, without any quality. None sees Him other than He—no sent prophet, nor saint made perfect, nor angel brought nigh[3] knows Him. His Prophet is He, and His sending is He, and His word is He. He sent Himself with Himself to Himself. There was no mediator nor any means other than He. There is no difference between the Sender and the thing sent, and the person sent and the person to whom he is sent. The very existence of the prophetic message is His existence. There is no other, and there is no existence to other, than He, nor to its ceasing to be *(fana')*, nor to its name, nor to its named.

And for this the Prophet (upon whom be peace) said: "Whoso knoweth himself knoweth his Lord." And he said (upon him be peace): "I know my Lord by my Lord." The Prophet (upon whom be peace) points out by that, that thou art not thou: thou art He, without thou; not He entering into thee, nor thou entering into Him, nor He proceeding forth from thee, nor thou proceeding forth from Him. And it is not meant by that, that thou art aught that exists or thine attributes aught that exists, but it is meant by it that thou never wast nor wilt be, whether by thyself or through Him or in Him or along with Him. Thou art neither ceasing to be nor still existing. *Thou art He,* without one of these limitations. Then if thou know thine existence thus, then thou knowest God; and if not, then not.

And most of "those who know God" (*al 'urraf*) make a ceasing of existence and the ceasing of that ceasing a condition of attaining the knowledge of God, and that is an error and a clear oversight. For the knowledge of God does not presuppose the ceasing of existence nor the ceasing of that ceasing. For things have no existence, and what does not exist cannot cease to exist. For the ceasing to be implies the positing of existence, and that is polytheism. Then if thou know thyself without existence or ceasing to be, then thou knowest God; and if not, then not.

And in making the knowledge of God conditional upon the ceasing of existence and the ceasing of that ceasing, there is involved an assertion of polytheism. For the Prophet (upon whom be peace) said "Whoso knoweth himself," and did not say, "Whoso maketh himself to cease to be." For the affirmation of the other makes its extinction impossible, and [on the other hand] that of which the affirmation is not allowable its extinction is not allowable. Thine existence is nothing, and nothing cannot be added to something, whether it be perishing or unperishing, or existent or non-existent. The Prophet points to the fact that thou art non-existent now as thou wast non-existent before the

Creation. For now is past eternity and now is future eternity, and now is past time. And God (whose name be exalted) is the existence of past eternity and the existence of future eternity and the existence of past time, yet without past eternity or future eternity or past time ever existing. For if it were not so He would not be by Himself without any partner, and it is indispensable that He should be by Himself without any partner. For His "partner" would be he whose existence was in his own essence, not in the existence of God, and whoever should be in that position would not be dependent upon Him. Then, in that case, there would be a second Lord, which is absurd: God (whose name be exalted) can have no partner nor like nor equal. And whoever looks upon anything as being along with God or apart from God or in God, but subject to Him in respect of His divinity, makes this thing also a partner, (only) subject to God in respect of divinity. And whoever allows that anything exists side by side with God, whether self-subsisting or subsisting in Him or capable of ceasing to exist or of ceasing to cease to exist, he is far from what smells of a breath of the knowledge of the soul. Because whoever allows that he is existent beside God, subsisting in Him, then in Him becoming extinct, and his extinction becoming extinct, then one extinction is linked to another, and that is polytheism upon polytheism. So he is a polytheist, not one who knows God and himself.

Then if one say: How lies the way to the knowledge of the soul and the knowledge of God (whose name be exalted)?

Then the Answer is: The way of the knowledge of these two is, that thou understand that God is, and that there is not with Him a thing. He is now as He was.

Then if one say: I see myself to be other than God and I do not see God to be myself.

Then the Answer is: The Prophet (may God bless him and give him peace) meant by the soul thine existence and thy reality, not the "soul" which is named "commanding, upbraiding," and "pacified"; [4] but in the "soul" he pointed to all that is beside God (whose name be exalted), as the Prophet (may God bless him and give him peace) said: "O my God, show me things as they are clearly," meaning by "things" whatever is beside God (whose name be exalted), that is, "Make me to know what is beside Thee in order that I may understand and know things, which they are—whether they are Thou or other than Thou, and whether they are of old, abiding, or recent and perishing." Then God showed him what was beside Himself, without the existence of what is beside Himself. So he saw things as they are: I mean, he saw things to be the essence of God (whose name be exalted) without how or where. And the name "things" includes the soul and other than it of things. For the existence of the soul and the existence of other things are both equal in point of being "things," that is, are nothing; for, in reality, the thing is God and God is named a thing. Then when thou knowest the things thou knowest the soul, and when thou knowest the soul thou knowest the Lord. Because he whom thou thinkest to be beside God, he is not beside God; but thou dost not know Him, and thou seest Him and dost not understand that thou seest Him. And when this secret is revealed to thee thou understandest that thou art not what is beside God, and that thou art thine own end and thine own object in thy search after thy Lord, and that thou dost not require to cease to be, and that thou has continued and wilt continue without when and without times, as we mentioned above. And thou seest all thine actions to be His actions, and all His attributes to be thine attributes. Thou seest thine outward to be His outward and thine inward to be His inward, and thy first to be His first and thy last to be His last, without doubting and without wavering. And thou seest thine attributes to be His attributes and thine essence to be His essence, without thy becoming Him or His becoming thee, either in the greatest or least degree. "Everything is perishing except His Face";[5] that is, there is no existent but He, nor existence to other than He, so that it should require to perish and His Face remain; that is, there is nothing except His Face: "then, whithersoever ye turn, there is the Face of God." [6]

It is as if one did not know a thing and afterwards knows it. His existence does not cease, but his ignorance ceases, and his existence continues as it was, without his existence being exchanged for another existence, or the existence of the not-knowing person being compounded with the existence of the knowing, or intermixing, but (merely) a taking away of ignorance. Therefore, think not that thou requirest to cease to be. For if thou requiredst to cease to be, then thou wouldest in that case be His veil, and the veil other than God (whose name be exalted); which requires that another than He should have overcome Him in preventing His being seen; and this is an error and an oversight. And we have mentioned above that His veil is His oneness, and His singleness is not other than it. And, thus it is permitted to him who is united to Reality to say, "I am the Truth," and to say "Praise be to Me." But none attains to union except he see his own attributes to be the attributes of God (whose name be exalted), and his own essence to be the essence of God (whose name be exalted), without his attributes or essence entering into God or proceeding forth from Him at all, or ceasing from God or remaining in Him. And he sees himself as never having been, not as having been and then having ceased to be. For there is no soul save His soul, and there is no existence save His existence.

And to this the Prophet (upon whom be peace) pointed when he said: "Revile not the world, for God—He is the world," pointing to the fact that the existence of the world is God's existence without partner or like or equal. And it is related from the Prophet (upon whom be peace) that he said that God (whose name be exalted) said: [7]

"O my servant, I was sick and thou visitedst Me not, I begged of thee and thou gavest not to Me," with other like expressions; pointing to the fact that the existence of the beggar is His existence, and that the existence of the sick is His existence. And when it is allowed that the existence of the beggar and the existence of the sick are His existence, it is allowed that thy existence is His existence and that the existence of all created things, both accidents and substances, is His existence. And when the secret of an atom of the atoms is clear, the secret of all created things, both external and internal, is clear, and thou dost not see in this world or the next aught beside God, but the existence of these two Abodes, and their name and their named, all of them, are He, without doubt and without wavering. And thou dost not see God as having ever created anything, but thou seest "every day He is in a business," [8] in the way of revealing His existence or concealing it, without any quality, because He is the First and the Last and the Outward and the Inward. He is outward in His oneness and inward in His singleness: He is the first in His essence and His immutability, and the last in His everlastingness. The very existence of the first is He, and the very existence of the last is He, and the very existence of the outward is He, and the very existence of the inward is He. He is His name and He is His named. And as His existence is "necessary," so the non-existence of all beside Him is necessary. For that which thou thinkest to be beside Him is not beside Him. For He will not have aught to be other than He. Nay, the other is He, and there is no otherness. The other is with His existence and in His existence, outwardly and inwardly.

The person to whom this description is applicable is endowed with many qualities without limit or end. But just as he who dies the death of the body loses all his qualities, both praiseworthy and blameworthy, so in the Sufi death all the qualities, both blameworthy and praiseworthy, are cut off, and God (whose name be exalted) comes into his place in all his states. Thus, instead of his essence comes the essence of God (whose name be exalted), and in place of his attributes come the attributes of God (whose name be exalted).

And so the Prophet (may God bless him and give him peace) said, "Die before ye die," that is, know yourselves before ye die. And he (upon whom be peace) said: "God (whose name be exalted) has said: The worshipper does not cease to draw near to Me with good works until I love him. Then, when I love him, I am to him hearing and sight and tongue and hand unto the end," pointing to the fact that he who knows himself sees his whole existence to be His existence, and does not see any change take place in his own essence or attributes, seeing that he was not the existence of his essence, but was merely ignorant of the knowledge of himself. For when thou "knowest thyself," thine egoism is taken away, and thou knowest that thou art not other than God. For, if thou hadst had an independent existence, so that thou didst not require to cease to be or to "know thyself," then thou wouldest be a Lord beside Him; and God forbid that He should have created a Lord beside Himself.

The profit of the knowledge of the soul is, that thou understandest and art sure that thy existence is neither existent nor non-existent, and that thou art not, wast not, and never wilt be.

From this the meaning of the saying, "There is no god but God," is clear, since there is no god other than He nor existence to other than Him, so that there is no other beside Him—and no god but He.

Then if one say: Thou makest void His sovereignty,

Then the Answer is: I do not make void His sovereignty. For He is still Ruler as well as ruled, and is still Creator as well as created. He is now as He was as to His creative power and as to His sovereignty, not requiring a creature nor a subject, because He is the Creator and the created, and the ruler and the ruled. When He called into being the things that are, He was [already] endowed with all attributes. And He is now as He was then. In His oneness there is no difference between what is recent and what is original. The recent is the result of His manifesting Himself, and the original is the result of His remaining within Himself. His outward is His inward, and His inward is His outward: His first is His last and His last is His first; and all is one, and the One is all. The definition of Him was, "Every day He is in a business," and there was nothing beside Him, and He is now as He was then, and there is in reality no existence to what is beside Him. As He was in past eternity and past time "every day engaged in a business," and there was no existent thing beside Him, so He is the same now as He was, "every day engaged in a business," and there is no business and there is no day, as there were in past eternity and past time no business and no day. And the existence of the created things and their non-existence are the same thing. And, if it were not so, there would of necessity be an origination of something fresh which was not [before] in His oneness, and that would be a defect, and His oneness is too sublime for that!

Therefore, when thou knowest thyself after this fashion, without adding a like or an equal or a partner to God (whose name be exalted), then thou knowest it as it really is. And it was thus he said (upon whom be peace), "Whoso knoweth himself knoweth his Lord." He did not say, "Whoso maketh himself to cease to be, knoweth his Lord," for he (upon him be peace) understood and saw that there is nothing beside Him. Thereupon he pointed out that the knowledge of the soul was the knowledge of God (whose name be exalted). That is, "Know that thy existence is not thy existence nor other than thy existence. For thou art not existent nor non-existent, nor other than existent nor other than non-existent. Thy existence and thy non-existence are His existence, and yet without there being any existence or non-existence, because thy existence and thy non-existence are actually His existence." So if thou seest things (without seeing another thing along with God) to be Him, thou knowest thyself; and, verily, to know thyself after this fashion is to know God, without wavering and without doubt, and without compounding anything of what is of recent origin with what is original, in any way.

Then if one ask: How lies the way to union, when thou affirmest that there is no other beside Him, and a thing cannot be united to itself?

Then the Answer is: No doubt there is in reality no union nor division, nor far nor near. For union is not possible except between two, and if there be but one, there can be no union nor division. For union requires two either similar or dissimilar. Then if they are similar they are equals, and if they are dissimilar they are opposites, and He (whose name be exalted) spurns to have either an equal or an opposite; so that the union is something else than farness. So there is union without union, and nearness without nearness, and farness without farness.

Then if anyone say: Explain to us this "union without union'; and what is the meaning of this "nearness without nearness" and this "farness without farness"?

Then the Answer is: I mean that thou, in thy stages of drawing nigh and of being far off, wast not a thing beside God (whose name be exalted), but thou hadst not the "knowledge of the soul," and didst not understand that thou art He without thou. Then when thou art united to God (whose name be exalted)—that is, when thou knowest thyself (although the knowledge itself does not exist)—thou understandest that thou art He. And thou wast not aware before that thou wast He, or He other than He. Then, when the knowledge comes upon thee, thou understandest that thou knowest God by God, not by thyself.

To take an example: Suppose that thou dost not know that thy name is Mahmud, or thy named Mahmud. Then if the name and the named be in reality one, and thou thinkest that thy name is Muhammad, and after some time comest to know that thou art Mahmud, then thy existence goes on, but the name Muhammad is cut off from thee, by thy coming to know thyself, that thou art Mahmud, and wast Muhammad only by ceasing to be thyself. And "ceasing to be" presupposes an affirmation of existence, and whoever posits an existence beside Him makes a partner to Him (exalted and blessed be His name). So nothing positive is taken away from Mahmud, nor does Muhammad cease to be in Mahmud, or enter into him or proceed forth from him, nor Mahmud into Muhammad; but as soon as Mahmud knows himself, that he is Mahmud and not Muhammad, he knows himself by himself, not by Muhammad. For Muhammad never existed at all, then how could anything that does exist be known through him?

So, then, the knower and that which he knows are both one, and he who unites and that with which he unites are one, and seer and seen are one. For the knower is His attribute, and that with which he unites is His essence; and the attribute and that to which it is attributed are one. And this is the explanation of the saying "Whoso knoweth himself knoweth his Lord."

So whoever understands this example knows that there is no union nor division, and he knows that the knower is He and the known is He, and the seer is He and the seen is He, he who unites is He and that with which he unites is He. There does not unite with Him other than He, and there is not separated from Him other than He. And whoever understands this is free from the polytheism of polytheism, and, if not, then he has not felt a breath of freedom from polytheism.

Most of "those who know" (who think that they know themselves and know their Lord, and that they are free from the delusion of existence) say that the Path is not to be traversed except by ceasing to be, and the ceasing of that ceasing. And that is due to their not understanding the saying of the Prophet (may God bless him and give him peace). And because they must blot out polytheism, they point at one time to the negation, that is, the cessation, of existence, and at another to the cessation of that cessation, and at another to effacement, and at another to annihilation. And all these explanations are unadulterated polytheism. For whoever allows that there is anything beside Him, and that afterwards it ceases to be, or allows a cessation of its extinction, he affirms that existence of something that is beside Him, and whoever does this makes a partner to God. May God guide them and us to the middle of the Path!

NOTES

1. Who believe in incarnations of God.
2. That is, phenomenal existence.
3. Koran, IV, 170.
4. For "soul" here we would say "flesh"; see Mr. Gibb's "*Ottoman Poetry,*" p. 198.
5. Koran, XXVIII, 88.

6.   Ibid., II, 109.
7.   To Moses.
8.   Koran, LV, 29.

Dialogue at the Day of Listening

Fairfax, California: May 22, 1991

Jean Klein: We cannot precisely say what this listening is, because it is not a function. It is without intention. Being free from intention also means being free from concentration. In both we are looking for a target, looking for a result, but in listening we are simply open, directionless.

In listening there is no grasping, no taking. All that is listened to comes to us. The relaxed brain is in a state of natural non-function, simply attentive without any specific direction. We can never objectify listening, because that would mean to put it in the frame of space and time. It is listening to oneself.

In listening to oneself there is no outside and no inside. It is silence, presence. In this silence-presence there is a total absence of oneself as being somebody.

In listening we are not isolated. We are only isolated when we live in objects, but free from objects we live our essence where there is no separation. In listening there is not a you and not another. Call it love.

Q. If the student and the teacher are one and the same does it not mean that you are a projection from my consciousness?

JK. When the teacher does not project himself as a teacher then there is oneness. Only in this oneness is teaching possible. Otherwise the teacher binds you, makes an object of you. When he makes an object of you, then you exist for his psychological survival and no teaching is possible.

Q.. Then who finds whom?

JK. The teacher frees you from discipleship. When he takes you for a disciple no transmission is possible. When the disciple is absent the teacher is absent. Otherwise you remain bound to the concept "disciple." It is a magical relationship.

It is only in absolute silence that we can speak of communication. Otherwise, there is no communication. It is the object which hurts communication.

Q. When the student gets too much taken by the form of the teacher, is it a serious obstacle?

JK. Yes, it is a hindrance. To be free from it keep your mind unfurnished. Then there is no representation. In love there is no representation.

As long as there is representation you are bound to what the mind represents. Free means being free from all objects. You are no longer tied to the object.

The intellect gives up when there is a clear representation that it cannot find what is beyond it. Then the intellect dissolves because it has no more role to play, and there is silence.

Q. Is that a slow development or sudden?

JK. The understanding is instantaneous. When you say, "I understand," see how the understanding acts on you. In the moment of insight you are nowhere, there is no one, there is simply understanding. But we are so accustomed to living in objects that we continually come back and make the understanding a representation. It is clearness about this that frees the mind. This clarity brings you to what you are by freeing you from what you are not.

You must live with the sayings of the teacher, who constantly points to the Ultimate, to the Self.

Q. What exactly is an *upaguru*?

JK. An *upaguru* informs the mind. But an *upaguru* is not really established in knowing. There is something contradictory in it. When the mind really knows its limits, you are ready. You are available. In this availability you are the waiting.

The formulation of the *upaguru* is still touched by the mind. The mind has not accomplished its possibility to not know. So one has not really understood what is beyond the mind.

Q. Why would an *upaguru* take himself for a teacher?

JK. The understanding of the truth does not immediately make one a teacher. You become a teacher when you first know yourself and then have the pedagogical quality to teach. You must know how best to present it to the disciple. Otherwise you are not a teacher. One can be a man of truth, but to transmit the truth on the level of the mind in space and time belongs to the quality of being a teacher.

Q. How does one know a true teacher?

JK. The teacher can never bring you to what you are because there are not two. He can only bring you to moments when you are free from objects. You know these moments, situations when you are completely absent.

I would say that when you leave the teacher, you must have a taste of freedom, a feeling of freedom in you. That is most important. The teacher is free, and echoes your own freedom. What remains in you is a taste, a shadow. And it is this shadow that can bring you back to its substance, its origin.

The teacher must be able to go into the deep conditioning of the disciple and proceed to teach according to this knowing of the deep conditioning of the disciple. The pedagogy is not the same for everyone.

Q. Does this require some familiarity between teacher and disciple?

JK. I think so. And also right observation on the part of the teacher.

Q. What are the qualifications of a student?

JK. When you have discovered the teacher, or rather when the teacher has discovered you, live really with the sayings of the teacher. Do not be dispersed. Really live the sayings, without touching them, without interfering with memory, without forcing the teaching. Simply live, really live with the question. The question brings you to the answer, because the question is the answer and the answer is the question. They are not two.

Q. Since I've met you and started to understand your teaching, I've sensed your teaching in nature and in other people. Is there any danger in looking for the same teaching in other places?

JK. You must be able to give all your heart to the teaching, the understanding, and you must be able to see how the understanding acts on you. The understanding must free you from non-understanding. It is a kind of feeling sensation you can even find in your body. You don't know where the feeling begins and where the sensation begins.

Q. Does the teaching sometimes have to go underground, as it were? Sometimes the teaching is vivid, sometimes it fades, then surfaces again.

JK. You must not take the teaching with intention. Let it come to you. There will be moments in your life when you spontaneously don't go into any intellectual formulation. In any case, you can never go to what you are; all you can do is to be ready to receive it, to welcome it. You can never say, "I have it," because there is no one to have it.

In a certain way, all that you do refers to the ultimate, because you can never really understand one object through another object. An object can never be totally understood by reference to another object. This is the limitation of scientific thinking. An object is always a fraction. You can only understand the object when it refers to its ultimate subject, Silence, if you like. So let the object become sacred and then it refers to silence.

Q. Would you say only one thing exists?

JK. It doesn't exist, it is.

Q. So when we use words that imply more than one thing, those words don't exist...

JK. We use words but before thinking, before doing, there is silence, and after thinking, after doing, there is silence. All that appears, appears in silence. All that appears in silence is of the same nature as silence. They are not two.

All that is perceived is perceived by consciousness, in consciousness. If all that we think and do did not refer to the ultimate we would not have music, poetry, painting, sculpture, and so on. There is music to glorify the ultimate, poetry to glorify the ultimate, painting to glorify the ultimate, and so on. There is music that comes from the ultimate. The glorified and the glorifier are the same.

Q. I have a friend who is dying and I feel fear.

JK. The question may be *"who* is afraid?" You are an object that appears in space and time. You are also the knower of the object. The knower is not afraid.

There is not a liver and not a one who dies. When we inquire deeply as to what is life, it is impossible that the notion of dying can come up. You cannot find out when you were born except maybe through hearsay or second-hand information. But really finding out when you were born is impossible.

You must go into it and question very deeply the idea of dying.

Q. What is the best way to assist a dying person?

JK. When you assist somebody who is so-called dying, you must die with him. You must free him from all kinds of qualification. That means you must free yourself from all kinds of qualification, live knowingly in all your nakedness. In this attitude you free the dying person from grasping memory, you free them from the past. You can only assist them with your entire love. This love is constant presence. It never disappears.

We should try to give up all qualifications, to die every evening.

Q. When we feel ourselves in globality when we're near a dying person, is that what you mean?

JK. Absolutely. No talking is needed, just being there. You are free from all thinking. Your openness strongly stimulates their openness. That is why the needy, emotive family should not be present. When you are present with that person you stimulate their giving up.

Q. The dying person will experience that anyway...

JK. Yes, but not knowingly. It is experiencing it knowingly that is important.

Q. You said that a child may have that realization in a certain sense, but it is not actualized. What is that actualizing process?

JK. The actualizing process is in you. It is not somewhere else. The apple tree is in the seed. There is water and sun and so on, but the tree is the apple seed. So it is important in which atmosphere you grow up. When you go deeply there is a profound desire to be autonomous, free from objects.

Q. When does this deep desire become known?

JK. It comes with maturity, and this maturity appears when you have touched the phenomenal world. Appropriation to the phenomenal world makes the child ask the question, makes him look for freedom. It is the innocent discovery of the child in the outer and inner world which makes him grow. Apparently it is biological survival but really it is all in view to free himself from his surroundings. The child appropriates the world in order to become free from it. He looks for autonomy.

Q. Is being free of objects the same as being free of desires?

JK. When you desire something, when your desire is attached to an object, the actual energy in the desire has nothing to do with the object. The object, at a certain time, merely stimulates the desire. So when you are able to free the desire from the object and live only with the pure desire in itself, you can be sure this will be the proof for you that it comes to you from what you most deeply desire, that is, desirelessness. So there is nothing wrong with living with your desire, objectless desire. When the desire is freed from the object, you will already have the perfume of what you most profoundly desire. Otherwise you will feel frustration.

Q. So if we take the desire that we have for an object and live with it, it leads us to our ultimate desire?

JK. You may for some time live with the desire for a certain object, then one day this object is attained. You will then see that at the moment of attainment the object is not present, and you are not present. There is only a non-dual state: happiness. Then you can see that the cause is not in the object and you no longer project any object. Then you are free from the desire for objects and a profound maturity arises: you are free from all projection, because you have clearly understood that the cause is not an object, that happiness is causeless. You must come to this experience.

When you become restless it is because you have identified happiness with an object. But happiness is not in an object. It is causeless. It comes when you are open. It is not in a red car, a beautiful house, a second marriage.

You must live completely in openness, and this openness is the happiness.

Q. Does an insight come a number of times before it becomes stable, before it becomes your real nature?

JK. The discovery is instantaneous. But then there are still residues in your body-mind.

You will have it in the absence of activity first. When an activity is completely accomplished there is this silence, but you usually attribute to this silence an absence of activity. You make the silence an object, because the absence of an activity is still an object. But this absence is presence. Later you will be solicited by this silent presence also during the activity. But do not make it an object. It is objectless.

There is nobody to be aware, there is only awareness. There is not a doer, only doing. Not a thinker, only thinking.

Q. What are these residues?

JK. They are residues of not-knowing which have accumulated on the psychosomatic plane. They are memory. It can take time for these residues to be eliminated. The insight into truth is once and forever but because we live on the phenomenal level it takes time for the insight to penetrate knowingly all levels of existence. But after the insight there is no substance in the residues. At every moment they point to the ultimate.

I remember when I first saw my mother after India and how clear it was to me that she was imposing old patterns on me. I saw from the ultimate perspective of freedom from an

"I" and a "you" how she imposed a relationship of mother-son, "I" and "you," and I saw in me the reflex to conform to that relationship. But the seer was no longer implicated and in seeing the situation clearly I knew that I, the seer, was free from it. So memory no longer had a hold on me. Every situation in life confirmed my ultimate freedom, every object points to the ultimate subject.

Likewise, happiness can leave its residue, its echo, in us because our real nature is happiness. We must be open to this echo which is a shadow of the real. I remember many years ago when I had just come from India, a lady made an appointment to see me. She said, "Sir, I am very unhappy," and she told me all about her problems with her mother, father, uncles, husband and so on. She said it was as if she were in a dark room with no ray of light.

I asked her, "Can you remember even a single moment when you were happy?" She said, "Yes. It was in Cannes, in the south of France, sitting in my chair, and I was waiting for my beloved who was expected to arrive from the airplane in twenty minutes. At this moment I was very happy."

I said to her, "Are you able to visualize it?" She said, "Yes, in visualizing this I find myself very happy." I said, "Keep it!"

Q. So you don't keep the visualization, the image or stimulus, just the feeling it evokes?

JK. Yes. Keep the extract.

Q. Is it that the teacher constantly reminds us of what is already there anyway?

JK. The teacher lives in not doing, but there is doing. He reminds you of your nearness.

Q. By his own being he reminds me of my own being?

JK. Yes, if you like...

He tells you in the most pedagogical way what you are not. You must follow this reasoning, this higher reasoning. There you will find yourself in the absence of any qualification, free from all objects. He empties you, in a certain way, of objects. All your objects are taken away, and all that is left is empty space, what you are fundamentally. It may not appear in the moment itself. It may appear the next day, or next month, or you may be crossing the street and suddenly see it.

Q. So your art is to transform our doings into not-doings?

JK. Yes. Doings can only have an object.

Q. Can absence not know it is absent?

JK. When there is total absence, there is presence. Absence refers to objects. When there is a total absence of objects, there is presence.

Q. Would an enlightened person know he/she is enlightened?

JK. When there is absence there is light. When you speak of enlightenment there is still an object, and there is a complementarity, a "non-enlightened state." In your total absence there is not a knower of the absence. The absence is its own knowing. The reference to absence refers only to objects, and you are not an object.

When you live this emptiness, you are completely vacant. There is no person who is vacant, there is only vacancy.

There are many states, but there is only one non-state: call it sahaja. In a state there is concentration. All the kinds of samadhis are concentration. In a non-state your ears, your eyes, your sense of smell, touch and taste are alive. There is no withdrawing.

Q. For realization to occur, does the crown chakra have to open?

JK. Understanding brings the spontaneous opening of the energy centres. You don't deal with these centres in themselves. You can, of course, open certain centres, but it will not bring you understanding. It is the understanding which opens you.

Q. If they are opened by understanding, do they stay open?

JK. They stay open.

Q. If the crown chakra is opened, does that mean that all the siddhis spontaneously occur to the realized?

JK. Yes. But it all comes from the understanding. They can be artificially opened, but it is only artificially. When it is really opened through understanding there is no longer any identity with the ego and no more taking yourself for a personal entity. It is a knowing that you are a channel, nothing more.

Q. What effects are there of the crown chakra being open?

JK. There is a certain transformation of the brain and muscle structure. There is a profound letting-go, a deep relaxation. There is no more taking, becoming, no more striving to attain. There is no longer eccentric energy to become, to obtain. You no longer live in the becoming process.

But all these phenomena are the result of understanding, not the result of any physical effort. These effects appear simultaneously with the understanding.

Q. Regarding siddhis… an individual can have abilities, but if there is no longer an individual to have them, does that mean siddhis go away?

JK. Absolutely. They have no more place.

Q. But if the crown chakra stays open maybe they could occur spontaneously, even though they are not occurring to anybody.

JK. Yes. Or no.

Q. Knowledge and understanding are not developed in infants. Is this why consciousness gets lost in the object?

JK. It is normal that the child first appropriates itself to its surroundings. It has already appropriated itself in the mother's womb and then the appropriation is the world around. That is biologically absolutely necessary.

We appropriate ourselves to our surroundings, to objects. But there must be a moment when there is understanding or else we remain stuck to the objects, not only stuck, but absorbed in the objects. There is a moment when the understanding must be understanding the real nature of the object. It is difficult to say at which moment in the life of a human being this occurs.

For me, it was when I was 16 or 17... When I read Karl Marx, Hegel, and so on, and became an anarchist and asked "What is Life? What is my reason for being?" I think, for me, that was my moment. It was the only moment that I seriously touched the Bible!

Q. What are the qualities of right knowing?

JK. The scientist starts with the known, memory. When he says "I know," his knowing is related to objects, including himself as an object. But when the truth-seeker says "I know," this knowing refers to the unthinkable. This knowing is not knowing. It is free from the known and his saying "I know" abides in silence.

Your Question

Q. During the months of the war in the Persian Gulf (1990-91), I found myself often feeling depressed. I felt helpless to help in any way. It was a moment when your teaching—to look first at the conflict in myself—seemed absolutely right (I felt responsible for the situation every time I argued with a friend or family!). At the same time the teaching seemed hopelessly ineffectual. I felt that far from entering a new world consciousness, the human race was once again proving itself to be in the dark ages with no sign of light or progress. Competition, greed and financial gain seemed again to be ruling the rulers. Lack of cultural exchange and dialogue was again apparent. The feelings of victory expressed with such pride by the Western powers involved left me cold because I felt deeply that the so-called victory had proved to be a loss on a much greater level, in terms of where humanity now finds itself at this moment. These feelings are still with me, and I wondered whether you could comment.

Jean Klein: You are the world. You are not isolated from the world. All that happens belongs also to you. The world appears according to your point of view. From the standpoint of the senses, the world is only sense perception. From the standpoint of mind, the world is mind. But when you take your stand in consciousness, in globality, the world is consciousness.

Your questions comes from a conflict and one conflict cannot solve another. You must see the root of the conflict, which is that you take yourself for an independent entity, in other words, a fraction. A fraction cannot see a whole fact but only a fraction, and any decision which emerges from a fraction cannot be harmonious. When this is seen very clearly, with one's whole being, we find ourselves, as we have said very often, outside the process. Then from this global point of view we should look at the situation again. This global point of view, free from you and another, permits us to allow the facts of the situation, the whole situation, to find a solution.

Every situation has its solution, which is always for the good of the whole. But we must wait without personal interference for the solution. It is like the man of Tao who acts according to Heaven. His volition is non-volition. His acting is non-acting. His practice is non-practice. It is the doctrine of non-doctrine. A man of Tao does not act according to codified morality, what society expects, or ideas and learned sentiments like nationalism, prejudice or economic or political ideals. In other words, there is no interference with what he has discovered in his global view of the situation. He is a citizen of the world, not a specific nation, and acts for the good of the world. He is the world and its suffering is his suffering. Its joy is his joy. The man of Tao, being without ego, is humble. And in this humility he never takes advantage of the weakness of others. Of course the ruler of a country should be a man of Tao as it says in Lao Tsu's *Tao Te Ching*.

Tao Te Ching
Lao Tsu

Whenever you advise a ruler in the way of Tao,
Counsel him not to use force to conquer the universe.
For this would only cause resistance.
Thorn bushes spring up wherever the army has passed.
Lean years follow in the wake of a great war.
Just do what needs to be done.
Never take advantage of power.

Achieve results,
But never glory in them.
Achieve results,
But never boast.
Achieve results,
But never be proud.
Achieve results,
Because this is the natural way.
Achieve results,
But not through violence.

Force is followed by loss of strength.
This is not the way of Tao.
That which goes against the Tao comes to an early end.

*

Good weapons are instruments of fear; all creatures hate them.
Therefore followers of Tao never use them.
The wise man prefers the left.
The man of war prefers the right.

Weapons are instruments of fear; they are not a wise man's
tools.

He uses them only when he has no choice.
Peace and quiet are dear to his heart,
And victory no cause for rejoicing.
If you rejoice in victory, then you delight in killing;
If you delight in killing, you cannot fulfill yourself.

On happy occasions precedence is given to the left,
On sad occasions to the right.
In the army the general stands on the left,
The commander-in-chief on the right.
This means that war is conducted like a funeral.
When many people are being killed,
They should be mourned in heartfelt sorrow.
That is why a victory must be observed like a funeral.

*

The Tao is forever undefined.
Small though it is in the unformed state, it cannot be grasped.
If kings and lords could harness it,
The ten thousand things would naturally obey.
Heaven and earth would come together
And gentle rain fall.
Men would need no more instruction and all things would
    take their course.

Once the whole is divided, the parts need names.
There are already enough names.
One must know when to stop.
Knowing when to stop averts trouble.
Tao in the world is like a river flowing home to the sea.

*

Knowing others is wisdom;
Knowing the self is enlightenment.

Mastering others requires force;
Mastering the self needs strength.
He who knows he has enough is rich.
Perseverance is a sign of willpower.
He who stays where he is endures.
To die but not to perish is to be eternally present.

Translated by Gia-Fu Feng and Jane English

Body Approach

Q. You say there is no phenomenal way out of the cage of the ego, but can we come to the deep relaxed state by first working on the body rather than waiting for an insight? What can we do on the body level to help us lose the idea of being an individual entity?

Jean Klein: The body is an object of our awareness; it is sensed; it takes place in our awareness. The body is in us, but we are not in the body. If we were we could not be aware of it.

Let us take an example. You feel icy cold. In this moment you are identified with the perception. You are lost in the sensation. Very quickly you think or say, "I am icy cold," and the perception is lost in the concept. You are now in defence, and you try to escape the cold in one way or another. But the moment you feel the cold as an object apart from "I," for example, "Here is a mass of cold," you are no longer escaping the perception and the sensation lives in your awareness. You know *you* are not cold, only an object is cold, so there is no longer the reflex to defend "yourself" against the cold. When your observation is free from any anticipation, the sensation can be felt and explored and dealt with as a fact.

Likewise, when we do the bodywork the sensation is felt and explored in our awareness. There is space between "I" and the sensation. You are no longer stuck to it, the object. The goal of the bodywork is to make us aware of this space between the "I" and the object, a space that is habitually cramped. This space between object and "I" is still in duality, but there comes a moment when the space is felt as our real nature, we abide in it, and the object, the sensation, appears in it.

There are a certain number of postures which are archetypes. By archetype I mean a gathering in one pose of many poses of the body, a concentration in one pose of many levels of the body.

One of these archetypes is the dead pose (*savasana*). The value of this pose is that one can feel and articulate the whole body. The body mass has its contact on the ground. What does "contact" mean here? Generally our contact with the ground is passive. But when we see that there is a contact and a counter-contact, that is, body and ground are interwoven—the body goes in the ground and the ground goes in the body—when this happens, there is no longer resistance or opposition. Then there is harmonisation of energy. Our body is no longer felt as separate from global energy, but is integrated in the living ground and the ground is integrated in our body.

LISTENING

Volume 5
1992

Gurvastakam 151
Sri Adi Sankaracarya
Translated by Peter Harrison

Excellence of the Gift of Love 160
St. Paul

Devotion 161
Jean Klein

Sadhana: *On Desire* 171
Jean Klein

Adoration of Ra 172
from *The Egyptian Book of the Dead*

Dialogue in Santa Barbara: February 16, 1992 177
Jean Klein

Your Question: *How can my life have meaning
and fulfillment?* 182
Jean Klein

Body Approach: *A guided relaxation* 183
Jean Klein

गुर्वष्टकम्

GURVAṢṬAKAM
"Eight Verses in Praise of the Guru"
Sri Adi Sankaracarya

Transcribed and translated from the original Sanskrit by
Peter Harrison

I

Though your body be perfect, ever free from disease,
Your honour unsullied, wealth high as Mount Meru;
If your mind does not dwell on the Lotus Feet of the Guru,
What then? What then? What then? What then?

ŚRĪRAN SURŪPAN SADĀ ROGAMUKTAM
YAŚAŚCĀRU CITRAN DHANAM MERUTULYAM
MANAŚ CENNA LAGNAN GURORAṄGHRIPADME
TATAḤ KIN TATAḤ KIN TATAḤ KIN TATAḤ KIM

शरीरं सुरूपं सदा रोगमुक्तं
यशश्चारु चित्रं धनं सेरुतुल्यम् ।
मनश्चेन्न लग्नं गुरोरंघ्रिपद्मे
ततः किं ततः किं ततः किं ततः किम् ॥ १॥

II

Dear wife, sons and grandsons, beloved relations,
Household and friends you may have in abundance,
But if your mind does not dwell on the Lotus Feet of the Guru,
What then? What then? What then? What then?

KALATRAN DHANAM PUTRA PAUTRĀDI SARVAM;
GṚHAM BĀNDHAVĀH SARVAMETADHI JĀTAM;
MANAŚCENNA LAGNAṄ GURORAṄGHRIPADMA;
TATAḤ KIN TATAḤ KIN TATAḤ KIN TATAḤ KIM.

कलत्रं धनं पुत्र पौत्रादिसर्वं
    गृहं बान्धवाः सर्वमेतद्धि जातम् ।
मनश्चेन्न लग्नं गुरोरंघ्रिपद्मे
    ततः किं ततः किं ततः किं ततः किम् ॥२॥

III

Though the whole Veda and Holy Tradition live on your lips,
And foremost amongst seers you write inspired verse and
  prose;
If your mind does not dwell on the Lotus Feet of the Guru,
What then? What then? What then? What then?

ṢAḌAṄGĀDI VEDO MUKHE ŚASTRAVIDYĀ
KAVITVĀDI GADYAN SUPADYAṄ KAROTI
MANAŚCENNA LAGNAN GURORAṄGHRIPADME
TATAḤ KIN TATAḤ KIN TATAḤ KIN TATAḤ KIM

षडङ्गादि वेदो मुखे शास्त्रविद्या
कवित्वादि गद्यं सुपद्यं करोति ।
मनश्चेन्न लग्नं गुरोरंघ्रिपद्मे
ततः किं ततः किं ततः किं तत किम् ॥३॥

IV

You may be fortunate at home and famous abroad,
Thinking no one excels you in the practice of virtue;
But if your mind does not dwell on the Lotus Feet of the
    Guru
What then? What then? What then? What then?

VIDEŚEṢU MĀNYAH SVADEŚEṢU DHANYAH
SADĀCĀRAVṚTTEṢU MATTO NA CĀNYAḤ
MANAŚCENNA LAGNAṄ GURORAṄGHRIPADME
TATAḤ KIN TATAḤ KIN TATAḤ KIN TATAḤ KIM

विदेशेषु मान्यः स्वदेशेषु धन्यः
  सदाचारवृत्तेषु मत्तो न चान्यः ।
मनश्चेन्न लग्नं गुरोरंघ्रिपद्मे
  ततः किं ततः किं ततः किं ततः किम् ॥४॥

V

Though your own lotus feet be worshipped by Emperors,
And by the hosts of rulers of this earthly globe;
If your mind does not dwell on the Lotus Feet of the
    Guru,
What then? What then? What then? What then?

KṢAMĀMAṆḌALE BHŪPABHŪPĀLAVṚNDAIH
SADĀSEVITAŃ YASYA PĀDĀRAVINDAM
MANAŚCENNA LAGNAŃ GURORAŃGHRIPADME
TATAḤ KIN TATAḤ KIN TATAḤ KIN TATAḤ KIM

क्षमामण्डले म्रूपभ्रूपालवृन्दैः
संदासेवितं यस्य पादारविन्दम् ।
मनश्चेन्न लग्नं गुरोरंघ्रिपद्मे
ततः किं ततः किं ततः किं ततः किम् ॥५॥

VI

Though your might and magnanimity be renowned in all
quarters,
And all worldly goods are in your grasp through the Guru's
grace,
If your mind does not dwell on His Lotus Feet,
What then? What then? What then? What then?

YAŚAŚCED GATAN DIKṢU DĀNAPRATĀPĀT
JAGADVASTU SARVAN KARE YATPRASĀDĀT
MANAŚCENNA LAGNAN GURDRANGHRIPADME
TATAḤ KIN TATAḤ KIN TATAḤ KIN TATAḤ KIM

यशश्चेद् गतं दिक्षु दानप्रतापात्
जगद्वस्तु सर्वं करे यत्प्रसादात् ।
मनश्चेन्न लग्नं गुरोरंघ्रिमध्ये
ततः किं ततः किं ततः किं ततः किम् ॥६॥

VII

Though it delights not in pleasure nor yogic powers nor
    extravagant ritual,
Nor in the beauty of a beloved's face nor in wealth;
If your mind does not dwell on the Lotus Feet of the
    Guru,
What then? What then? What then? What then?

NA BHOGE NA YOGE NA VA VĀJIMEDHE
NA KĀNTĀMUKHE NAIVA VITTEṢU CITTAM
MANAŚCENNA LAGNAṄ GURORAṄGHRIPADME
TATAḤ KIN TATAḤ KIN TATAḤ KIN TATAḤ KIM

न भोगे न योगे न वा वाजिमेधे
  न कान्तामुग्वे नैव वित्तेषु चितम् ।
मनश्चेन्न लग्नं गुरोरंघ्रिपद्मे
  ततः किं ततः किं ततः किं ततः किम् ॥७॥

VIII

Though your mind does not turn to the forest, nor to
    your own household,
Nor to duty, nor the body, nor to all that is precious;
If it does not dwell on the Lotus Feet of the Guru,
What then? What then? What then? What then?

ARAṆYE NA VĀ SVASYA GEHE NA KĀRYE

NA DEHE MANO VARTATE ME TVANARGHYE

MANAŚCENNA LAGNAṄ GURORAṄGHRIPADME

TATAḤ KIN TATAḤ KIN TATAḤ KIN TATAḤ KIM

अरण्ये न वा स्वस्य गेहे न कार्ये

न देहे मनो वर्तते मे त्वनर्घ्ये ।

मनश्चेन्न लग्नं गुरोरंघ्रिपद्मे

ततः किं ततः किं ततः किं ततः किम् ॥ ८ ॥

IX

The virtuous one who recites this eightfold praise of the Guru,
Whether an ascetic, a king, student or householder,
Whose mind lives always with the sayings of the Guru,
Will attain the desired state known as Brahman.

GURORAṢṬAKAÑ YAḤ PATHATPUṆYADEHI
YATIRBHŪPATIRBRAHMACĀRĪ CA GEHĪ
LABHEDVĀÑCHITĀRTHAM PADAM
   BRAHMASAÑJÑĀM
GURORUKTAVĀKYE MANO YAJA LAGNAM

गुरोरष्टकं यः पठत्पुण्यदेहि
    यतिर्भूपतिर्ब्रह्मचारी च गेही ।
लभेद्धाञ्छितार्थं पदं ब्रह्मसंज्ञं
    गुरोरुक्तवाक्ये मनो यस्य लग्नम् ॥९॥

Excellence of the Gift of Love

If I speak in the tongues of men and of angels, but have not love, I am a noisy gong or a clanging cymbal. And if I have prophetic powers, and understand all mysteries and all knowledge, and if I have all faith, so as to remove mountains, but have not love, I am nothing. If I give away all I have, and if I deliver my body to be burned, but have not love, I gain nothing.

The First Epistle of Paul to the Corinthians

Devotion

Q. What is devotion?

Jean Klein: It is being in the total absence of oneself. It is the deep feeling of one's homeground, one's origin where the devotee and devoted are not two. In the absence of oneself there is the global feeling of our dwelling place. So devotion means to free ourself from what we are not. When we are free from ourself, what we are shines. Devotion means offering what we are not, offering for the love of offering, without anyone who offers anything to anyone.

Q. What is the place of devotion in the path of knowledge?

JK. Devotion is the driving power to understand that the seeker is the sought. Devotion is an energy, a forefeeling that brings us to the devoted. It is a global feeling, not fractional like thinking. When knowledge is not integrated in our totality, our global sensation, it remains an intellectual representation. So devotion integrates knowledge in being knowledge.

Q. So using the beautiful words of Sankaracharya, what does it mean "to dwell on the Lotus Feet of the Guru"?

JK. In the absence of oneself there is presence. Dwelling on the Lotus Feet of the Guru means being present. The Feet are the reminder of what you are.

Q. If one has everything one could want on the phenomenal plane but one does not dwell on the Lotus Feet of the Guru, what meaning does life have?

JK. The phenomenal only has meaning when it refers to the

Ultimate, because then it becomes sacred. When an object refers to the Ultimate it loses its objectivity. On the phenomenal level an object refers to another object, but this does not give it its full meaning. The phenomenal is wet with the noumenal, that is why the phenomenal gives the forefeeling of the Ultimate.

Q. Is there a place for attachment to the person of the guru in devotion?

JK. No. If, at the beginning, you are attached to the physical guru it is because you are accustomed to a hold in the objective world. Your mind must be free from any object. One day you will see that you have mistaken the source of your desire, that you have stopped inquiring. It is only in inquiring further that you give up all projections. That is why the guru doesn't give a hold for attachment to his person.

Q. On what basis can one choose a guru?

JK. The first meeting is the most important, because at that moment you are free from reference and the guru points you to what you fundamentally are. The pointing is not always in words but sometimes is in nonvisible ways. Later you may feel you were simply given the freedom to be.

An empty mind at the time of meeting is essential. When the mind is full of ideas and projections one is not open to the flavour of the guru. An empty mind, an open mind, calls for maturity and maturity means being without conditioning, free from the known, open to the unknown. In the freedom from all ideas you meet the freedom of the guru which is your own freedom. And you will be convinced. In an open mind you can see the facts, whether or not he or she truly concerns you. Discrimination comes from an open mind.

Q. It sometimes happens that one thinks one has met the guru and then one becomes doubtful. How can we be sure?

JK. Only when the disciple is free from attachment to the physical guru can there be real relation which is non-relation, where there is no "me" and "he." In being free from the object there is transformation. It is a profound independence.

When you are attached in an object-object way, you will inevitably be disappointed because your deepest desire is not fulfilled. You must inquire what you desire really. Desire is the driving power, the impetus in self-inquiry. The guru is not a person but the Ultimate, so dwelling at his feet means to be constantly, knowingly, in identity with this Ultimate. In dwelling in your most profound desire you free yourself from objects and become one with the desired.

Q. So it is not enough to simply be aware of desire, we must really follow it?

JK. Yes, you must follow it. Only following the desire with all your being—dwelling at the feet of the guru—can purify us.

Q. What exactly is purified?

JK. Wrong thinking is purified. When we clearly see the process, how we function, it brings us to right thinking. Only from right thinking can we see wrong thinking. We cannot define the right, only the wrong, because we fundamentally are the right. We can only be stimulated, transformed, by the right. Wrong thinking can never stimulate the question in us.

When we look innocently it is right thinking. It is pure perception—looking free from end-gaining.

Q. How can one who does not already dwell on the Lotus Feet of the Guru have the opportunity to do so?

JK. To come to this depth of truth-seeking one must question all the situations and circumstances in life. Question free from any conclusion. Take note and live in the taking-note. When the taking-note appears in your freshness there is questioning without reference. Generally, questioning has a reference but in simply taking-note with an innocent mind there is no reference, no comparison or judgment or conclusion. It is welcoming. When you are earnest nothing escapes you.

Q. How does one become earnest?

JK. By seeing beauty and love in things around you. You are built of beauty. There is the seed of beauty in you, so you can know beauty in your surroundings. Follow this beauty, seek it out. Cultivate it.

Q. When the seed is covered in earth, how can we find it? Must we not first get rid of the earth?

JK. Forget the earth. See only the beauty. It is seeing the beauty that frees the phenomenal. First you must feel concerned. It belongs to you as a human being to feel concerned. A baby is concerned. You can see it expressed in the vitality of all his movements. He is enthusiastically interested in exploring all his surroundings. When you see what is vital to you as a human being you automatically become concerned.

Q. But not everyone is equally concerned...

JK. Of course, heredity and conditioning play a role and some are more tamasic than others, but to be concerned is your human inheritance. The fact that you are reading this, that it has come into your hands, shows that you are concerned. It is looking for you.

Q. Even though we may be concerned intellectually and be very interested in self-inquiry, there is often a kind of laziness in us, a desire to postpone the search for Truth. We might say, "When I have enough money to retire, I will turn my energy to self-inquiry" or "When I find the perfect mate we will inquire together." In other words, "Save me, Lord, but not yet." What is the origin of this procrastination?

JK. Fear. One hundred percent fear. Fear of the unknown. Fear of giving up what one already knows and has and likes. Fear of giving up what one can hold onto. Deep down it is the fear of dying. As Plato said, "Can anyone be courageous, a warrior, who has the fear of death?" And this fear of dying is only there when we don't know life.

Q. So if we feel we are postponing earnest self-inquiry, you suggest we first face our fear of the unknown?

JK. Yes. Explore it, and when it appears to you, don't emphasize it—the fear, the seen—but refer to consciousness—the seer, the knower of it—which is Life. This bringing back of the seen to the seer is a purifying of the fear.

Q. Is not a certain fear of the unknown a biological inheritance because there may be a tiger lurking around the corner? In this sense isn't instinct or biological survival at odds with realization?

JK. Yes, as long as the body is conditioned. But when the body is really integrated, there cannot be biological fear because the body finds its ground in the Self. The real body is without boundaries and this is the forefeeling of paradise.

Q. If I may recapitulate, you've said that we can come to dwell at the Lotus Feet of the Guru by questioning the situations in our lives without forming any conclusion; by cultivating earnestness through seeing beauty and love in our surroundings; by facing our fear of the unknown which causes us to procrastinate a ruthless self-inquiry; and by following one's most deep desire. I'd like to talk more about this last way, or sadhana, if you allow me to call it that. What happens when we follow our desire?

JK. You desire something and, finally, attain it. What happens in that moment when the desired object is attained? There is a moment of desirelessness where there is no object and no you wanting it. This moment of fulfilment is an absolutely non-dual state. In this moment there is no cause. It is the timeless present. This is your real nature.

Q. But it lasts such a short time, or our living in it does. Very quickly, the reflex to feel it, to know it, to bask in it, to say "I'm so happy," "this is oneness," etc., comes up.

JK. Exactly. You put it in the subject-object relation and make a state of it. When you say, "I'm happy or content," you put a curtain between yourself and the non-state and you close yourself off from the spontaneous upcoming, from grace.

Q. Then somewhere in us we feel a lack and we begin to wonder whether we are happy after all and we again begin looking for a way to return to that fulfilled state. We look for something, a cause, to bring it to us.

JK. This non-understanding brings you to live in the becoming process. So the first thing is to understand the process, see its mechanical functioning. When we see it clearly—and it strikes us as an insight—in this moment of seeing we are out of it, free from the process. This movement of freedom annihilates the old patterns.

Q. But then we slip back into it again. How can a temporary moment of understanding help us?

JK. Because the understanding belongs to the timeless, to what is permanent in you. And this leaves an echo in us which beckons from time to time. The insight is a window in the dark room, a break in the pattern.

Q. What is this echo, this residue of the Truth?

JK. Matter is energy in movement and at the moment of insight, the instant of understanding, there is a shift in this energy, a reorientation. It is distributed differently, so that when the reflex to go in the old pattern comes up the body-mind remembers its correct position, its right thinking, its new way of being. In real understanding the patterns of non-understanding change to understanding, wrong thinking to right thinking, as we said earlier.

Q. After the insight leaves an echo in us how do we face it? Should we consciously welcome it, remember it, cultivate it, or forget it? And if we forget it, might the echo not simply fade away? How can we keep the echo alive in us?

JK. Live with the insight, keep it in its freshness as a sensation, otherwise it becomes mind-stuff. Let yourself be solicited by the echo of the insight. Be available and it will push you to a new moment.

Q. How does one keep it as a sensation? Do we water it, treat it delicately?

JK. Don't be heavy with it. Do not remember it in relation to anything. Keep it in its purity. Do not keep it in memory. Let its flavour pervade you.

Q. So one way to approach desire is to see how we attribute a cause to the desireless moment and how we are then in the chain of causes. Can you talk more about what you call the purification of desire? As I understand it, we take any desire we might have and live with the feeling, thought, emotional and psychological attachment, the sensation of the desire, while letting go of the actual object of desire.

JK. Yes, we keep the flame of desire but drop the object of desire and in this way we are brought to the essence of desire. When you let go of the object you are in the energy of desire. It is no longer eccentric towards an object, it has no more direction. You are then in a directionless state, a state of waiting, free from any representation, free from the past and from intention.

Q. But it is not a passive waiting state, is it?

JK. It is alive, consuming all that could be attained, all that could be an object. Then you find yourself in your nakedness, your timeless presence, in the Now. Not the thinkable now, the being Now.

Q. And is this Now full of life?

JK. It is not full of life. It is Life itself. It has no dynamism. It is Consciousness.

Q. If one is full of desire for a woman or a man or a new job or money or a house or a guru or to be a teacher or to be a good doctor, how can one just let the object go?

JK. In the understanding that this object is not your ultimate desire, that it is not what you are really looking for, the object is spontaneously let go. When you desire an object you are fixed towards it. Your whole structure is contracted in grasping, taking. The energy only stops grasping when the object is either in your hand, attained, or when you let go of the object. In either case the eccentric energy has no more role to play and it returns to stillness.

Follow your desire to its end as you'd follow a stream to the ocean or an echo to its origin. The beginning and end of desire is one and the same.

Q. Where is the desire localized?

JK. Desire is a thought and the thought process is in the forehead.

Q. Can it be of help then to consciously relax this area which is the factory of desire?

JK. It is only in an unencumbered mind that desire is not blind. The whole head must be fully sensed and then you will see how you are localized in the forehead. When it is sensed, it becomes relaxed. When it comes to you, relax your forehead and you will see that the whole brain becomes relaxed. In deep relaxation there is no object of desire. You are free from memory and anticipation.

Q. So when we desire something it means we are not relaxed?

JK. Yes. It means you are not oriented. When you are oriented there is objectless desire and then this desire points to your heart without centre or periphery.

Q. That state where the desire is purified of its object, is that pure perception?

JK. Yes. It is a thoughtless state, the Now.

Q. You said that understanding is the only means by which change occurs. And this understanding is sudden. Does the change take time?

JK. Yes, the current may be switched off, but the fan keeps turning for a while. The old pattern has a residue of momentum to live out but as there is no new stimulation for it, it will quickly die.

Q. You said that the seed of beauty and inquiry is in all of us. Will it be realized in all of us?

JK. We cannot help but look for autonomy. We will look until we are free, free from the "me," the "I," free from ourself.

Sadhana: Purify the Desire

A *sadhana* means living for a time in intimacy with, and inquiring deeply into, an aspect of the teaching.

Sadhana
On Desire

Jean Klein: The deep desire in us is to be, to be free from ourself, from the person, from all boundaries. When we follow the essence of this desire it brings us to the Desired.

In our absence the Desired awakens, beckons. We cannot look for it. It looks for us, or rather, it is looking, eternally, for itself.

Desire freed from an object is purified desire. All that you can look for is only an object. But the Desire of desires is to be in the Objectless. The seeing of this is a flash of light in our darkness, a conviction that leaves not a shadow of doubt. What we are looking for is the looker; the seeker is the sought, the sought is the seeker.

Adoration of Ra
from
The Egyptian Book of the Dead

Rejoicing in the houses. The sound of brass bells on dancing ankles. The hips of women sway through dusty streets. Day upon day the sun is risen. Day upon day the sun will rise. Day upon day this heat on adobe walls and the splay of light on Osiris. Morning stars and eventide. Chants ring through the valley and across the sands to rise to the altar of heaven. The soul of Osiris walks with wind into the temples of gods. He sets sail in the boat of morning sun. He comes to port at eventide. He twists and twines through star-studded waters, the sound of his oars the ssh-sssh of wind. The sun beats on and on like a tireless heart.

Blessings on thee, hawk, fierce and beautiful as love, whose horizons are the edges of memory so vast a man gets lost. Blessings on thee, beetle sun, which rolls into life every day kicking six legs and humming your shiny ball of song. This world is a little patch of ground you travel with no haste. The sun has burst upon the land, light yellow dust on the head of a bee. The gods are all drunk with light and singing. They crown each other king. The lady of the great house weaves garlands on his forehead. Vines and flowers of the twelve cities meet themselves. "My lord," she says, "the sun is bright today. It hovers between your shoulders." The idea of himself travels with him, affixed like the figurehead of a ship. His enemies beat themselves with sticks, tumble and sink beneath black waters. From the netherworld the dead arise to glimpse his shining face. The sea is pregnant with form. And the belly of the sky is beautiful.

Every day, the sun. Every day. And I walk east in the garden to see you, west through the country to be with you. Oh sun, my head fills with light. Do not turn me from your easy lust, whole in the sky, white in the heat. Do not bind me in sheets of darkness, a worm in the brown cake of earth. My hands are bread I have made every day. The sun spins into my heart, a place where sparrows nest. I am ridiculous and rolling on the ground, pleased with such company. Every day, the sun on the wall, light lingering on a ripe fig. I am he who worships the sun, a space in my heart a bird could fill. I am one who listens to the grass speaking in the garden. May I chew the green blade of eternity in a garden filled with sun. May I walk into fire and be burned like kernels of wheat, ground into the pulp of existence. May the sun pound and bake me brown as bread. May I rise like bread every day.

In the field with my cattle, my shadow sinks into black earth and rises. The smell of things growing. The sky and horizon part like waking lovers; like a child, the sun rises from their sleep. The world watches its steps—old man, old child, old king, sun passing in the sky, light of all that can be said, shadow of hidden things. Every face watches, every eye turns; resplendent dawn and evening. Such passion is existence. Every day my liege rides his boat, glory dripping like water from an oar. Every day the streets churn with people, every face turning. Such power can not be measured. Such love cannot be told. Unspeakable grace in the fields and cities. I dip my bread in milk and eat.

Mantis, this landscape is hidden from all but the most holy eye. Oh sun going out to the sea's edge over the crest of mountain, what might a weary man call home but the light in his head, the scroll in his heart? What darklings wait with blood-red teeth within the walls of his sacred home? Such country the sun has seen, truth like memory or love. Such colours of robes some women wear, more mauve than grapes their gowns and eyes. What is hidden belongs to the sun. It is too much for a man to know. It is Ra who gathers the world together, who holds and beholds with his eye, this juxtaposition of vegetation and air, the thousand colours of prayer and stone. Having sprung from formless water, he takes his shape in fire. He springs from the mouth of the horizon as if he were the first word he uttered. May he string his words into song. May he roll through the heavens like music. And for as long as the sun is shining, may the strings of my soul hum like a lyre.

Sun, your number is one multiplied by millions. I am but a man with my thousand longings for unity. May we never cease to be. May there be no time in which a man must count the days toward some end. Oh, that life could be more than its fragments. No before and no after, no exaltation but in the timeless one. The sun strides over heaven crossing distances of millions of years and the hundreds of thousands of millions... one day of the sun. He set-rises, set-rises over thousands of cities, trees and mountains and men. The distance of the instant. He has made an end to hours and likewise counted them. In the morning earth fills with light. Law and baptism. The one of us all endures. It is our work under the sun.

Speak of the rising heart of carnelian. Red heart of a living god, old priest in an ancient tomb, an image scratched into muscle and blood. On this stony plateau we stand, all our days like beads of lapis strung on the throat of sky. We stand—existent cities washed with colour, ash of night fallen underground. The great world pours out its unguents and the little world is made great. A shout among many people rises on a day of splendour when the sun folds back on itself. He deepens and lengthens and thickens, moulding his body with light. The sun grinds itself like corn. Tendrils of fire seek their limits of light. This is the colour of time, the joy and pain of a birthing mother. He is born in the form of Ra. He creates himself on his mother's thigh.

May I reach an everlasting heaven and walk in the legend of mountains with thoughts quiet as deer. May I meet myself in every vegetable and rock quickened by tendrils of light. Holy and perfect is the world which lives by fire in the embrace of the carnelian heart. May I walk with the sun until eventide, forgetting the reason of hours. May I burst into light like a purple flower remembered by a lover.

The sun has risen like gold or wheat, aurora in the land of his birth, splendour in a country of sky. His mother is draped in a gauze of air, the disc revolves in her hand like a bowl of meal. Egypt will be fed. Great light bursts on the horizon and men who've slept in the dark with stomachs empty as night rush into the streets hungry, happy to eat morning. Ten thousand thousand fingers wash in the flood, ten thousand thousand grapes and olives feed on living water. In the towns and in the temples there is a festival, flood of wine and flowers, one song many lutes are playing. A woman suckles her baby, while her husband drunk with meat and beer lies in the shade of a fig tree, singing praises to her inner thigh.

Might of might. Splendour of splendour. This is the terror inherent in love: that such power may exist without reason, that death may be feared and lusted for as a woman, that passion gives rise to passion. I am moved by desire as if a boat transported me from horizon to horizon. What I have done for love, let it be held against me. I am a man whose heart is full. I am a man empty of sin. It is life I desire. My lust for it and I enter the heart of the mountain together. Together we are judged by shining beasts and they say, "There walks he who loves his life."

One day with a shout I'll rise through the sky. My voice will mingle with air. I'll cross horizons. With silver wings I'll enter the realm of magic. Within the temple of mountain and sky, corn grows amid earth's yellow scars. This is the sacred cathedral of Ra into which men long to enter. My name recalls the countless stars under which new lovers kiss. Death ferries me to a distant shore while striped fish spawn on turquoise waters, while black fish leap in white rivers.

The universe is drawn in circles. The memory of chariot wheels clacking across small stones foreshadows the sap's death as he wraps himself around the wheel. He is crushed by its embrace. The air crackles when Ra is within. And sailors who've known only cities by the sea and the whip of the rope and sail, come to moor at last amid a crush of flowers and rejoice and weep and go on. The days before and the days after fill with the odour of pomegranates. The heart ripens like fruit, falls and breaks. Sweet meat for the lips of god. On such a day one glances into the sky and finds the eye of Ra looks back. One finds loaves of bread on fine reed mats and the eye of Ra looks back. The air crackles. The sun beats on and on.

Translated by Normandi Ellis

Excerpt from Dialogue,
Santa Barbara, California: February 16, 1992

Jean Klein: When there is teaching, you must follow the line free from expectation and anticipation—as in the same way when you trace the route on the map it brings you to your destination. It is very deeply rooted in the body-mind that there is something to achieve, to become, to attain, and this brings us absolutely away from what we are. It takes us in the opposite direction. So we must first face our body-mind, accept it, explore it, get to know it. In this exploration there comes a moment when you are no longer interested in what you explore but live in the exploring itself. The explored is in the exploring, but the exploring is not in the explored. In other words, the known is in the knowing, but the knowing is not in the known. Otherwise, there could not be knowing.

By "explore the body-mind" I mean sense the body-mind. And by "sense" I mean have the sensation of it. Systematically go through all the parts and let each part become sensitive. In this way you become aware of your body. The body is only known through the five senses so let it come up to your five senses. The most obvious of all the sense faculties is sensation or feeling. We know our bodies mostly through sensation. In sensing the body you become free from the reactive body, free from mechanical functioning. So the moment you explore, sense, your body you no longer feed its conditioning. There's no longer an accomplice to it, to its tension, expectation, aggression. There's a letting go, a deep relaxation. Then there's a moment when there's no more emphasis on the object, the body-mind, and there's a switchover so that the observer-subject-explorer is emphasized. You find yourself objectless, no longer in relation of subject to object—abiding completely in stillness, in beingness. That is self-knowing.

Become free from undertaking, from doing. Not doing is also an undertaking. Doing and not doing are movements in the mind. And the mind, like all objects, has its roots in the self, in our highest principle. It is only in this higher principle that there is a conversion between doing and not-doing. In this conversion there is no more left and right, yes and no, like and dislike, doing and not-doing; you are free from duality, there is really wholeness, completeness. It no longer has anything to do with the mind.

Q. Is that living intelligence?

JK. When you are free from psychological survival you are also free from psychological memory. There is still functional memory but there is no longer memory which revolves around the "me." So, free from this restriction, our brain cells are completely open to the universe, to the Ultimate; then there is intelligence. And then there is no more repetition. As long as there is psychological survival there is no intelligence.

Q. In that state we could do, but we would know we're not the doer.

JK. Yes.

Q. You don't have to sort of not do.

JK. There's nothing to do, there's only being open, being available. In this present moment, for example, we should see that we are still stuck to knowing. Free from the knowing we live our not-knowing, our emptiness. But see what this emptiness means. Generally when people speak of emptiness, it means to be empty of something. This emptiness refers to something of which we are empty, and not to emptiness itself. Do you see the difference? When you understand it, visualize it; it is important that we represent this understanding very often. In visualizing this emptiness it goes in our total structure. We *are* this emptiness.

Q. It seems that often this emptiness retains something of the flavour of the teacher and his sayings. Eventually does this flavour dissolve as well?

JK. When there is understanding, you see clearly that there is nothing to teach. As there is nothing to teach, where is the teacher? When there is no teacher and nothing to teach, there is teaching. And then in this absence there is a perfect availability of a meeting between the so-called teacher and the so-called ignorant one. One cannot teach you to sit on a chair when you are already seated. A teaching that tries to teach you how to come to what you are, takes you away from what you are. Simply live without end-gaining, daydreaming, intention, live without projection, in complete openness. This openness is not an object, it is nowhere, it is not localized. So, become open to the openness. This is the seventh direction. In other words, knowing ourselves in consciousness. All that is perceived is in consciousness.

Q. Ordinarily when we see objects we refer the object to the known. It's like a projection—that's a tree and there are the characteristics of the tree. But when the object appears in globality, does it then refer to nothing, to the space around the tree?

JK. There is no seen without seeing. There is nothing heard without hearing. The seen refers to its seeing. Outside of the seeing there is nothing seen. You create the world every moment when you think of it. When the body-mind wakes up in the morning, the world also wakes up. The world is, exists, in yourself. It is you who create the world, because the world is nothing other than your five senses and the sixth sense...

Q. Conception.

JK. Conception. But... when you look at the tree, it is sense perception. You see it, you smell it, you touch it, and so on. And then you conceive it. But the moment you conceive it there is no longer the perception, because the perception and conception cannot occur together. So that when the perceiving is over, there's a conception, and when the conception is over what remains? The identity that you have with the tree.

Q. The identity that I have with the tree?

JK. Your real nature and the real nature of the tree are the same; there's no difference. First you give up the idea of body and then you give up the mind and then you are one with it. That is love. In this moment all is and nothing is.

Q. In which case, I don't understand the nothingness. When you're everything, where is the nothingness?

JK. There's no more conceptualization. There's no more object. Before you wake up in the morning, what happens? You know this moment. You have the profound feeling that you are, yet you are free from all objects. It is a transition from deep sleep to the waking state. It is a very important moment, this moment before the body wakes up. Take note of it.

What is important is that the mind is oriented, that it knows that there is something beyond the mind. Only this allows you to be available to change. It is the same as when somebody says that there are seven directions but you know only six: in front, behind, left and right, up and down. But somebody you trust says there are seven. So the mind, in a certain way, is open to it. The mind knows nothing but it is open to something completely new.

Q. Receptive, then.

JK. Yes. It is only in this receptivity that you can come to the understanding that there is a seventh direction: that is the heart. So it is very important that the mind is informed.

Q. What do you mean by "heart"?

JK. It is not properly speaking a direction but the centre from where all directions flow. It is the Self.

Q. In the morning before the mind is really free-wheeling and engaged…? There's little chance there?

JK. Because what we call the body-mind is more or less a superimposition on what is. The body-mind exists in time, but what is, is timeless. Consciousness is. The body-mind is only a superimposition, like the three states of sleeping, dreaming, waking—superimpositions on this timeless continuum.

Q. In relationships with people, it's always as if they're pulling to identify with the person. Most conversations seem to revolve around that whole self-centred kind of movement. How can one be in a healthy relationship with everyone, friendly with everyone, without allowing that self-centred movement and yet not ignoring people completely. How does one deal with people who are identifying with themselves? How to be in good relationship with them?

JK. Friendly and good relationships are the result of understanding. There are many people who seem to be good or friendly, but one can never be truly friendly or good through acquired behaviour. Good and friendly are the result of understanding. When you are really good and friendly, you are not friendly and good. Think about it.
Thank you for listening.

Your Question

Q. For many years I have given all my time, energy, knowledge and power to my family and to my business. My life was completely oriented towards bringing up and giving advice to my children and earning my living. Now my children are grown up and no longer need me and I am retired from business, and I feel a certain loss of orientation and an emptiness that was previously filled with all kinds of activities. How can my life have meaning and fulfilment?

Jean Klein: See things as they are now, not as you wish them to be. See only the facts, free from all psychology. Look at your feelings of lack, boredom, loneliness, desire, confusion. See how all these feelings of confusion and absence are related to the fact that you have taken yourself for a parent and a worker. Now these self-images have no more role to play. Your colleagues no longer need you and your children no longer look to you for advice. See how you still take yourself for a parent, for somebody, and this is a fraction. Become free from the self-image. Then you can have a non-objective relationship with your children and your surroundings. When there is no longer any reference to being a parent you are open to the facts, what actually is.

Live in the perceived not the conceived. Only the perception is right. The concept is wrong because it is memory. So give no more place to the concept. In the absence of psychological behaviour there is no reference to old brain patterns and only then is there intelligence which is the awakening of all your resources. Then you will have a new relation to your surroundings. It is no longer one of object to object, but of love. There is no longer an "I" and a "you" but only oneness. When there is no superimposition on your children and surroundings, every moment is joy. Life is joyful and in the absence of any patterns of behaviour there is only friendly togetherness.

Body Approach
A Guided Relaxation

Jean Klein: Feel the contact of your feet on the floor.

Give up the weight of your legs. Put all the weight on the contact with the ground.

Feel the contact of your bottom on the chair. Put all the weight on this contact.

Feel the lower part of your lumbar region. Feel the spinal cord. Let the feeling rise up step by step, vertebra by vertebra. In other words, let your spinal cord become straight through the feeling.

Contact the left knee with your left hand; contact the right knee with your right hand. Put all the weight on this contact with the knee. You have three contacts: with the ground, with the chair, with your knees. Let it be one contact.

Feel your shoulder and shoulder blades. Let your left elbow and right elbow go down as far as you can, so that the shoulders are taken with them. In other words, explore how far down your shoulders can go. Be aware, when you feel the rising up of your spinal cord, that simultaneously your shoulders go down. Feel the cervical region. Bring your neck a little backwards horizontally like opening a drawer. Feel as though you touch the wall behind you. And the chin goes a little in the direction of the sternum. Have the feeling now of the whole body structure.

Feel the cavity of your left eye. Feel the eye itself. Be aware of the tension, the defence there. Feel the cavity of your right eye. The right eye itself. Feel the left and right eyes dropped several inches down in front, detached from their cavities.

Feel your right brain. Feel the top of your head. Make it feeling. Feel it in the same way as you listen to waves. Feel the left side in the same way. Feel the waves of the left brain.

Feel the left brain and right brain like water falling down over the neck to the shoulders. Feel your eyes and both sides of your brain taking rest on your shoulders.

Feel the space in your mouth. Feel all the walls which constitute your mouth. Let them be feeling. Feel the roots of your tongue. Let the tip of your tongue rest behind the lower teeth.

Feel your left ear. Feel the architecture of your left ear. Go deep in. Be aware if there is any tension, grasping, taking. Feel the architecture of your right ear. Go deep in, in the ear canal. Let the music of the sound waves come to you. Let the feeling come up that the left ear occupies the whole of the left part of your body and the right ear occupies the right part of your body, in other words, the whole body becomes one ear. Hear with your whole body the sound of the waves. Hear now the sound waves without any selection, without any choice.

Be only awareness, only hearing without a hearer. There is nothing heard, only hearing.

*

In the beginning it may be difficult to really sense all the different parts of your body. But after doing it for some time you will see that it is very easy.

When your shoulders are completely down, the lower part of the shoulder blades move towards each other, and only then do you feel that your shoulders are really down. As feeling—sensation—brings the spine to rise up vertebra by vertebra and at the same time the shoulder blades to go down, it feels like two elevators, one going up, the other going down. The right position of the head is important because at the seventh cervical vertebra there is a kind of break and the head tends to drop down in front. That should be avoided.

The moment you become aware of the tension in your eyes, you will experience some deep relaxation. The eyes are a very important sense organ in our structure. They are conditioned to grasping, taking.

There is also grasping in the hearing. All these tensions in the organs of seeing and hearing are very deep obstacles to a quiet mind. So do not go to the object. Let go of taking the object. Let the heard come to you and the seen come to you.

At first you will feel only the deep relaxation of your body, but later you will find certain new qualities, a kind of dynamism, a kind of elasticity. And then what is perceived is not a passive mass but a current of energy. This is the original body, a body impregnated by life.

So, in the beginning it takes time to really come to the right position of the psychosomatic body, but, as we said, there is an organic memory of the original unconditioned body. Later you will be able to integrate and go, knowingly, immediately, into this natural state.

When your brain is completely relaxed it can be sensed like a sponge in constant vibration. The more you can sense an organ, have it really in your hands, the more you can relax it completely. When, for example, you relax your eyes, you feel the difference between looking with the sensation that the eyes are in front grasping towards the world, and looking in a completely relaxed way from behind you. You should experience the distinction between these ways of looking. I will not explain exactly what the difference is; you will feel the difference.

Of course, all these suggestions are more or less crutches, so don't put too much weight on them.

LISTENING

Volume 6
1992

Bringing the Perceived back to the Perceiving 189
Jean Klein

Tripura Rahasya 198
The Mystery Beyond the Trinity

Songs of Kabir: Number 20 207

On Welcoming 208
Jean Klein

Approach on the Body Level: *Sensing the Brain* 210
Jean Klein

Your Question: *Is studying the mind beneficial?* 218
Jean Klein

Bringing the Perceived back to the Perceiving

Q. One of the pedagogical devices—as you call them—that you say is essential to the direct path is to bring every object back to the perceiving; the heard to the hearing, the seen to its seeing, the felt to the feeling and so on. What exactly does this mean?

Jean Klein: The first thing is to understand that when something is perceived it is perceived in consciousness by consciousness. Nothing is perceived without a perceiver. The perceived has all its reality, its existence, its potentiality in the perceiver. The perceived has no separate existence. There are not two; there is only one.

Q. Sometimes you say the perceived is in the perceiving and sometimes you say the perceived is in the perceiver. Is the perceiver the same as the perceiving?

JK. I am using the term perceiver in the sense of the ultimate perceiver which is not a thing, a subject. It is perceiving itself, or consciousness. When you look deeply, there is nothing "outside" consciousness. There is no observer, only observing, no hearer, only hearing.

Q. In our everyday perceiving, when I hear a car, for example, there is "I" the perceiver and the car—the perceived...

JK. You take the "I" for an object, but the "I" is not an entity. If you try to think of "I" with no qualifications, simply "I," you cannot. This unqualified, unthinkable "I" is not an entity.

Q. What is it then?

JK. It is our universal being, consciousness.

Q. And is the car perceived by this universal being?

JK. Yes, absolutely. By the "I am."

Q. How can I feel what you are saying? How can I be convinced? It is still an intellectual, a philosophical idea.

JK. It is only in being it that you can be convinced. It must be seen by the undivided mind. Let us first be clear about the difference between living in the divided mind—reasoning and choice— and living in the undivided mind—openness and globality. You can never come to the apprehension of truth through reasoning. Reasoning belongs to the subject-object relationship. The apprehension of truth belongs to the whole mind. The whole mind is free from any point of view.

Q. The mind usually functions through reasoning, in a divided way, subject-object. How can we come to the point where the mind functions from wholeness?

JK. It is only in your openness that the undivided mind comes into its own. In openness you find yourself in a constant questioning where there's no conclusion. You live without reference. The mind is empty. All your body is in this wholeness. It is relaxed, expanded. There's no fixation. You live physically and mentally in non-localization, non-volition.

Q. What is the difference between living in non-concluding and simply drifting?

JK. In drifting you are identified with, stuck to, the body, senses and mind. You inevitably have ideas, goals or intentions of one kind or another. You are in the situation and see yourself in relation to the situation. Perhaps you have an image of yourself in a certain situation. You still see things from the split-mind.

In living in non-concluding, which is living in openness, the situation is in you but you are not in the situation. The situation is never seen in relation to desires, aims and so on. In the Tao there is no reference to an "I". There is volition in non-volition. That means it is the situation that asks for action. You live only with facts and act according to the facts. In the Tao, insight is more important because when there's not fractional seeing, there's global seeing which brings its own conclusion.

Q. If I live free from the divided calculating mind, and I practise bringing the perception back to the perceiving, what will I learn? How will it help me?

JK. When everything seen and heard goes back to its home-ground, seeing and hearing, it is glorified, made sacred. An object sanctified is no longer an object.

Q. What do you mean "goes back to"?

JK. When the object is referred to its origin, it brings you back to your homeground.

Q. Is the reason, if we can call it a reason, to bring the object "home" to the perceiving, just to show us our own Home?

JK. Yes, it is very important that you have this glimpse.

Q. When I look at something, especially a familiar object, I'm aware that I don't see it as if new. I see it with my memory. But when I see a completely new object, don't I spontaneously look without reference?

JK. Free from reference, looking is always new. It is reference which brings previous experiences into the present situation. This is looking from the divided mind. Free from reference you look from the whole mind.

Q. In looking from the whole mind is there no thought at all?

JK. There is no thought. There is no choosing. The whole mind is a state of pure openness. It is beyond positive, negative and all complementarity.

Q. What is the physical pre-condition for this state of open mind in which objects are simply received?

JK. When you are free from reference, your body and senses are in a state of availability. In this state of welcoming, of waiting, the muscles and nervous systems are in their original relaxed state where there's no grasping and no refusing. It is really our Adamic state, a state of complete relaxation, expansion, of readiness in all directions.

Q. And in this readiness the object appears as it really is—free from our projections?

JK. In the state of availability there are not two, no "I," no "it," no barriers. The object appears in this openness and disappears in openness. The objectivity of a thing is maintained only by the divided mind functioning in subject-object relationship. When the subject becomes pure, becomes innocent, free from all striving, then it disappears and with it, its object—and what remains is only openness, being.

Q. Openness is beingness and beingness is openness?

JK. Absolutely. Our openness is awareness.

Q. When objects appear in beingness, how do they appear to us?

JK. They are sanctified, as we said. They are no longer things. They are sacrilized by the direct contact with their source. They partake directly of their origin and are not separated from it. This original Beingness is consciousness, ultimate awareness.

Q. Or welcoming, openness or availability?

JK. Yes, welcoming is presence and in this presence you are absent as a perceiver. There is only perceiving with no perceiver and nothing perceived. When there is no divided mind, no "I," no chooser, no thinking, no qualifying, then there is pure perception.

Q. And when the pure perception refers to the perceiving...?

JK. That is an apperception of reality, of your Self. It is direct perception.

Q. So when I look at the flower free from all interference it is a pure perception and when the flower looks at me, reminds me of me, of myself, it is a direct perception?

JK. Absolutely.

Q. When I look without reference, without thought, will I remember what I am looking at? If I walk along the beach and the seen, heard, smelled, felt comes back to its seeing, hearing, feeling, etc., will I be aware of the sand, gulls, salt air, and will I later be able to write a poem about them?

JK. In the moment when the seen is back to the seeing there is no more duality. You are not aware of things nor can you recall them because you are not in memory. You are living only in your glory. But this moment is very brief.

Q. Is it a kind of blank state from the point of view of the phenomenal world?

JK. It is blank in that it is empty of objects, but the absence of yourself is not a blank state because when you are absent there is Presence.

Q. So our glory is our consciousness, perceiving without an object?

JK. Yes, it is seeing where nothing is seen. It is consciousness without objects. The sense organs function but they take themselves in charge. There is no controller, no perceiver, no one aware.

Q. So the only reason for the initial object of perception, no matter what it was, is to bring us back, to act as a pointer, as you say, to our beingness?

JK. Yes, to its homeground which is our isness.

Q. And you suggest that we become familiar with bringing the seen back to the seeing, the object back to consciousness, only to make us aware, for a moment, of our real being?

JK. Yes. Yes, it reveals our real nature which always is.

Q. It seems, then, that the moment we are talking about now, the moment when we live our glory, our being, where consciousness knows itself by itself—this moment is like the no-mountains in Zen, because it is consciousness aware of itself in the absence of objects. But "then there are mountains again." How can we live our real being and also live in activity?

JK. The moment when the seen brings you back to the seeing is a timeless moment when you live in your glory. At first the reflex will be there to go again to the object, but after the moment of glory you now have a feeling, an echo, that the object is in you. After several of these moments, you will feel clearly that there is no separation, that time is in the timeless.

Find yourself in the absence of objects and there comes a moment when objects appear in you. You will feel activity is in you but you are not in it. The activity is constantly purified; it is sacred at every moment. This is enlightenment: where presence is constant, based in the timeless, presence in all activity.

Q. Is there a sudden moment when the smell of the sea appears in awareness, when objects appear in our glory, their glory?

JK. There is one moment when you are knowingly in it. How the timeless begins again to flirt with time is not in the brain's power of explanation to describe because it is the timeless and takes place in it.

Q. I'd like to clarify this, if I may.

JK. Of course, go on. I like being pushed into the corner.

Q. Is there, then, a moment when in living in the seeing, in the hearing, in consciousness without objects, suddenly objects appear in our being, in consciousness? And is this felt on the physical level as a sudden expansion—when the whole world is in us?

JK. Yes, it is a switch over. But first you abide in beauty, you are attracted by beauty because you are beauty and beauty looks for beauty. So live in it, dwell in it, take it to yourself and then there comes a moment when you are it. It is a total expansion.

Q. Is this threshold, living in consciousness without objects, an essential moment for the truth seeker on the direct path?

JK. To know consciousness without objects is essential to everyone. Until we know our Self without objects we cannot know objects in our Self. We must become alive to the fact of our eternal Self without objects.

Q. And, of course, this absence of objects when the perceived dissolves in the perceiver has nothing to do with the introversion of the mind and senses.

JK. It is very difficult for people to be presence without any object at all. They always need some subtle object, a vibration, a body sensation, a light, a feeling of transcendence or expansion. But when the senses are accepted totally, welcomed, they open and there's a deep relaxation. In this deep relaxation they are integrated into our being. If, on the other hand, they are refused, as happens with introversion, their grasping reflex remains because the sense organs automatically look for existence. So there is no deep expansion and no integration.

Q. If we still find subtle objects, vibrations, feelings and so on, does it mean we have practised introversion?

JK. Yes, because you are still trying to achieve something. There is still intention in your doing. Why try to be an angel? An angel is still something, a sage is nothing.

Q. Would you say, then, that the practical essence of enlightenment is integration?

JK. Yes. There is nothing to refuse and no one to refuse. All is consciousness perceived by consciousness in consciousness.

Q. So to make it quite clear: when the seen is brought back to the seeing (or the heard to the hearing and so on) one lives in consciousness, perceiving. The sense organs are open and functioning but as awareness is no longer directed, on the level of perception it seems there is a blank. There are no sensations, no colours, no vibrations, no light, no feeling. Phenomenally there is no object at all and yet there is in this absence a full presence. Is this so?

JK. Yes, absolutely. Even though the senses are open you don't hear, see or perceive anything, even subtly. You are simply in the openness. And then you come to the absence of the absence.

Q. When we are in openness without objects is there still a kind of localization, a localization in the absence, a localization in our own self-awareness without objects? Or is this a contradiction?

JK. The absence or presence of objects in no way affects perceiving consciousness. When the object abides in perceiving consciousness then it is something else because it is no longer related to the ego, it is related to the ultimate.

Q. So those teachings which say that consciousness with mountains is more advanced or higher than consciousness of oneself in the no-mountains...

JK. These are all suppositions. I am talking from experience. When you know yourself you know that the world is in you. It is not a stage, it is an unfolding. The world is not separate from you. There is only one truth: when you see the truth you know it on all levels.

Tripura Rahasya
The Mystery Beyond the Trinity

This dialogue between Prince Hemacuda and Princess Hemalekha was also a favourite with Ramana Maharshi.

After their marriage, Prince Hemacuda and Princess Hemalekha lived happily for some time in the royal palace. But gradually the Princess became remote and indifferent to everything. The distressed Prince asked her the reason for her change of attitude.

Hemalekha: Oh Prince, listen to me. It's not that I don't love you, but one thought keeps tormenting me. I cannot understand what's good or what's bad for people in this world. I've thought about this for a long time now, but how could a woman like me find the answer? Please teach me.

At these words, Hemacuda burst into laughter and replied: They are right in saying women have little judgment. Even the four-footed creatures and the birds and insects know what's good and what's bad for them. It's obvious that all these creatures tend to seek out the pleasant and the good, and turn away from the rest. What is good gives pleasure, what's bad causes pain. My dear, this isn't really a great problem! How could it have bothered you for so long?

Hemalekha: You've expressed it well. We women lack judgment. That's why I'm prepared to surrender to your explanations. Explain all this clearly and I'll drop my musing to enjoy life by your side. You said that what is good is pleasurable and what is bad is painful, yet it happens that the same thing sometimes gives pleasure and sometimes gives pain, depending on the circumstance. Fire, for example, is pleasant in the winter, but hard to bear in the summer. It can also be pleasant in small doses and unpleasant in large amounts. Think of your father, the king. He has everything he could wish for: power, gold, a palace, elephants, a harem, a lineage. Why then is he always sad, while others, who don't have all of this, live content? Isn't it true, as well, that pleasurable objects don't always exist everywhere and in unlimited supply, so that even kings constantly encounter the deception of "not enough" or "too much," or "not yet" and "no more so soon"? Isn't it true that desire sharpens with enjoyment, like a fire stirred by the wind? And the more a being is conscious, hence amenable to pleasure, the more he's vulnerable to pain, such as the eye is irritated by the tiniest speck, so that man could well be the most miserable creature in the universe?

Having heard these words, the Prince sank into melancholy. Accustomed as he was to pleasure, he could neither denounce it completely nor continue to indulge in it limitlessly, without reservations. Again, he spoke to the Princess.

Hemacuda: Oh dearest one, until now I never appreciated the depth of your mind. Now your words haunt me so much that I'm like a man who has been condemned to death and can no longer taste the dishes placed before him. Let me learn from your wisdom. Tell me what I must do to attain true happiness.

Hemalekha: The only important thing is that you come to know what constitutes the essence of your being.

Hemacuda: But can you tell me how to know who I am?

Hemalekha: All you need is to be ready for it. Begin by purifying your intelligence for we need it to understand the nature of the Self. In some way it is already known by all, from gods to the most infinitesimal creatures, but it never presents itself in a visible form. This is why, strictly speaking it can't be taught. It's as if you asked someone else to show you your own eyes. All a master or teacher can do is indicate the way and means. The method lies in discriminating between what is mine and what is I. Retire to a quiet place and try to systematically eliminate all that could be called "mine." The residue, which can never appear as "mine," will be the Self. For instance, you see me and know me as your wife. This means I could be called "yours" in terms of a certain relationship, but this wife-relationship doesn't belong in any way to the essence of your being.

After hearing these words, the Prince, without delay, withdrew to his palace. He gave the guards, posted at the entrance to the grounds, orders to prohibit all visitors and leave him undisturbed. Then he climbed up the nine floors of the palace to the terrace from where a view stretched far over the surrounding countryside. There he sat on a mat and, concentrating his mind, began to reflect: "Truly the whole world is mad. No one knows himself and yet everyone pursues various activities convinced they will benefit by them. Some spend their time studying the Scriptures, others the laws; some are busy accumulating wealth or ruling kingdoms; some fight the enemy while others give themselves up to pleasure. All this is done in complete ignorance of who they really are. Even I have done just the same until now. It's time for me to meditate on my real nature. I don't recognize myself in any of these things surrounding me: the wealth, the harem, the elephants or goats, the palace or even the whole kingdom. All this is purely and simply "mine." But surely this body is myself? It seems so. I was born into a royal family: I'm slender and have a clear complexion, etc. This is what I am."

Yet, pursuing this meditation, he changed his mind: "No, I am not my body. Made of blood, flesh, and bones, it is changing from moment to moment. Not one atom from when I was a child, exists today. Yet I am conscious of being "the same" as during my childhood. Further, while I pass through all kinds of experiences while dreaming, this body remains as inert as stone. How could it then be myself? Yet, it's a fact that I exist. Otherwise, how could I remember having slept and dreamt? Unless I don't exist, at all, in any way. Yet no, that's impossible. If that were so, who would have had the dream experience? Who then would be seeking right now to know his essence? So I am something conscious and different from the body. Could I be the vital breath which produces all the body's movements? No, for in deep sleep, the breath persists, yet one no longer knows anything of surrounding things. Perhaps, then, I'm the mind (*manas*)? But this is made up of thoughts which follow each other unceasingly, like waves breaking on the shore. Why should I identify with this thought rather than that one? It's the same for the intelligence (*buddhi*), the organ of judgment and decision. How many different judgements sweep us along in the course of a single day! Yet I'm conscious of remaining the same from morning to night. What is more, I can't, at any moment, imagine myself as non-existent. The body, breath, mind, discrimination, all are "mine." There's no doubt I am something who knows, but I can't see through what means I could in turn know this Knower in me. And yet it seems that through this very stop in understanding I am already a little closer to my real nature. How strange this all is! One could say that what I seek to know recedes when I try to grasp it with thought and draws nearer the moment I relax the tension of my mind."

Hemacuda then abandoned all thought activity. Immediately he found himself surrounded by dense darkness. Thinking this was the essence of the Self, he was gripped by anguish. Returning to himself, he resolved to make another attempt. Controlling himself by Hatha-Yoga, he found himself in front of a strange diffuse light which did not seem to come from any direction. Then, in a further effort, he fell asleep and had all sorts of dreams, some pleasant, others terrifying. Scarcely awakened, he resumed his concentration and in a split-second plunged into a fathomless ocean of joy. But, once again, he returned to ordinary consciousness. His confusion was immense: Had he only dreamt, or had he reached the Self, and, if so, was the Self light or darkness, bliss or a chaos of images? Incapable of coming to a definitive conclusion, he resolved to once more consult the Princess.

Hemacuda: Dear wife, I've done everything that you recommended. I've immobilized my mind by suppressing all of its activities, those directed inwardly as well as outwardly. I've successively encountered darkness, light, dreams, and profound joy. But in all of that, where is the essence of the Self?

Hemalekha: You have done well to seek to be free from your mind. Without this, no one could ever possess Self-knowledge. But, oh dearest husband, you must realize that these means in themselves don't give access to the Self, since the Self is always present, always attained. If it were something to attain, hence something external and foreign, how could it be called "Self?" One cannot know how to attain it. By its very nature it is "out of reach." Let me give you an example. Suppose a certain object is in the dark and can't be seen. Then a lamp is brought and the object is discovered as if it had only just been produced on the spot. Or again, imagine that I have, absent-mindedly, forgotten where I put my bracelet. The only thing 1 have to do is to remember by eliminating every other thought. I will then find the bracelet exactly where 1 left it, but as if it appeared in this spot for the first time. Thought activity serves here only to remove the obstacles to remembering. It's the same in the case of the Self.

The truth is that ignorant as we are of the nature of the Self, and therefore incapable of recognizing it despite its continual presence, we vainly seek it outside ourselves. You know the story of the simple man who, one evening, makes his way to the royal palace which is all illuminated. Around him are people discussing the beauty of the illumination, but he, not knowing the meaning of the word "illumination," asks for it to be brought to him, and placed under a torch so that he can see what it is. Your case, dear husband, is exactly the same! Now listen carefully: You say that after having suspended every movement of your mind you found yourself in dense darkness? Well, all you need to do is try to receive the moment between achieving the suppression of thought activity and the appearance of darkness for the essence of the Self to manifest more clearly than before. It's just here that those whose eyes are habituated to contemplating the external world are easily deluded, exhausted, victims of hallucinations, and don't succeed in finally recognizing the Self. There are many wise men,, versed in Scriptures, but almost all of them remain enslaved by suffering because they haven't succeeded in discerning the Self. For this, learning to interpret Scriptures isn't enough.

The Self isn't something distant so that attaining it requires crossing this distance. It's not something the intellect is capable or incapable of illuminating. Just as one could never unite with his shadow by running after it, so there's nothing to "do" to attain the Self. As a small child sees a thousand things reflected in a mirror placed in front of him, but doesn't see the mirror as such, so men see the infinite phenomena of the world reflected in the mirror of the Self, but have no idea of the real nature of this Self. It is like those who ignore space itself, only seeking things in this space and thinking space is a great receptacle. The whole world—oh dearest one—is formed by activities of knowledge on the one side and by objects of knowledge on the other. But between these two, absolute consciousness, Self-hood, remains self-revealed and self-subsistent. That's why no instrument is required to know it. Perhaps someone might ask how one comes to know something like absolute consciousness exists. But it's not even necessary to answer this question: If consciousness doesn't exist, then both the question and answer vanish. Consciousness is beyond doubt, one can't even imagine its non-existence. It's limited neither by time nor space, for time and space are the first things to be reflected in its mirror. It is your essence and whosoever realizes this truth in all its breadth becomes creator of the universe.

Let me tell you how it will be less difficult for you to realize this. You meet it, for example, in the instant separating being awake from being asleep, and being asleep from being awake, in the instant the intellect jumps from one thing to another, in the stupor a face to face encounter with something terrifying provokes, or the sudden meeting of a friend you no longer expected to see again. Meditate on all that and, once you have understood, you will no longer be fascinated by anything else. Everything rests on this consciousness, dense and homogeneous as the polished surface of a mirror, and the apparent unreeling of the universe in space and time is just due to ignorance of this fact. The Self is neither the knowing subject nor the known object, but their common base. It is the supreme Lord men sometimes call Vishnu, sometimes Siva, sometimes Brahma. Try to realize this for yourself. Ignore your senses, turn your thoughts to their source. Drop even the attempt to grasp or not to grasp this truth, and what will then arise will be the Self.

Thus directed, the Prince soon reached the state called "concentration devoid of mental constructions." At the end of several hours he returned to a state of ordinary consciousness and again experienced the world surrounding him. Immediately he felt the desire to return to his concentration, and for this, he closed his eyes. Then Hemalekha took his hand and said to him:

Hemalekha: Oh dearest husband, what are you doing? I don't understand you! What have you to gain by closing your eyes or to lose by opening them?

Hemacuda: Dearest, after a long search I have finally reached the realm of eternal peace. Where could I find, in this cold and arid world full of suffering and misery, such a place of repose? All these mundane activities seem to me now as tasteless as the remains of sugarcane after the juice has been extracted. Unfortunately, I've never before experienced this state of bliss. I see that I was like a man who makes a tour of the world, begging food, forgetting the treasure buried under the ashes in his hearth. Never having noticed the ocean of bliss always within me. I dispersed myself in pleasure-seeking. I believed these to be stable and solid—though they come and go like lightning—and that's why I suffered. How strange! Everyone wants to be happy and yet they do exactly the contrary to what could bring them happiness. Today, dearest, my suffering ended. I desire nothing else than to dwell in this state of unsurpassable bliss. But I pity you who, after knowing such a state, still continue to participate—like an insane person—in the routine of mundane pursuits.

Hemalekha: Dear husband, I'm deeply sorry that you again haven't really understood. This supreme bliss which, once known, prevents one ever again being fascinated by this world, is still for you a distant horizon. Everything you've learned up to now is worth practically nothing. Do you think the apprehension of Reality has anything to do with opening or closing your eyes? How can you consider the absolute as a state attained by practising some determined activity, or in abstaining from this activity? Might Reality suddenly appear through the mere lowering of these eyelids wide as four grains of rice?

As long as these knots in you haven't been unravelled, you won't taste this supreme felicity. These knots have been made from the rope of Illusion—ignorance of our own essence. The major knot is believing that the body is the Self. Innumerable secondary knots are linked to this. Believing that something like the Self exists outside the world forms another knot. Only the one who has cut through these knots is free. So stop imagining you can attain this by closing your eyes. There is nothing other than your own essence and it's identical with absolute consciousness which remains even after the dissolving of every form. You can't even call it a "state." Can you tell me where and when it is not? Isn't the mirror present everywhere reflections exist? A time and a place when absolute consciousness isn't present is as non-existent as the son of a barren woman. Then how could that which never and nowhere is absent—disappear when you open your eyes?

So, dear husband, tell me where you cannot find supreme consciousness, like fire that consumes everything at the end of each cosmic era? This supreme consciousness makes all our activities similar to itself, our physical activities as well as our mental ones, just as fire, in consuming wood from the fig-tree to sandalwood, makes these similar to itself. One who has understood this truth no longer feels the least inclination to open or close his eyes. So drop this futile obstacle to identifying with this consciousness by controlling your mental activities. And slice through this knot of believing the cosmic emanation is something different from your own essence. The entire universe is reflected in consciousness like the vast heavens in a hand-mirror. Realize this and then behave like an ordinary person. Don't retreat into solitude; stay here where you are and let drop even the feeling that you are on the way to reuniting with absolute consciousness.

After having meditated at length on these words, Hemacuda was finally relieved of his last illusions. He no longer dreamed of withdrawing from the world, and he lived for a long time in Hemalekha's company. His father died, so he ruled the vast kingdom, administering justice, assuring security to all, going to war when it was unavoidable. He no longer wasted any opportunity to dig wells and reservoirs, to plant trees along the roads, to build shelters for the pilgrims. He loved to hear talks by ascetics and saints of all denominations, and he made it possible for his people to hear them, too. While amassing riches, he didn't seek to fill the royal treasury, but performed great solemn sacrifices like Ashvamedha or Rajasuya. He regarded rich and poor, wise and ignorant, men and women, children and aged, with equal eyes. He neither leapt for joy when in success nor lamented in adversity. He fulfilled his royal duty like a good actor plays the role of a king on stage. He always seemed retired in himself during the numerous court intrigues, yet at just the right moment he exposed any conspiracies and did exactly what the circumstances demanded. In short, he led the existence of a person liberated in this lifetime.*

(Tantric text from the 10th century: *Tripurarahasya*, ch.IX-X)

*The editors chose to omit one last paragraph where the whole kingdom, "ministers, generals, merchants, scholars, artisans, shepherds, prostitutes, thieves, and executioners realized the Self," because its sentimental element detracted from the power of the denouement.

SONGS OF KABIR

No.20, man tu pār utar kānh jaiho

To what shore would you cross,
    O my heart? there is no traveller
    before you, there is no road;
Where is the movement, where is the
    rest, on that shore?
There is no water; no boat,
    no boatman, is there;
There is not so much as a rope to tow
    the boat, nor a man to draw it.
No earth, no sky, no time, no thing, is
    there: no shore, no ford!
There, there is neither body nor mind;
    and where is the place that shall
    still the thirst of the soul? You
    shall find naught in that emptiness.
Be strong, and enter into your own
    body: for there your foothold is
    firm. Consider it well, O my
    heart! go not elsewhere.
Kabir says: "Put all imaginations
    away, and stand fast in that which
    you are."

                    translated by Rabindranath Tagore

On Welcoming

Jean Klein: Are there any questions?

Q. Would you be kind enough to say something about the word "welcome"? I find it rather difficult in certain situations to welcome the situation!

JK. In welcoming you are completely open, and your whole body is in a state of receiving. In welcoming there is no anticipation of any kind; you are ready, available to receive, to accept. You are in a state of listening. In welcoming you are beyond the mind, beyond choice, and you are free from the complementarity of good and bad; you receive in love. In welcoming you are free from the person.

When you become more established in welcoming you can really say you welcome the welcoming. This means you no longer emphasise what you welcome, but you emphasise the welcoming itself. This is being the welcoming. In being welcoming there is no place for the person, for an entity, so it is not in subject-object relationship. You cannot objectify the welcoming; the welcoming is open to its welcoming.

These are only words, but when you make them your own so that they are not only intellectual but you are really in the state of welcoming, you will feel a very big difference on the level of the energy. In a state of waiting the energy is still ready to perceive; it is ready to be directed. But when we come to welcoming for its own sake, when the welcoming is itself what we welcome, then the energy is completely at rest, rests in itself. In this perfect equanimity, there is no more thinking, for thinking is matter, vibration of energy in movement. But when we are in welcoming, what we welcome is our own welcoming, and we are beyond the mind. The mind is energy, but when we are in the timeless, free from the mind, that is the supreme availability, the supreme equanimity. It is beyond all perceptions. It is the background, it is the light.

We may first feel it in its total nakedness free from any activity or function, or we may feel it in the interval between two activities, two functions. Then it will appear in us during the function and during the activity. It appears as a feeling of space, of room, between ourselves and the activity. We are no longer stuck to the function. We have the feeling that all activities, all functions are in our total absence, that we are not in the function, not in the activity. When we say, in ordinary terms, that we must take some distance, it is artificial and the distance is not natural. But in absolute availability there is no reference to any object from which we need to be distant. There is no reference at all. It is pure seeing, pure hearing, pure acting, thinking without a thinker, doing without a doer, hearing without a hearer; it is absolute spontaneity. In this absence of a centre, absence of a controller, we live perfectly appropriately in all situations. In perfect availability we have a non-objective relationship with ourselves and with our surroundings. We are free from complicity with our surroundings, no longer an accomplice to any situation. It is an absence of all affectivity, but it is the presence of affection, of love.

In living in welcoming, reasoning and thinking have no more role to play. In welcoming we are free from psychological memory, and in being free from psychological memory there is intelligence. This intelligence does not function through reasoning. It is a profound intuition, an insight. It is only this insight that can change the situation, that makes transformation possible.

Approach on the Body Level:
Sensing the Brain
from dialogues in Grasse, October 3rd and 4th, 1992

I

Jean Klein: When the muscles are sensed, they are freed from conditioning because the sensing liberates the tension and reactions. They are brought to their natural state. You can sense the brain in the same way, although this is ignored in neurology. When the brain is sensed it relaxes completely and all its vibrations slow down.

When the brain is deeply relaxed there is no more localization so there can be no conceptualization. You cannot think because thinking is localization, mainly in the forehead. So there is no need to defend ourselves from thinking but simply to come to the absolutely relaxed brain.

Function and activity belong to the mind and the mind functions in space and time. In deep relaxation you are free from thinking and thus free from space and time which are only thoughts. When we are free from space and time there is only a constant presence which cannot be found, described or localized. I only speak from my own experience in saying it is constant presence where nobody is present and nothing is present. It is dangerous to express it even in a poetical way, but the most appropriate expression for me is that it is a constant current of love.

When the brain is really sensed we are taken away from fixation, localization in the brain. We have the impression that we are in the expansion of our body. This feeling of expansion is the beginning of meditation. Meditation is not the act of relaxing the brain which is still doing something.

Just as we can free the muscles from conditioning, the

residues of the past, in the same way we can free the brain from function and activity. You may already have some experience of this. Before the brain conceptualizes, finds words and thinks, there is a pure perception. But we are so accustomed to the reflex of analysis, comparison and so on that we have little knowledge of what is a pure perception.

There are many tricks to stop us from thinking but these only cause a fixation on some subtle object, whereas meditation is completely objectless. Meditation does not begin with achieving a state. It begins with the objectless non-state. This non-state is the current, the presence which is not affected by the functioning of the mind. It is only ignorance that attributes this presence, this bliss, to the absence of objects. If you remain convinced that tranquillity lies in the absence of objects you will never become free from duality. Presence is beyond the presence or absence of objects, beyond the mind, beyond the brain. All these appear and disappear in limitless presence which is not an object.

When you sense the brain as you sense your muscles, it is not with the intention to interfere with the functioning of the brain. It is simply feeling, sensing the brain without looking for a result. It is an innocent looking free from calculation. It is this innocent looking that frees the brain from the brain. It brings you to be free from the meditator, the doer, which is a brain construct, nothing else. So just as when we deeply sense the body we are in the expanded body, so when we sense the brain we are in expansion, and then meditation is something entirely different. Most techniques, many practised in certain monasteries, emphasize the stopping of brain function. We may then be free from the contents of the brain but the contents are not the problem. The real issue is to explore not the contents but the container. The container is not an absence of contents just as the taste of the mouth itself is not the absence of other tastes.

So when there is an absence of activity in the brain, don't live the absence of brain activity but live the presence. Be in identity with the presence which is not in subject-object relationship. When you come out of the subject-object relationship and live in identity, then something happens in the body, in the brain. The energy no longer moves in the old way. There's a sudden rectification.

You are presence, not the stillness of the mind, so the brain functions when it needs to function. If called upon to think, it thinks. When there is nothing to think it has no more role to play. The brain is an organ like any other. It takes itself in charge. In its relaxed state the brain is empty but you are so accustomed to having an object in your mind that often you ignore the empty mind. There are many moments in daily life when the mind is free from thinking, but the reflex to connect with objects and go away from the empty brain is very strong because this empty state is considered a blank state. In the blank state one emphasizes the absence of thinking, the absence of the object, instead of consciousness without an object, presence. Generally we only know consciousness with an object, being conscious of something, even if it is consciousness of tranquillity, peace and so on. These are still objects, states, and keep you in the frame of duality. Consciousness without objects is unknown to you, yet it is your nearest, your real nature, what you are. This presence cannot be experienced as joyful or not joyful. It is without any quality. It simply is.

The stillness of which we speak, which is beyond the non-functioning of the mind, is a result of understanding. When it is very deeply understood that there is nothing to attain, nothing to achieve or become, that all you are looking for is right here like the chair on which you are sitting, only this can bring you to silence.

I have been talking about a practical approach to coming to this understanding, through sensing the brain, like a scientist who shows you the steps that brought him to his convictions. Take note that you are constantly in a state of achieving something or becoming something. It is enough that you see it. Then you are out of the automatic, mechanical reflex. When you become aware of the reflex, the awareness is itself out of the function. Be with this innocent looking.

The brain is an object perceived as you perceive your ear. It is a sensation like feeling the hand. When you explore the sensation of your hand you come to different levels of feeling. It is the same with the brain. The brain is, in a certain way, dependent on the other organs, especially the eyes. When we look at things in a grasping way, as we usually do, it affects the brain. The optic nerves are very near to the brain so when the eyes are in tension so is the brain. The letting go of tension in the eyes and the brain is a science to be learned. Giving up brings you to a state of availability. You are ready, available, innocent, completely in the welcoming state.

Q. When we feel the relaxed body we first feel it as heavy. Do we also feel the brain as heavy?

JK. Yes, it is first felt as a weight and then one feels expanded vibrations. You can feel the energy brain as you do the other organs. In contacting the sensation of the brain there is no longer an accomplice to the conditioning and it goes into its generic state. In sensing there's no room for a doer, a thinker, an "I," because when you are one with the sensation you cannot have another thought.

Q. Would you talk more about the moment at which meditation begins?

JK. In the moment of the absence of the thinker, the doer, there is meditation.

Q. Is there meditation even when there are thoughts in the mind?

JK. Yes, because meditation is beyond the activity of the mind. The eyes, ears, all the sense organs are open but there is no emphasis on them. There's audibility, visibility and so on, but not something heard or seen because the hearer or seer is absent.

Without a subject there is no object. In meditation there is no introversion of the senses. When you undertake "meditation" from 7 to 8, you practise introversion. This is not meditation. In meditation nothing is excluded.

Q. When the brain organ comes to its natural state where there is nothing more to hear or think, is this meditation?

K. No, emptiness of the brain is still a state. The mind has moments of perfect silence but this is a silent mind, it is not meditation. What you are is beyond mind.

Q. Is the presence that is present in the silent mind meditation?

JK. Yes, it is the *sahaja* state, eternally present, in which the mind appears silent or in motion, and you accomplish what life asks of you but you are constantly in your timeless being. It is an active life which functions according to the situation without a me or "I".

II

JK. When we are present we are not localized.. We are localized in non-localization. We are simply open where nothing is objective. At a certain moment in living in this openness there's a switch over and we are open to the openness. This is real meditation where there is no meditator and nothing to meditate on.

The body is only memory. It is not the real body which wakes up in the morning. It is only memory, pattern. But when you listen to the body, listen without any intention a whole palette of sensations appear. When the body is listened to, when it is completely sensed, it loses its consistency and becomes expanded. It feels more liquid, more fluid, there's no border, no centre. This light, fluid body is the organic body and when you once become aware of it, it will solicit you. The organic memory of expansion will one day be completely integrated in the global expansion.

Sensing the body is healing the body because defence, reaction, tension and fear are contractions. When we speak of fear or anxiety we have already felt it on the body level as a sensation. But we conceptualize it. We go away from the perception into the name fear. So to face fear we must go back to the original perception of it on the body level. In sensing the body, we do not, however, emphasize what we sense, the tension, but we emphasize the listening, the awareness.

We may be quite accustomed to relaxing our shoulders or our arms but it is new to relax the brain. In sensing the brain we first feel its weight. Then it loses all substance and we feel as if there is no longer a head. The head is completely expanded and disappears. When the head is really sensed, most of the organs are also completely relaxed, especially the eyes which are constantly in grasping, looking for security.

If you cannot feel the brain directly then begin with the eyes. Sense their cavities and follow the optic nerves into the brain. When the brain is relaxed there will be a feeling of space surrounding it. Make this an object of your consciousness and you will dissolve in space. In the end there is a fusion of the observer and the observed, and there is only presence.

Q. When the brain is deeply relaxed there is a sensation of peace, of bliss, of...

JK. These are pleasurable experiences, it is true, but pleasure is degenerated happiness. Real happiness is in the disappearing of the "me," being one with the cosmos. Happiness is expansion, pleasure is contraction. In pleasure there is still the person experiencing something.

Q. So even though certain states may make me feel very good, you would recommend avoiding them?

JK. Yes, because you still attribute your good feeling to a cause. In the moment of true happiness there is no cause and no one who is happy. There is only happiness. Later the mind says "I am happy because of this or that state." Looking for states is an escape, a compensation. It binds you to the object.

Q. If we sense the brain fully just before going to sleep will we wake up in the alertness that is the natural state of the brain or can the brain go into its old habits of contracting during sleep?

JK. Yes, the brain can go back to its old states. But if you relax the brain in the evening and sense the brain in daily life, seeing when it is tense, then there will absolutely come a moment when it will function normally. When you drive your car and notice how your shoulders are tense, you may rectify it ten times, but then one day it doesn't appear any more. Then you are functioning really appropriately to the work of driving or seeking.

Q. So when you say, as you often do, that the body wakes up in the morning in consciousness, are you saying that the body also wakes up in the alertness of the relaxed brain?

JK. Absolutely.

Q. When we bring an object seen back to the seer, at some moment there is a switch over from the object to seeing, itself. But when that object of perception is the relaxed, expanded, alert brain is there still a switch over to being the perceiving or is it more like a growing, an expanding of awareness?

JK. Absolutely. Expansion, yes. Flowing in. When you sense the brain you bring it to its normal relaxed state because it must be relaxed in order to be sensed. Many parts of the brain are blocked because they are constricted through habitual use of the I-image. We employ only a fraction of our brain. The attention you bring to sense the brain is not attention with intention.

When this happens there's fixation. Attention must be free from all intention. When you think you are being attentive you are not attentive. Simply explore innocently.

Your Question

Q. If the personality is a tool, and in a sense our relationship with it is similar to our relationship with our body, then why wouldn't it be useful to examine this "tool," try to understand how it functions, why it behaves the way it does, what its compensations are, etc.? The mind and body are intimately connected, but I don't think one can understand the mind just by studying the body.

In my own case, I can, for example, experience depression as a definite physical disability (the grayness of perception, the lack of motivation, the death wish), but I cannot understand why, when I am faced with a choice between behaving in a way that I know is beneficial and behaving in a way that is self-destructive, I choose the latter.

Jean Klein: Awareness of the body is awareness through body-sensing. At first the body is emphasized, but in the end awareness is emphasized. What is the difference between examining the mind or the body? Both are objects. When I feel anxious, I take note of it.

Q. For you taking note is enough, but what about us complex and conditioned creatures who have many hidden motives and compensations? Is it not useful to examine the roots of our behaviour?

JK. But all these roots have one root: the I-image. I agree, examine the existence—or rather, non-existence—of this I-image. To examine the mind you must first examine the examiner. No matter how much you discover about motives for behaviour, it will not radically change anything. The mind cannot change the mind because the mind is conditioned. Only the higher principle can change the mind.

Q. How can I contact this higher principle?

JK. You need a teacher, of course. You have to see the source of every question, the source of thinking. When a question comes up see the source of the question. When you look beyond superficial motives and compensations, you will see the source of all questions is the I-image. So the only useful way to explore the mind is to become familiar with this robber.

Q. Robber?

JK. Robbing joy.

Q. How can I face the lack of motivation and general depression?

JK. See where this passivity is localized. When you examine the body fully in this way, you will be outside it. But there are moments when you are not identified with the passivity. The fact that you are aware of the lack of motivation means that this awareness does not belong to it, is independent from it.

Q. Where does the death wish come from? It does not seem to be the desire for the I-image to die, but a real urge to have an end to physical existence. So I choose the most self-destructive way of behaving.

JK. Ask yourself who would like to die. Who? You would like to die to find something else. It is always to find something else. See that you want to find something else.

Q. It feels more like a desire for total annihilation.

JK. For whom? When you see for whom, there will be an awakening. You will not find any "who" who wants annihilation, and in this stop, this not-knowing, this silence, there's awakening. As it is so strong it is easier to see it.

Q. But it seems to be a biological urge beyond my control.

JK. But there's nothing to control. Controlling in view of what? A controller stops life. Trying to control is violence. It is making war on yourself. This causes depression. See that the controller is a fiction and it will dissolve. Life does not need any controller. The observer of all this is not in it. Focus on the knower of it, and you know it well or you could not ask all these questions.

Come back to the knower of the state and leave the state to itself. Don't be taken by the state, any state. What you are is not a state so don't waste energy trying to understand states. Give all your energy to the perceiving.

Q. Perhaps I am afraid that if I do not control life in some way it will become chaotic or I will go mad.

JK. It is the fear of letting go, letting go of the image of yourself. It is the fear of not conforming to your image, maybe the image of the non-conformist. It is the fear of disappearing. But there is no one to disappear! There is no one to be the same, no one to be different, no one to go mad, no one to be depressed. Turn around! Be the light. Be in the Now. There is nothing else. Give up your presence and be the Presence.

LISTENING

Volume 7
1993

On Love 223
Jean Klein

Love and Marriage 225
Jean Klein

Poem from *The Love Songs of Chandidas* 238

Sahaja 239
Ananda K. Coomaraswamy

Poem from *The Love Songs of Chandidas* 249

Living in Oneness 250
Jean Klein

Sadhana: *Love* 263
Jean Klein

Poem from *The Love Songs of Chandidas* 263

Your Question: *I find myself in moods that are
beyond my control* 264
Jean Klein

Approach on the Body Level: *The relaxed body
and the energetic body* 266
Jean Klein

On Love
Jean Klein

Love is the greatest emotion.
Love is the only emotion.
Love is eternal.
All emotion arises and dies in love.
Everything else is emotivity, states,
    transitions, all feeling that is in
    time and space, bound to an object.

Love is without object.
It is completely unconditioned.
The heart of all existence is love.
All that exists is in our heart.

Love is unexpressed.
The radiation of love comes from love and
    brings you back to the unexpressed.
When you love you come back to yourself.
You love yourself, not your person.
You love your own love, free from body,
    free from senses, free from mind.

In love there are no negative feelings,
    no hate, no fear, no moods, no anxiety,

no compulsion, no conflict.
Love is beyond the split mind, beyond
    high and low, beyond complementarity.
The heart has no division.
The one you love is yourself.
The one you hurt is yourself.

There are glimpses of love when
    you are free from the I-image.
Remember the glimpse.
Remember the moment of no-relationship,
    no other.
When you love yourself, you love another.
When there is no you, there is no other.
Only love.

You must be ripe to love. Be ready.
Knowing yourself in your absence of self.
Love is only when there is no you.
Love is in your total absence.
In total absence is total presence.
Is Love.

Love and Marriage

Based on the video *Love and Marriage, an interview with Jean Klein*

Q. From a spiritual perspective, what is love between a man and a woman?

Jean Klein: You can never objectify love. It is indefinable. You cannot put it in the frame of the mind. The question arises, "How can I find and experience love?" You must explore, in yourself, what love really is. You will see that when you love someone, in reality you love the ultimate in them. You love the divine in them. Then you may also say, I'm attracted to you, and I love you. But first you love the divine in them. To really see the divine love in another, you must exist knowingly, yourself, in divine love. Then there are no longer two, but only one. I think it is important to understand the oneness in a love relationship. There are not two.

Q. Even though there are two personalities in two different bodies, there's really oneness?

JK. Absolutely. The essence is one. It is the essence that is the transformer, giving shape to the love.

Q. In the beginning, when two people meet, for a very brief moment they sense this oneness. Then it seems to fade away, and they say they've lost it. Can one lose love?

JK. Never. When you meet somebody, you have a first impression. It is a global impression. That means the analytic mind does not come in. All that exists is a sense of beauty, a sense of love. It is the aesthetic, the intuitive mind that comes into play. Then you go on and talk. You face the intelligence and formulation of the other, the harmonious gestures and beautiful voice, and so on. This makes you say you are in love or attracted to this person. As long as this background of the first impression remains, you are in love. But very often this background is forgotten. The background is the subject but when the object is emphasized, when the physical appearance is emphasized, the background, the first impression, is forgotten. Some people forget the love. They emphasize what is only an expression of love. They forget that the body-mind is an expression of love.

Q. Could you tell us what you mean by the body-mind?

JK. When you love somebody, your whole psychosomatic being is affected by it, struck by it. This feeling belongs to real love. You must keep alive this background of love because it is this background which nourishes the physical relationship.

Q. Should the couple remember very often what brought them together?

JK. Yes. Feel again the first impression. Think of it. You don't always need to talk about it, but, of course, you can talk about it.

Q. But so often it seems the negative images that develop in a relationship are accumulated into the love—the times we're disappointed or annoyed. Those images pile up, and we no longer see our beloved as we first did.

JK. The first impression is the love you need. You need your own love, because you are one in that love. Generally our listening, looking, and seeing are only patterns that we superimpose on our beloved. There is repetition. In the end you say, "This is my husband," or "This is my wife," and you see only what you have projected. You do not see your husband or wife. It is important that there is fresh seeing, fresh discovery from moment to moment.

Q. How do we do that? How does a couple keep the moment-to-moment freshness alive?

JK. When there is humility and simplicity, you will discover the background of love. In humility and simplicity you see things as they are. When, in this simplicity, you explain your feelings to your partner, your partner is affected by this simplicity. They speak in the same way, in simplicity. In speaking this way, putting facts on the table, there is oneness. In this humility and simplicity, both come together.

Q. When you say simplicity, what do you mean?

JK You are free from memory, completely in freshness. The ego is not pronounced. You are back in your nakedness. You are back to the first love when you, as you, were not there. It is only the present moment that is real. Everything else is memory.

Q. In our relationships, then, we need to put aside memory?

JK. Absolutely. Otherwise when you come home, you see that your partner has become an object. You have superimposed certain qualities, characteristics on them. There is repetition. You must see this. When you really see this, take note of your reaction. You must see that you have superimposed the same qualities that you superimposed yesterday, a year ago, and so on. There is no longer fresh seeing, new seeing. It is only when you see it that there is transformation. Feel your reaction to seeing the fact.

Q. Would you say that when this quality of seeing exists, the relationship is a mirror in which one's inner being is reflected?

JK. Absolutely. Then you are really on the stage of life. You can only see what you are when you are on the stage of daily life, in contact constantly. When you are alone in your kitchen, all things are perfect. But when you are on the stage in a relationship with your wife or husband, with your surroundings, your neighbours, then you see what you really are and are not.

Q. A difficulty comes in, however, because we human beings have trouble with our feelings. Especially when they're negative or angry feelings. We're not able to see clearly then. It's difficult for a husband and wife to see each other in this freshness, humility and simplicity when this anger exists. Why do we have so much trouble with feelings, all kinds of feelings, but especially negativity?

JK. When you live in simplicity, in humility, you see facts. In this factual seeing hate and anger disappear. When you are really in love with your partner it affects your aesthetic, intuitive mind. When you are in love and in humility, the I-image is no longer used. Then there is simplicity and beauty. We must cultivate beauty in our life.

Q. You're saying that maybe we can be helped in dealing with our feelings if we create beauty around us?

JK. Absolutely. We should live mainly in feeling, not in thinking. It is the thinking mind which disturbs the feeling mind.

Q. In beauty, the thinking mind takes a rest?

JK. Yes. Let it come into the picture only when it is needed.

Q. How does a couple do this while living in the modern world of distractions and disturbances, obligations, bills, children, in-laws? How do we create beauty? How should we structure our life?

JK. When you come together, there is a certain art to freeing yourself from your preoccupations. Don't bring home the problems of business. Set aside, every day, time to be in intimacy, in loving stillness, not so much speaking.

Q. But most of us, unfortunately, don't know that Stillness. Our minds are chattering all the time.

JK. l agree. We are occupied in continuing the striving from the day. But we must find the possibility to stop it. Before going to sleep, you set all of your clothes aside; in the same way set aside all of your preoccupations, your qualifications.

You will find yourself in your nakedness. Keep this feeling of nakedness, of being free from qualification. It is this stillness, this togetherness in love that harmonizes the rest of the relationship. When there is caressing and coming close together, there is no thinking. You cannot think and caress at the same time. The two functions are completely different.

Q. You would agree, then, that our relationship can be a vehicle to help us nurture our spiritual inclinations?

JK. Absolutely. When you love somebody there is only loving. It brings you back to your homeground, love. You can never make it a thought. It is a global, whole feeling. There is nobody who feels it. There is only love feeling. You don't love the husband for the husband, but for the divine in him or her.

Q. Of course, if a relationship is filled with a lot of ego residue, such as competition and conflict, then we wouldn't expect it to be much of a vehicle for the manifestation of our spiritual sides. Could you tell us, on our level as beginners, what we can do to claim our true nature?

JK. Generally the relationship between two people is more or less on the level of object to object, personality to personality, man to woman. On that level there is conflict. When you go deeply, there is only asking and demanding. The image we have of ourself is maintained only in certain situations. It looks constantly for situations, and is constantly in insecurity. We must see that in this kind of relationship, person to person, male to female, there is conflict.

The concept of a man is a restriction. The concept of a woman is a restriction. A man is more than a man, and a woman is more than a woman. Before the woman appears, there is the divine. Before the man appears, there is the divine. When you take yourself for a man or a woman you mutilate your totality or globality.

Q. We are more than just a woman or man.

JK. There is a level where the man and woman disappear, and there is only love. When you see your beloved from this point of view, if you can call it a point of view, he or she is completely different. When the relationship is not of object to object there is imagination and improvisation. The love relationship can be creative on the psychosomatic plane, and the man and woman can express themselves in the most unexpected ways.

Q. Are two people in conflict relating object to object?

JK. Yes. And an object can never free itself from another object. It is stuck. There are moments when you are completely absent of the I-image. These are moments when you act spontaneously. When the I-image is present, everything is intentional. You project and anticipate. When you are no longer concerned with the I-image, then there is spontaneous action. In spontaneous action there is right action. It is only in spontaneous action that there is loving action. Otherwise you are only looking for practical, psychological survival.

Q. We must be careful that we haven't trapped ourselves into an image. We must see past that.

JK. Exactly. When you are free from the I-image your personality is freed. Your personality will then act as required by a situation, but you are no longer identified with it, not stuck to it.

Q. So just as I must take care not to project an image onto my partner, I must see that I don't do the same to myself.

JK. Absolutely. And your partner will not feel imprisoned. Otherwise you put him or her in a certain pattern. It is uncomfortable. You can see when children are put into a pattern, they are not free and can't wait for the vacation to begin! With a partner, it is the same.

Q. What do I do when I'm locked up in my ego, seeing that I have petty reactions of envy or jealousy or annoyance? What is the best way for me to deal with those upheavals?

JK. Practically speaking, go back in your room, sit down, and listen to these reactions in yourself. Feel them on the body level. When you say you are hungry, the words are only concepts. Free yourself from the concept of hunger. Hunger is really an actual feeling in your body. Similarly, witness the feelings you've just described. You will see the feelings no longer have an accomplice, and the energy dissolves in your freshness.

Q. In the freshness of witnessing, observing, and looking, it dissolves.

JK. It is very important that you have this reflection. And not just the reflection, but this life in your daily living. You must also ask the question, "What is the deep relationship that I have with my beloved in this moment?" It is important to keep it alive, keep the flame alive.

Q. There must be the awareness to keep the flame alive, and then from that the motivation to listen.

JK. Yes. All harmonization, on all levels, comes from this. If you don't see this from this level, but only from the level of the mind, it is exhausting.

Q. Then there's all the conflict and tension and battling.

JK. Yes. The moment you see these reactions, sit down and say, "Here is a mass of reactions." I am aware of these reactions. It is an awareness without any expectations of anything. Just see it, like a child sees for the first time the rising or setting sun.

Q. What happens to my personality, my patterned way of expressing myself? Do I give that up?

JK. It gives you up. When you need your personality in different circumstances it is there and you act. But it is no longer a frozen personality. It is a free personality.

Q. In a relationship, if one partner has realized his or her true nature, can the marriage be maintained?

JK. Absolutely. The moment you feel yourself in completeness, in wholeness, your partner will feel it. You can only form society by beginning with yourself.

Q. If one of two people is truly looking for harmony, there cannot be a clash or conflict.

JK. The moment you integrate your simplicity, your humility, there is no longer an idea of correctness, justification or condemnation. There is simply seeing facts. You say what you feel in relation to another. You don't justify. There are no accusations. There are only facts. The partner will be astonished by this simplicity. And you can be sure there is a moment when everything moves together.

When you see the facts the seeing is unconditioned as when

you go to a gallery and look at paintings there is only seeing. There is not a seer and something seen, but only seeing. When you listen to the other, the listening is unconditioned, as in a concert there is only one listening. You feel yourself in this listening, in this love. It is very important that we cultivate beauty, very important. In beautiful behaviour, in the absence of the person, there is intelligence. Intelligence exists only when the I-image is absent. Then there is sensitivity and imagination, creation. You create a relationship with your beloved in this moment. Otherwise, you only project patterns and repetition. One day that will become boring. The moment you see that it is becoming boring you must ask, "Why is this? How can I change this?"

Q. The moment we find ourself stuck and bored and irritated we have to act immediately.

JK. Absolutely. Don't postpone the solution. There is nothing to postpone. Proceed in the moment itself. Come together in this humility and simplicity. It is very interesting when you wake up in your humility, how you feel yourself in humbleness.

Q. What is humility?

JK. It is being free from the mind, free from being this or that. It is being free from being anything. Be nothing. In this nothingness there is fresh seeing, new seeing. In this emptiness there is fullness. It is very important to see that in love there are not two, but only one, one background which is constantly witness, in a certain way. It is the light of the relationship. The woman and man appear in this background.

Q. So the two, the man and woman, live in the one awareness?

JK. Yes, when each lives in the background, love, consciousness, there is only togetherness and in this the man and woman appear from time to time.

Q. This way of living together is very mature. What would you suggest for couples who may not live so harmoniously?

JK. To remember from time to time to find the love, their homeground. To refer their love to the ultimate love. To see that there are moments when the male and female, the person, is not there, and that in this absence love surges up. To welcome these moments where there is nobody with nobody. In this absence there is really presence, amour, love.

Q. You said there's humility when we get away from the mind. And yet, most of us have to spend a considerable portion of our time rooted in the mind. You said once that even the person who has found oneness still meets their daily obligations. To come to our true nature, is it necessary to step out of the stream and leave society and go off somewhere to lead the simple life?

JK. The problem is the same wherever you go. It is dressed in a different way, I agree. There are new colours, new forms, but the problem is the same anywhere.

Q. So the changes in structure don't matter?

JK. I would say, when you come back from activity, remain sitting in stillness. Stillness means that you objectify, in a way, your stresses and reactions, that you become relaxed. You become really relaxed. To come to this relaxed state you must listen to your body. When your body is completely relaxed, then your mind is still. Then a love relation begins with your surroundings. Otherwise you are constantly in the becoming process, with anticipation. You are never in the now. When you believe yourself to be a person, when you cling to the I-image, you are never in the now. You are only in the future. And what is the future? The future is only the past. Live in the now. It will change, completely, your relationship with your partner. Your body-mind is an object of your observation. You are the observer, but you are not the body-mind. To the observer, the observed is divine.

Q. Divinity is in us as a natural fact. There's nothing to do, nothing to look for.

JK. Absolutely. You must only integrate it knowingly.

Q. What happens sexually between two people? Is there divinity in that, too?

JK. Absolutely.

Q. How so?

JK. In this love there are not two. It is inherent to the biological and psychological structure to live this moment of oneness on the physical plane. When two partners come together on this level, they are not two, but only one. The relationship on the sexual plane is a celebration of this oneness on the physical plane. When the physical relation does not come from the divine, then there is repetition. When there is repetition, one day there will be no more excitement. It is only the divine that constantly gives freshness.

Q. So it's important sexually not to see object to object. Because object to object will eventually get boring and the passion will be lost.

JK. Absolutely. There is no more discovery. There is no more imagination

Q. If we're calling one type of relationship object to object, might we call the other subject to subject?

JK. There is no longer an object. There is only the subject.

Q. At the subject to subject level of oneness, you say it's inherent in biology to manifest oneness at the physical level.

JK. Exactly. It is not only on the so-called sexual level. It is in a look. You look in your beloved's eyes, or give them a caress. Rather than sexuality, I prefer the term lovemaking. Every moment there is love. You touch their hand. Every word is love giving. The woman is attracted, affected by the look of the man. And she shows that she loves the look. She appreciates it. Because of this appreciation, the man comes to look more deeply.

Q. The woman wants to be looked at, and the man wants to be appreciated.

JK. But not merely on the psychological level. The look of the man sees beyond the woman to the divine, and in this deep looking the woman expands and feels her divinity. She spontaneously shows her appreciation of this looking without a looker and the man expands in her appreciation, appreciation of the divine in him. It is the ultimate forgetting of the female and male.

(Pause)

Q. To return to my practical concern, at the end of the day when I've been buffeted by the world and the identifications that strengthen my ego, I need to take the time to sit down and relax.

JK. And this relaxation comes automatically the moment I listen to it, am conscious of it, am aware of it. There is no directing or using it.

Q. It must be effortless.

JK. Exactly. It is the seeing and listening of a child. It is completely innocent, without anticipation.

Q. And that's the way two people need to communicate, as well, in innocent listening.

JK. Absolutely. In innocence there is nothing else but the divine.

Q. Of all the things we've spoken about, what is the one thing that couples should take with them from this discussion?

JK. That they are not two, but only one. But do not only understand it as a concept, an idea. Make it a feeling. Believe me, this feeling is known the moment you free yourself from being this or that, free yourself from the I-image. In living in the absence of the image there is creativity. It is important to have creativity in a relationship. Creativity can only come when there is silence, when the mind is free from all knowing. It is only in this not knowing that there is the knowing of love. Because you can never love the known. The known is thinking. But in the absence of knowing is plenitude, fulfilment, and absolute security.

Find your match
In a worthy love
Before you lose your heart.
Love is a jewel
To be guarded with care
When lovers are equal
In maturity…

from *The Love Poems of Chandidas*
translated by Deben Bhattacharya

Sahaja
from
The Dance of Shiva
Ananda K. Coomaraswamy

The following article is included, even though it is not *sruti* (the heard in silence, in Being), because of the truth and beauty of most of its ideas.

The last achievement of all thought is a recognition of the identity of spirit and matter, subject and object; and this reunion is the marriage of Heaven and Hell, the reaching out of a contracted universe towards its freedom, in response to the love of Eternity for the productions of time. There is then no sacred or profane, spiritual or sensual, but everything that lives is pure and void. This very world of birth and death is also the great Abyss.

In India we could not escape the conviction that sexual love has a deep and spiritual significance. There is nothing with which we can better compare the "mystic union" of the finite with its infinite ambient—that one experience which proves itself and is the only ground of faith—than the self-oblivion of earthly lovers locked in each other's arms, where "each is both." Physical proximity, contact, and interpenetration are the expressions of love, only because love is the recognition of identity. These two are one flesh, because they have remembered their unity of spirit. This is, moreover, a fuller identity than the mere sympathy of two individuals: and each as individual has now no more significance for the other than the gates of heaven for one who stands within. It is like an algebraic equation where the equation is the only truth, and the terms may stand for anything. The least intrusion of the ego, however, involves a return to the illusion of duality.

This vision of the beloved has no necessary relation to

empirical reality. The beloved may be in every ethical sense of the word unworthy—and the consequences of this may be socially or ethically disastrous: but nevertheless the eye of love perceives her divine perfection and infinity, and is not deceived. That one is chosen by the other is therefore no occasion of pride: for the same perfection and infinity are present in every grain of sand, and in the raindrop as much as in the sea.

To carry through such a relationship, however, and to reach a goal, to really progress and not merely to achieve an intimation—for this it is necessary that both the lover and the beloved should be of one and the same spiritual age and of the same moral fibre. For if not, as Chandidas says, the woman who loves an unworthy man will share the fate of a flower that is pierced with thorns, she will die of a broken heart: and the youth who falls in love with a woman of lower spiritual degree will be tossed to and fro in great unrest and will give way to despair.

Because the stages of human love reflect the stations of spiritual evolution, it is said that the relationship of hero and heroine reveals an esoteric meaning, and this truth has been made the basis of the well known allegories of Radha and Krishna, which are the dominant motif of mediaeval Hinduism. Here, illicit love becomes the very type of salvation: for in India, where social convention is so strict, such a love involves a surrender of all that the world values, and sometimes of life itself. When Krishna receives the milkmaids, and tells them he owes them a debt that can never be paid, it is because they have come to him "like the *vairagi* who has renounced his home"—neither their duties nor their great possessions hindered them from taking the way of Mary. The great seducer makes them his own.

All this is an allegory—the reflection of reality in the mirror of illusion. This reality is the inner life, where Krishna is the Lord, the milkmaids are the souls of men, and Brindaban the field of consciousness. The relation of the milkmaids with the Divine Herdsman is not in any sense a model intended to be realised in human relationships, and the literature contains explicit warnings against any such confusion of planes.

The interpretation of this mystery, however, is so well known as to need no elaboration. But there is a related cult, which is called Sahaja, which constitutes a practical discipline, a "rule," and what we have to speak of here concerns this more difficult and less familiar teaching.

In Sahaja, the adoration of young and beautiful girls was made the path of spiritual evolution and ultimate emancipation. By this adoration we must understand not merely ritual worship (the Kumari Puja), but also "romantic love."

This doctrine seems to have originated with the later Tantrik Buddhists. Kanu Bhatta already in the tenth century wrote Sahaja love songs in Bengal. The classic exponent, however, is Chandidas, who lived in the fourteenth century. Many other poets wrote in the same sense. Chandidas himself was called a madman—a term in Bengali which signifies a man of eccentric ideas who nevertheless endears himself to everyone. He was a Brahman and a priest of the temple of Vashuli Devi near Bolpur. One day he was walking on the river bank where women were washing clothes. By some chance there was a young girl whose name was Rami: she raised her eyes to his. There was a meeting of Dante and Beatrice. From this time on Chandidas was filled with love. Rami was very beautiful: but in Hindu society what can a washerwoman be to a Brahman? She could only take the dust off his feet. He, however, openly avowed his love in his songs, and neglected his priestly duties. He would fall into a dream whenever he was reminded of her.

The love songs of Chandidas were more like hymns of devotion: "I have taken refuge at your feet, my beloved. When I do not see you my mind has no rest. You are to me as a parent to a helpless child. You are the goddess herself—the garland about my neck—my very universe. All is darkness without you, you are the meaning of my prayers. I cannot forget your grace and your charm—and yet there is no desire in my heart."

Chandidas was excommunicated, for he had affronted the whole orthodox community. By the good offices of his brother he was once on the point of being taken back into society, on condition of renouncing Rami forever, but when she was told of this she went and stood before him at the place of the reunion—never before had she looked upon his face so publicly—then he forgot every promise of reformation, and bowed before her with joined hands as a priest approaches his household goddess.

It is said that a divine vision was vouchsafed to certain of the Brahmans there present—for Rami was so transfigured that she seemed to be the Mother of the Universe herself, the Goddess: that is to say that for them, as for Chandidas himself, the doors of perception were cleansed, and they too saw here divine perfection. But the rest of them saw only the washerwoman, and Chandidas remained an outcast.

He has explained in his songs what he means by Sahaja. The lovers must refuse each other nothing, yet never fall. Inwardly, he says of the woman, she will sacrifice all for love, but outwardly she will appear indifferent. This secret love must find expression in secret: but she must not yield to desire. She must cast herself freely into the sea of contempt, and yet she must never actually drink of forbidden waters; she must not be shaken by pleasure or pain. Of the man he says that to be a true lover he must be able to make a frog dance in the mouth of a snake, or to bind an elephant with a spider's web. That is to say, that although he plays with the most dangerous passions, he must not be carried away. In this restraint, or rather, in the temper that makes it possible, lies his salvation. "Hear me," says Chandidas, "to attain salvation through the love of woman, make your body like a dry stick —for He that pervades the universe seen of none, can only be found by one who knows the secret of love." It is not surprising if he adds that one such is hardly to be found in a million.

This doctrine of romantic love is by no means unique: we meet with it also at the summit levels of European culture, in the thirteenth century. "And so far as love is concerned," says a modern Russian (Kuprin), "I tell you that even this has its peaks which only one out of millions is able to climb."

Before attempting to understand the practice of Sahaja we must define the significance of the desired salvation—the spiritual freedom (*moksha*) which is called the ultimate purpose, the only true meaning of life, and by hypothesis the highest good and perfection of our nature. It is a release from the ego and from becoming: it is the realization of self and of entity—when "nothing of ourself is left in us." This perfect state must be one without desire, because desire implies a lack: whatever action the *jivan mukta* or spiritual freeman performs must therefore be of the nature of manifestation, and will be without purpose or intention. Nothing that he does will be praiseworthy or blameworthy, and he will not think in any such terms—as the *Mahabharata* says, with many like texts, "He who considers *himself* a doer of good or evil knows not the truth, I trow." Nothing that the freeman does will be "selfish," for he has lost the illusion of the ego. His entire being will be in all he does, and it is this which makes the virtue of his action. This is the innocence of desires.

Then and then only is the lover free—when he is free from willing. He who is free is free to do what he will—but first, as Nietzsche says, he must be such as can will, or as Rumi expresses it, must have surrendered will. This is by no means the same as to do what one likes, or avoid what one does not like, for he is very far from free who is subject to the caprices or desires of the ego. Of course, if the doors of perception were cleansed we should know that we are always free ("It is nought indeed but thine own hearing and willing that do hinder thee, so that thou dost not hear and see God")—or the world itself is manifestation and not the handiwork of the Absolute. The most perfect love seeks nothing for itself, requiring nothing and offers nothing to the beloved, realizing her infinite perfection which cannot be added to: but we do not know this except in moments of perfect experience.

Very surely the love of woman is not the only way to approach this freedom. It is more likely by far the most dangerous way, and perhaps for many an impossible way. We do not, however, write to condemn or to advocate, but to explain.

In reading of romantic love we are apt to ponder over what is left unsaid. What did the writers really mean? What was the actual physical relation of the Provençal lover to his mistress, of Chandidas to Rami? I have come to see now that even if we knew this to the last detail it would tell us nothing. He who looks upon a woman with desire (be it even his wife) has already committed adultery with her in his heart, for all desire is adultery. We remember that saying, but do not always remember that the converse is also true—that he who embraces a woman without desire has added nothing to the sum of his mortality. Action is then inaction. It is not by non-participation but by non-attachment that we live the spiritual life. So that he in Sahaja who merely *represses* desire, fails. It is easy not to walk, but we have to walk without touching the ground. To refuse the beauty of the earth—which is our birthright—from fear that we may sink to the level of pleasure seeker—*that* inaction would be action, and bind us to the very flesh we seek to evade. The virtue of the action of those who are free beings lies in the complete coordination of their being—body, soul and spirit, the inner and outer man, at one.

The mere action, then, reveals nothing. As do the slaves of passion impelled by purpose and poverty, so do the spiritually free, out of the abundance of the bestowing virtue. Only the searcher of hearts can sift the tares from the wheat; it is not for mortal man to judge of another's state of grace.

When we say that the Indian culture is spiritual, we do not mean that it is not sensuous. It is perhaps more sensuous than has ever been realized—because a sensuousness such as this, which can classify three hundred and sixty kinds of fine emotions of a lover's heart, and pause to count the patterns gentle teeth may leave on the tender skin of the beloved, or to decorate her breasts with painted flowers of sandal paste—and carries perfect sweetness through the most erotic art—is inconceivable to those who are merely sensual or by a superhuman effort are merely self-controlled. The Indian temperament makes it possible to speak of abstract things *même entre les baisers*.

For this to be possible demands a profound culture of the sexual relationship—something altogether different from the "innocence" of Western girlhood and the brutal violence of the "first night" and the married orgy. The mere understanding of what is meant by Sahaja demands at least a racial if not an individual education in love—an education related to athletics and dancing, music and hygiene. The sexual relation in itself must not be so rare or so exciting as to intoxicate: one should enjoy a woman as one enjoys any other living thing, any forest, flower or mountain that reveals itself to those who are patient. One should not be forced to the act of love by a merely physical tension: minutes suffice for that, but hours are needed for the perfect ritual. What the lover seeks should be the full response, and not his mere pleasure: and by this I do not mean anything so sentimental as "forbearance" or "self-sacrifice," but what will please him most. Under these conditions violence has no attractions: in Arabia, Burton tells us, the Musulmans respected even their slaves, and it was "pundonor," a point of culture, that a slave, like any other woman, must be wooed.

Lafcadio Hearn has pointed out the enormous degree to which modern European literature is permeated with the idea of love. This is, however, as nothing compared with what we find in the Vaishnava literature of Hindustan. There, however, there is always interpretation: in European romantic literature there is rarely anything better than description. That should be only a passing phase, for the real tendency of Western sexual freedom is certainly idealistic, and its forms are destined to be developed until the spiritual significance of love is made clear.

Under the sway of modern hedonism, where nothing is accepted as an end, and everything is a means to something else, the preconditions for understanding Sahaja scarcely exist. Sahaja has nothing to do with the cult of pleasure. It is a doctrine of the Tao, and a path of non-pursuit. All that is best for us comes of itself into our hands—but if we strive to overtake it, it perpetually eludes us.

In the passionless spontaneous relation of Sahaja, are we to suppose that children are ever to be begotten? Certainly not of necessity. It is true that in early times it was considered right for the hermit who has renounced the world and the flesh to grant the request of a woman who comes to him of her own will and desires a child. But this is quite another matter—and incidentally a wise eugenic disposition, removing an objection to monasticism which some have found in its sterilisation of the best blood. The Sahaja relation, on the contrary, is an end in itself, and cannot be associated with social and eugenic ideas. Those who are capable of such love must certainly stand on the plane of the "men of old," who did not long for descendants, and said, "Why should we long for descendants, we whose self is the universe? For longing for children is longing for the world: one like the other is mere longing." We cannot admit such a longing in Sahaja. It is, however, just possible that such a relation as this might be employed by the Powers for the birth of an avatar: and in such a case we should understand what was meant by immaculate conception and virgin birth—she being virgin who has never been *moved* by desire.

The Sahaja relation is incommensurable with marriage, *categorically regarded as contract*, inasmuch as this relation is undertaken for an end, the definite purpose of "fulfilling social and religious duties," and in particular, of paying the "debt to the ancestors" by begetting children.

Those whose view of life is exclusively ethical will hold that sexual intimacy must be sanctified, justified or expiated by at least the wish to beget and to accept the consequent responsibilities of parenthood. There is, indeed, something inappropriate in the position of those who pursue the pleasures of life as such and evade by artificial means their natural fruit. But this point of view presupposes that the sexual intimacy was a sought pleasure: what we have discussed is something quite other than this, and without an element of seeking.

It is only by pursuing what is not already ours by divine right that we go astray and bring upon ourselves and upon others infinite suffering—to those who do not pursue, all things will offer themselves. What we truly need, we need not strive for.

It will be seen from all this how necessary it is that sexual intimacy should not in itself be considered an unduly exciting experience. It is more than likely also that those who are capable of this spontaneous control will have been already accustomed to willed control under other circumstances: and a control of this kind implies a certain training. We may remark in passing that in "birth control" we see an objection to the use of artificial means—an objection additional to what is obvious on aesthetic grounds—in the fact that such means remove all incentive to the practice of self-control. Those who have good reason to avoid procreation at any time, should make it a point of pride to accomplish this by their own strength—and in any case, no man who has not this strength can be sure of his ability to play his part to perfection, but may at any time meet with a woman whom he cannot satisfy.

How is one to avoid in such a relation as Sahaja the danger of self-deception, the pestilence of suppressed desires, and even of physical overstrain and tension?

For very highly perfected beings it may be true that those subtle exchanges of nervous energy which are effected in sexual intercourse—and are necessary to full vitality—can be effected by mere intimacy, in a relation scarcely passionate in the common sense. We read, indeed, of other worlds where even generation may be effected by an exchange of glances. But it is given to few to function always on such a plane as this. Are we then to forbid to those who need the consolation of mortal affection—are we to forbid to these the passionless intimacy of Sahaja? Why should we do so? Even for those who cannot renounce the sheltered valleys of the personal life for ever, it is well sometimes to breathe the cold air of the perpetual snows. We should add that to whom chastity is difficult, it is to be dissuaded: in order to be sure of our ground we should not attempt the practice of a degree of continence beyond our power. We should also be careful not to "mix our planes" or to make one thing an excuse for another. We must recognize everything for what it really is—the relative as relative, the absolute as absolute—and render unto Caesar those things, and only those, which are lawfully his.

We are now, perhaps, in a better position to know what is meant by Chandidas when he speaks of the difficulties and the meaning of Sahaja. What he intends by "never falling" *(sati)* is a perpetual uncalculated life in the present, and the maintenance not of deliberate control, but of unsought unshaken serenity in moments of greatest intimacy: he means that under circumstances of temptation none should be felt—that temptation should be merely overcome. And to achieve this he does not pray to be delivered from temptation, but courts it.

Here nothing is to be done for one another, but all for love. There is to be no effort to evoke response, and none to withhold it. All this is far removed from the passion and surrender, the tricks of seduction, and the shyness, of the spiritual allegory and of the purely human experience.

One who pervades
the great Universe
is seen by none
unless a man knows
the unfolding
of love…

On the earth
rest the water,
on water
rest the waves
and on the waves
afloat is love…

Love, love and love.
This four-letter word
carries a multiple
of opinions.
But if you adore it
and go deeper and deeper,
you will find that
it is the only One—
Wholly love.

from *The Love Poems of Chandidas*
translated by Deben Bhattacharya

Living in Oneness:
A Practical View

The following article is an edited compilation of questions and answers from the talks at the Santa Sabina Center, July 2 to 5, 1993, and from the spontaneous questions of many people during conversations with Jean Klein.

Jean Klein: You can never say "I love this person" before loving yourself. I do not mean the self that you believe yourself to be, the person: body, senses and mind, but the real self which cannot be objectified, which cannot be known like an object, which is what you fundamentally are.

Think really what it means to love your Self. There is only one Love and it appears when you, as you, are not. When you are not, there is no other.

So-called love is not love. This love is a fashion. In two years you sell it because it no longer feeds you. When you say "I love this woman," five years later you are discussing maintenance. That is not love. The love of which we are speaking here is without any origin. It is causeless. It is your own love. That you can really say "I love this woman or this man" means that you know your own love. You really live in presence. In this presence there is an absence, the absence of yourself, the absence of your phenomenal self.

To be really related with our surroundings one must first be related with oneself. One should have a non-objective relationship with oneself. One must not see oneself through an image. Free from this object image, we come also to a new seeing with the other and with our surroundings.

Q. But when you say you love yourself, how is the yourself in that love different from the yourself that you are aware of before you had love?

JK. Before, it is an object. People told you that you are beautiful, good, handsome and so on. You know yourself only as an object. But you are not an object. You can only say "I love myself" because you *are* yourself. Yourself is love.

Q. Is there a difference between loving which is unconditional and being in love which is selective and a state?

JK. Most people love only certain attributes in the man or woman. They are completely identified with the body-mind and do not know themselves, so they cannot see the distinction between being love and the expression of love. They have not discovered love in themselves. You cannot achieve love, you can only discover it.

Q. How can you discover it?

JK In your solitude, in your stillness. This love never changes. It is a continuum.

Q. When you say in your solitude, do you mean one must be alone or do you mean a solitude in oneself?

JK When you are free from thinking, you find the seed of love. At first you may think only of your beloved's attributes but there will come a moment when they are exhausted and there is only feeling. Sustain this feeling.

Q. Yesterday you said there is no other. I can understand that as a concept and I have moments of living it, but even if I don't know it, is it a good idea to live as if I did, to act with other people as if there were no separation? It's like practising something that hasn't been realized yet as a way to be open to other people.

JK. When you meet somebody, you make him immediately objective. This is memory. You don't meet him. When you know your Self, it is not objective. It is original perception, feeling. You meet another in this relationlessness; then there is no other. There you can talk about life. Then when you meet somebody and they leave, there is no more reference to objects. There is really purity. As long as you consider you're somebody, there is also another. So first free yourself from being somebody. The living then is completely different. It is in silence. You must be absent yourself, then you meet the absence of the so-called other. In this absence there is presence, there is life, there is reality, there is consciousness.

Q. Can you love someone without liking them?

JK. Like is on the phenomenal level. Love is universal. If the love in you is weak then you will focus on liking. But liking is never forever.

Q. So when you try to be someone's friend, are you still thinking and comparing on the object-object level?

JK. Until there's a glimpse of love, no friendship is possible. Friendship is when there are two admirers. It grows from the glimpse of love. One should not face the lack of friendship in oneself by trying. Simply have a relationship without naming it, a relationship which refers to one's own glimpse of love. In our mundane society we speak very often of friends.

Q. The other day I was in the company of people who were socializing and talking in a way that made me feel completely estranged. I even felt as though my more sensitive layers were being violated. How should I face this kind of situation?

JK. You are living in the split mind. When you live in the split mind there's reaction. But the question is, how to face it? See, free from judgment, how the situation you're in acts on you. Then you will act in the right way.

Q. There is an expression often used: "I don't have anything in common with this or that person." Is this a valid observation or is it missing the point, namely, that our essential nature is in common with all?

JK. The expression comes from the divided mind, from living in sympathy and antipathy. Don't forget that you belong to this humanity. You are nothing else. It is only your right attitude that changes the society.

Q. The other day I was feeling in openness and then a friend struck out at me in anger and I felt constriction in my heart area as if my heart were closing up trying to protect itself. How can one stay in openheartedness and still not have the heart damaged?

JK. When you are not identified with your body-mind, you cannot be affected by it. When you live in the mind, there is constantly hate, reaction. When you stay in the mind there is duality. You love, you hate and so on. Go beyond hate and love. Look again. Looking, seeing is consciousness. On this plane you are beyond hate and love. In your real self there is no place for hate and for sympathy, what we call love.

Q. It often happens that I open my heart and women fall in love and make demands on me. How can I deal with that?

JK. In your case, see that you live in wishful thinking. This wishful thinking is an obstacle for real love. You are identified with your body, what you believe it to be and expect it to achieve. To live in this imagination is a poison, the greatest parasite that prevents you from seeing things as they really are. We must purify love from imagination. Opening the heart does not take place on the affective level. When one shows love and there is anticipation of phenomenal love, then one must give no hold at all. Be yourself completely free from the male. Then the other will find there is nothing to grasp.

Q. Because this anticipation of achieving something is an obstacle to receiving pure love.

JK. Absolutely. Because love cannot be achieved. We can only be available for it.

Q. There are people who are completely content on the phenomenal level and society admires them. Do you?

JK. They have forgotten what it means to be a human being, to have a human life.

Q. Which is to find one's true nature?

JK. Yes. To be related to one's origin and to act from this position.

Q. Does this mean that we cannot really love someone unless we are living in our true nature?

JK. We can have a purified love before we are established in our true nature. This love is free from wishful thinking, open to all that life brings, free from expectation. A purified love changes our whole psychosomatic nature. When you project desires, the unexpected is prevented from happening. The unexpected only comes to an open, an empty mind. The expected is memory, the unexpected comes from heaven.

Q. Are you talking about unconditional love?

JK. Yes. It is a relation where there's no asking. In the right relation between mother and child, as symbolized by the Virgin Maria and her child, all things are given, are perfect. There's no demanding. It is a current of affection. The oneness of love is tangible. There are not two, only one. I think this mother and child relation, when the mother is free from being a mother, is the purest expression of love that we have. The child lives in the mother's love and the mother lives in the child's love. It is a symbol of non-duality. But the mother must be free of the mother-image. Then she is ready for it. It is rare.

Q. Is it different with a father-child relationship?

JK. The father is the symbol of the phenomenal manifestation. He brings the right attitude, an earnest outlook for facing the world. The mother gives the joy of living. Goethe said it beautifully, "Vom Vater hab ich die Statur, des Lebens ernstes Führen. Vom Mütterchen die froh Natur, die Lust zum Fabulieren." [1]

Q. Do you think that, ideally, one should have a glimpse of oneself before getting married?

JK. That is the logical way, but our animal nature will not allow it.

Q. So what is the best compromise?

JK. To see that there is no flavour, no elevation in an object-to-object relationship. It is the relationship itself which brings you to question it.

Q. So the relationship can be a teacher?

JK. Yes. It shows you how you live superficially. Live with the question and one day it will clearly make an impact.

Q. Coomaraswamy said that the partner must be of the same spiritual and moral fibre as oneself.

JK. Of course, but it is rarely possible. You must trust life. It is only life which can bring you to the living answer.

Q. What if, for example, you get married at twenty-three and find out seven or ten years later that you have grown differently? Maybe children are involved. The usual reaction is to separate.

JK. It is true, but only understanding can harmonize the past. The ego-mind can never come to an answer because it lives in choice based on the personality. Free from the ego-mind, free from choice, you discover life. It is only life that brings you to right action.

Q. So if we find ourselves wishing we were out of a situation that we got ourselves into earlier, you would say look at the situation free from the ego, the person, see the facts and be open?

JK. Yes, have a purely impersonal look at the situation.

Q. What about your own past? Would you do it again in the same way?

JK. One can never repeat life. Life is unexpected. But there is no conflict in me. I am out of the vicious circle.

Q. But even if we all share the background of love in all that we do, don't the needs of day to day living require a certain compatibility of lifestyle and values? For example, tastes in music or food, or the importance of the spiritual in one's life.

JK. In our profound being we all desire the same: to be in oneness, and not live in fraction. Look at what brought you together. It is this oneness. It all depends on how you live with your partner. Do not confine him to the need to be a certain way, have a "spiritual dimension," have your interests, etc.. One man might be open through nature, climbing mountains and so on. Another may express his openness through travel and exploring different cultures, another may love art or music or children. It is not children he loves but what is in them, not the phenomenal structure, but the innocence and beauty they encapsulate. Everyone is interested in something. One must find it out. If he has a sense of beauty then that is enough to build a relationship on. And the fact that he fell in love means that he has a sense of beauty. Go back to the seed of that love.

Q. But there may be situations when, no matter what you do, it is still a completely incompatible relationship.

JK. You must be humble and simple and put everything on the table without any accusation. Then wait, be patient. Feel the love that brought you together. Act from that background. Then put all the facts on the table again, in humbleness. Listen. Then wait. There may, even after some years, come a moment, a conviction, that you must go. Then go. But the act is not from the mind, from intention. It comes like a pulsation.

Q. Do all our preferences disappear in our real self? And if this is the case, how does the real self discover a beloved? Aren't all his beloved?

JK. Choice does not pass through the mind. There is no choice because there is no chooser. When you feel love, your whole nature is present. The composition of our phenomenal being is more attuned to one than others. The companion, the beloved, is the most perfect expression of the oneness of Love according to our phenomenal nature, body, mind, sensibility, talents and so on. Love is one, its expressions are multiple. We experience only a fraction of our phenomenal richness. When we are free from ideas, we have a much greater palette for our expressions of love.

Q. Could a realized being live with many beloveds?

JK. It is not in his desire to find many beloveds. When he finds one who touches him deeply on all levels, it is enough. In any case, their relationship is based on one relationship, the divine.

There is no more outside or inside, no more me and you. It is beyond the mind. There are many things the world cannot understand.

Q. What do you see as the purpose for getting married? What is marriage?

JK. It is a social convention that gives psychological security, the security that the man will not look for other women and the woman will not look for other men. It can give consistency to the relationship because there is a stopping of dispersion. It may bring two useless people together.

Q. Because they will be less dispersed and perhaps more oriented spiritually?

JK. Yes. In their living together something useful may come up! There is nothing inherently sacred in marriage. Sacredness appears when you are married to the divine. It is not for the sake of the husband that you love the husband, but for the Self. It is not the wife that you love, but the divine. When you love the attributes of your beloved, you can be sure you will soon be in conflict. But Love is eternal.

It is life that shows you the real meaning for being together. Life is the most important guide of all. Do not refuse it in all its manifestations.

Q. Where does the desire to have children come from? Is it the desire for immortality as Plato says, although he finds it a less noble way than becoming immortal through works of art, for example?

JK. It is a gift, an offering, from the lover to his beloved to show how much he loves her. This love which is a union is, in any case, immortal.

Q. What do you think of the conscious use of sex to create a child? Certain religious traditions encourage couples to only have sex for the procreation of children.

JK. Feeling oneness on the body level must be spontaneous. It must not be used for an achievement, a goal or a result. When there is anticipation or projection of a result, there is contraction. If a child is to appear, he must appear in expansion, in freedom from all projection. The moment of conception is very important and should not be mechanized or mechanical. Most couples are not ripe to have children because their love is not complete. To have a child takes very great maturity on the part of the man and woman. Maturity means to see things not from the point of view of the male and female, but from the view that is beyond woman and man. The only teacher that is beyond the human mind is life, and you must be open to life.

Q. Is the discipline followed by professional celibates, religious orders, or yogis a valid spiritual path?

JK. The monk, nun, priest know the power of the instinctive nature and have adopted a certain discipline not to fall in the trap of this nature so that they are not distracted. It is the same with the yogi who practises powers. He needs his power and does not want it dispersed. But all that is achieved through discipline is an illusion, a misunderstanding. A disciplined mind or body is not a free mind or body.

Q. What is the real meaning of brahmacharya?

JK. To keep the energy for the Ultimate, all kinds of interference are renounced by the yogi. Brahmacharya is not a giving up, but a renouncing of all activities that take you away from being one with the Ultimate. It does not refer only to renouncing on the sexual plane, as is often emphasized, but to the conservation of energy in speaking; not speaking nonsense, gossip or hate. It is the renouncing of all useless activities. It is the orientation of energies toward the relationship with the Ultimate. So go away from all dispersion. You should be brahmacharya until you are oriented concerning your real self.

Q. Would you say it is not the giving up of activity but the selection, the use of discrimination, in activity?

JK. Yes, that is my use of the word brahmacharya. In India it has a much more restricted meaning. There, the brahmacharya becomes passive in all daily activities.

When there is a strong desire to realize the divine, being serious is more or less effortless. But it is a waste of time forcing someone, through discipline, to live seriously when they are driven by their instinctive nature. When there's love for something there's no discipline. It is functional like practising the violin. When there is no love, discipline is violence.

Q. Regarding conserving energy, many artists and athletes have said that they practise actual celibacy at times when they are performing.

JK. To play Hamlet or to give a concert asks for so much presence, so much energy, that you cannot use any energy for anything extraneous to the role, dance, piece at hand.

Q. An intimate relationship inevitably brings out all the aggressive and fearful feelings that might have been hidden. Very often people do not want to face all this turbulence and prefer to "not get involved." Is this an escape or a true path?

JK. It is a refusal to be open, a fear of facing the unexpected, the unknown. It is a lack of faith in life, in what life brings. When you know yourself, your body, its vibration, its sensuality, you recognize it in another. It has nothing to do with object to object sexuality. It is something secret, magic. It burns on a very deep level. This should never be refused. But few people know the love in themselves well enough and are mature enough to know this deep love. Such a love is chaste, in the true sense of the word, pure love.

All expressions of pure love belong to love. But most of the so-called expression of love, in the form of sexuality, is a perversion.

Q. Because it comes from an object to object relationship?

JK. Yes.

Q. So pure love can have the most passionate and unconventional expressions?

JK. Absolutely. Or it may all be expressed in one glance.

Q. Is a profound compatibility essential to a harmonious relation? I ask this because the other day you told a woman not to share a bed with her lover, and you have said to other couples that they should not sleep in the same bed. Yet to others you say the contrary. What is your reason for suggesting sleeping alone?

JK. In sleep there is an escape of certain energies and vibrations which may affect the other in a negative way so that deep rest is not possible. It depends on the nature of the man and the woman. There are those whose muscles never rest and all the nervous energy is given to the companion. Such a person needs to take advice on how to let go, give up, become free from tension before sleeping. The companion must not be a waste basket for all these residues!

Then there are couples whose relationship will not survive if they sleep together because they are bad lovers (*laughs*) or have not enough energy for the day and the night. In these cases the relationship may quickly become boring. And what is attraction? It is an energy which can, in many cases, diminish with too much proximity. The impossibility of sleeping together, without knowing the negative effect, certainly brings divorce to many couples. And it is more difficult to come to the absolute state of relaxation through letting go when you are not alone. But there is a kind of togetherness that is com pletely different. It is not spoken. It is secret. It is sacred. And it is often unrecognized.

Q. Unrecognized by...?

JK. People may say "Why are they together?"

Q. But they are in tune in daily life and in the oneness of deep sleep?

JK. Absolutely. When you live without compulsion then life is harmonious in all its states. Life is inexhaustible. A woman is inexhaustible, a man is inexhaustible. Life is living in openness without memory, without superimposing patterns on the other. It is life that brings both together, that brings us all together. It is very important that we live together, live related. It is the joy of living.

Q. So we must trust life?

JK. Yes! But even when you don't have faith in life, life has faith in you!

NOTES

1. "From my father I get my stature and earnest nature.
From my dear mother, my blithe nature and love of story-telling."

Sadhana
Love

Jean Klein: Remember every morning and every evening before going to sleep, that your original nature is love. Feel how this remembering acts on your psychosomatic structure. And be one with, in identity with, this feeling—without observer and observed.

How can I describe
what is love
and when it is born
and where it is seen
and who found it
and how?

A connoisseur
draws out love
with tender care
from the pulsation of leaves,
from the rays of the flowers...

from *The Love Poems of Chandidas*
translated by Deben Bhattacharya

Your Question

Q. I often find myself in moods that are beyond my control. I may be very high, then very low. Sometimes I feel melancholic or depressed without really knowing why. This obviously upsets the harmony of my relationship with those near to me. How can I come out of this tendency to moods, high and low?

Jean Klein: Moodiness appears when you live in dispersion, when you live in relation to objects. If you look closely, you will see that you live in hoping, in wishful thinking and you are bound to the becoming process, the so-called future, to wanting, obtaining, grasping. You hope that an object will bring you peace, joy, but an object can never bring you beyond the object. When you are moody refer to the inner insight. Only this insight can free you from moody states.

Q. Which insight do you mean exactly?

JK. The insight that the glimpse of your real nature has taken place in you, and has given a new direction to your phenomenal life.

Q. I'm not sure that I've had this absolutely clear glimpse that I can refer to. What can I do then?

JK. Look. Come back to your looking. When your looking is free from wanting, attaining, you'll free yourself of the moodiness. Feel this distance, this space from the moodiness. See in the actual moment itself how knowingly being in this distance acts on you, on your whole nervous system. It is being knowingly in this space relation that is the highest transformer of all kinds of moody states—up or down. What is important is to be this distance, not merely know it intellectually. In other words, see how it has acted on the negative level of your being. The impact alone will lift you. Eventually all your brain patterns will come to a new integration. You must come to a state of equilibrium in all circumstances.

Q. You said that to have the glimpse of your real nature you must be mature. Must I completely rid myself of my moods before having the glimpse?

JK. When you are free from wishful thinking, come back to the facts. It is only in looking at the facts, seeing things as they are, not as you wish them to be, that you can become free from conflict. You live in wishful thinking because you believe you have free will. The idea of free will is an illusion. You have no choice because there is no chooser. You cannot free yourself from conflict by choice, by free will, but only by accepting all parts of the situation in the absence of a chooser, a willer. Only this accepting will give you the solution. Living with the facts brings you to a healthy stand.

Out of moodiness spring jealousy, argument and hate. See that you live in dissatisfaction. Moodiness is the result of striving that has not been achieved, when the desired state has not been attained. When you see this clearly, the extremes of moods are reduced and are consumed in the seeing. Don't hurry the impact. Let it act on you.

Approach on the Body Level

Q. You have spoken about the relaxed body as a dead body and, yet, I thought the energetic body was also relaxed. What is the relation between these two and should I experience both when doing the yoga?

Jean Klein: The body is conditioned through all the residues which come from previously using the body in a not absolutely functional way. By conditioned I mean that the muscle, bone and nervous structure are in tension, contraction, and do not function correctly. This tension has accumulated because it was not completely released after an action. In other words, the action did not appear and disappear in the totally relaxed, organic state. So a chronic tension is maintained. This tension paralyses the energy body and normal functioning. Look at how the octopus moves effortlessly with all its limbs as one, or the panther running, and you will feel how restricted your vital body is.

When you think of and feel your body you think of and feel the conditioned body. This is all you know as body. It has become memory. It is not possible for the energy body to wake up in tension. First all residues, contractions and tensions must be released. This deep letting-go brings a profound relaxation, a feeling of weight. The muscle-bone structure is felt as heavy; it is the weight of the actual structure. What is emphasized at this point is the relaxation, the sensation of the released structures falling into the ground. This is the dead body.

This deeply relaxed dead body is sensed first in its separate parts, then as a mass without frontier. In this sensing a vibration comes up where there is no residue of the boundaries of the body. Sustain the vibration and play with it. You can give it different directions, different sizes and so on. You can feel it expanded in all directions in various postures.

Q. Can you feel the dead body in all the positions or only in *savasana* (the dead body pose)?

JK. You can feel it in all the positions, but lying on your back with all points touching the ground is the easiest way to feel it.

Q. What about the light body, the quality of lightness in the body?

JK. The vibration, the energy body becomes so fine and subtle that it is felt as light. When we come to the light body we have found the original empty body, free from all weight, all objects. When you are familiar with the life-energy body, you can go directly to it without passing through the dead body. Then the organic memory of the energy body solicits you directly.

Q. When you say "you can go" to the energy body do you mean become aware of it, turn your attention to it?

JK. Let me give you an example. You are shaving in the morning and you become aware that you are employing too much energy and tension for the act. When you are already familiar with the light energy body it will come back to you in the moment itself and your act will be freed from tension. All actions must have the appropriate energy.

Q. Is your special way of teaching awareness through body movement one way to become familiar with the energy body?

JK. Yes. You can become aware of using too much tension at any moment. The teaching on the physical level facilitates this awareness and the awakening of the energy body.

Q. Can one be living in the light body without being aware of it—before one has learned of it from a teacher?

JK. Yes, absolutely. But the teacher can be any incident in life which plays the role for the awakening, the being it knowingly.

Q. When you are in bed before going to sleep you have said to put aside all qualifications, all the residues of the I-image. Should we go directly to the relaxed energy body before going to sleep or stay in the dead body?

JK. When you are free from the I-image you are spontaneously in the life body. But, as we said, if you have not had a glimpse of the vital body then you need to go through the dead body.

Q. If you go to sleep in the relaxed dead body state how do you wake up?

JK. It is not sure that you wake up in the same relaxed way because the process of elimination is not completed and residues may come in during the night.

Q. And if you go to sleep in the vital life body, how do you wake up?

JK. Then you wake up in the life body because it is empty and there is no hold for the psychic body.

LISTENING

Volume 8
1994

Beyond Politics 271
Jean Klein

Sadhana: *Reference to the I-Image* 285
Jean Klein

The King's Dohas
Translated by Herbert V. Guenther 286

Your Question: *Why have our meetings lost their impact for me?*...295
Jean Klein

Awareness Through Body Sensing: *Breathe and meditation* 297
Jean Klein

Beyond Politics
(1993)

Jean Klein: When talking about a united Europe, one must first look at what it means to be united. The underlying reality of all human beings is one, consciousness, manifested in very similar ways. Whether we are black, white, yellow, red, or British, German, Belgian, French, we all have the same body structure, same liver, same breathing systems, and these are affected similarly by the same fears, anger, hate, jealousy, sexual urges, anxieties, and so on. The body can be treated universally, the psyche and soul can be healed in universal ways. Humanity is profoundly one. We are in any case united. We only need to be aware of it. Without feeling this oneness we can never come to a united Europe.

There are two aspects to the unity I mean here: actual oneness and multiplicity in oneness. The most important is the recognition that our very homeground, our origin is one. It is not a composed oneness, but actually is oneness. It is called by many names, consciousness, stillness, our original nature. It is present when all aspects of individuality are absent. When there is no more object, it is there as presence. Presence in the absence of anything.

We are, however, educated to take the absence of objects as an absence of awareness. This is a profound error. We have identified with the world of referents and only know ourselves in relation to objects. We know only the qualified I, as in "I am English, I am French, I am a lawyer, a man, a woman," etc. But our original nature which we have in common with all, is when the I stands without any qualification. This unqualified I is presence, consciousness. It is our homeground out of which all phenomenal existence arises and into which it returns. Before we can be united, or even truly related, we must accept intellectually, even before we have the living experience of it, that our homeground is one. This is the only *a priori* conviction that can ever work in solving the conflict in our world society. It is the only workable structure, because it is the only truth. Out of this truth comes authority. Truth is the only sovereign. Truth is ethical, functional and aesthetic. It is the fundamental knowing that consciousness without objects is our original nature and that to take ourselves for individual personae is the sole cause of conflict and suffering.

Every undertaking of a human nature must have, as its background, that which binds everyone together, which all have in common, which gives support to the phenomenal world, consciousness. The expression of this deep conviction is love, openness, humility, and the seeing of facts as they are, not the seeing of the products of wishful thinking and illusion based on the misconception of the existence of a personal entity. True thinking comes from non-thinking, from Silence, from stillness, from this background. Thinking that comes from thinking is obviously based on memory, on past conditioning. And all thinking that is creative must be fresh, new, and free from preconceptions. It is not thinking that can change society, but a looking away from thinking.

On the level of objects and ideas, there can be no solution to any situation. We turn in the vicious circle of the divided mind, caught up in endless choosing and arbitrary decision-making, arbitrary because the premise is arbitrary that there is a chooser, someone to decide. There can be no authority based on arbitrariness. When we take ourselves for individuals we take ourselves for a fraction. No situation can be clearly seen from the fractional point of view. No facts can be clearly put on the table when clouded by the idea of the person. In the absence of a personal entity the situation unfolds in all its possibilities and the facts are presented. The person can never bring a solution. It is the situation itself that brings its own solution, the right solution. It may not be pleasant for the ego, but it will be ethical, functional and aesthetic. The truth is never personal. Right thinking, right acting and right feeling are not personal. This impersonal vision is the ground of all harmony.

An harmonious society must be built on the inner state of every human being. This inner state is not an appropriation of moral, spiritual and functional rules, but the building of an inner foundation grounded in knowledge and love.

In observing the seed of truth, unity will evolve inevitably, not as something constructed by the mind in an arbitrary fashion, but as an organic happening. A united Europe is an inevitability. In 1928 students in Berlin, myself included, were shouting in the streets for a pan-Europe, a unity. Our deepest desire is to be united. If it is not today, it will be tomorrow, because it belongs to the survival of the human race to unite, to unite in love. So, before embarking on uniting Europe, the perspective must be clear.

The perspective of a united Europe cannot become clear in an evening! It is a kind of living together, living with the question, the inevitable question. When the perspective is clear, all practical issues will be resolved. Economic and political unification cannot take precedence over, but is a result of, a clear perspective based on the oneness of humanity.

The second aspect of unity is multiplicity in oneness. It is clear that when we realize, in the absence of the notion of an individual, that the original homeground of all phenomenal existence is consciousness and that we are all essentially one, the cause of conflict disappears. The great majority of conflict is caused by psychological survival, the attempt to protect one's ego, or national ego, in its many forms and extensions. In the absence of the person as chooser, judge, comparer, there is a welcoming of life and all that life brings.

This welcoming and openness is love. It is only in love that the infinite diversity of life's expressiveness can co-exist harmoniously. Love cannot be adopted or attained. It is what we fundamentally are. Each person and nation must come to the understanding of this underlying principle we call love. It is an experience without an experiencer. When the experiencer is absent there is no more conflict. Differences are faced purely functionally without psychological involvement. Differences are respected. When one nation faces another nation with historical not psychological memory, it appeals to its greatness, its richness of culture, language, tradition, and so on. And the power of a united Europe lies in maintaining the different traditions, cultures, languages, myths of each country. It is the dynamism of a country that keeps it alive, virile, powerful; otherwise, it calcifies and loses all vitality and interest. In any case, true culture belongs to no one and to all. It is, as we said, the same humanity in many aspects. Whether expressed in religion, art or language, it is all from the same origin. Orchestras, paintings, etc., have long been cross-cultural. There needs to be a coming together of selected people to expose the seeds of culture in each country. But to be identified with cultural traditions is the beginning of unification. It is in learning about and respecting the great thinkers and artists of one's own country that one can learn to admire the cultures of other nations. Basing unity on economics is doomed to failure because it emphasizes the object rather than its origin. In a society based on acquisition, on greed and consumerism, a species of competition is born which has nothing to do with creative production and beauty. But when we live intelligently, without anticipation and end-gaining, the roots of our society will change. The object will no longer take priority, but emphasis will be given to the ground from which it comes.

A new Renaissance is only possible when art and science, culture, is an offering to the Ultimate. Without a feeling of the Ultimate, it is not possible to create a cultured and happy society.

And no society can be happy when it is culturally stagnant, when it has nothing to offer, nothing to be proud of, nothing to be admired. In adoration there is togetherness. In listening to music there is togetherness. In seeing painting or dance, there is togetherness. In the act of admiring we are one without admirer or admired.

By the Ultimate, I do not mean a personal or conceptual God. Although this was a beautiful pretext for creativity and offering in the Renaissance, today's God language is purely conceptual, a nuisance which prevents new knowledge and new discovery. God can only be discovered, never attained. The European God is a sleepy person responsible for two great wars. Today, we must find what is beyond objects, and to find it we have to look where thinking cannot take place.

Each one of us must find our true nature, not based on contrived morality and beliefs. It is this true nature which is the only sovereign. Sovereignty based on self-image, religious, political or any other, is completely hypothetical, an illusion. It will inevitably bring conflict. No nation in the world today can live in isolation. Real sovereignty is not based on competition and self-image but on knowledge and love. It is the superiority, not of others but of oneself. There is only spiritual authority. Temporal authority flows from this knowledge, this love.

There is only one authority and it is not authoritarian. We need a kind of Academy of people who are rooted in this spiritual authority and who are educated and cultured and who can see facts as they are, free from interpretation and wishful thinking. What is called for is an exchange between people of competence with knowledge and experience in all aspects of culture. The united Europe currently under discussion is a purely intellectual construct that has no basis in real knowing, no basis in reality. Goethe said to Linne: "Da hast du die teile in der hand, fehlt leider das geistige band." (You have details/pieces in your hand but unfortunately no spiritual band/tie/binding.) The present rule of bureaucracy where the so-called leaders are void of culture, authoritarian without authority, and acting from the personal point of view, can never bring harmony. One cannot construct unity on the phenomenal level. There is no mental or phenomenal way out of the situation we are in. Only unity based on the non-phenomenal principle is consistent. There is only one sovereign authority, but it is not authoritarian.

Loving and giving to our surroundings must be beyond the personal, as it was in the Renaissance. An Academy approaching things through knowledge, beauty, kindness and love is the only way to a united Europe. For beauty has its own authority.

Education will then come out of love. One learns because one loves it. Then we will be able to give, to share what we have loved and learned, and which is the inheritance of all humankind. Ultimately, when we have acted on the principle that binds us together as human beings, there will be no nations, but the cultural traditions will remain in all their richness. When our wrong thinking, a thinking that is based on acquisition, is righted, we will live in offering and openness. The new Renaissance will be based on what is actual, on real knowing, not the accumulation of fundamentally unrelated facts. When we no longer take ourselves for an image inevitably arguing with other images, there will be no more talk of blending the practical with the spiritual because the spiritual is the only practical way. Nothing else works.

Q. You say that competition is essentially a negative way of functioning, but it seems to be an integral part of today's society. Is all competition to be avoided or is there a constructive competition?

JK. Society can only be changed by each one of us because it is we who make up society. Competition is based on quantity not quality. Quantity is war. When production is based on quality, not quantity, everything will change.

Q. It is truly hard to visualize a non-competitive society, no economic competition, no Olympic games, no team sports. Or

can these things be accomplished with another human feeling?
JK. When our work is approached through quality, intelligence
and creativity are called upon. Emphasizing quality makes
you grow as the producer. It emphasizes the sattvic state and
consequently the product brings out the best in the consumer.
In living in quantity the society degenerates completely. When
a society is based on quality it grows in love and beauty, art,
culture, betterment and so on.

Q. How should education proceed?

JK. Children closely watch their parents and the society. We
must understand very deeply the nature of the child and educate
according to the age of the child and not another age. We should
not push the child into achieving, completion. This is only an
extension of the parent's ego. One must expose the child at an early
age to art, music, painting and dancing. It brings harmonization.
Sports must be undertaken in a new way. Sport is usually violence
as in the much acclaimed "competitive spirit." We need only show
our own possibilities, not in relation to others.

Q. Do you feel that the reign of quantity is responsible for an
escalation in society's problems, violence, boredom, etc.? Perhaps
because there is a deep lack of satisfaction.

JK. Certainly. Many factors in modern society contribute to
violence, especially noise, television, a complete elimination of
the value of psychological and physical space, and the objecti-
fication of the man-woman relationship. This leads to a deep
reaction and frustration which looks for outlets. A new society
begins with education. It begins with our children. How is it
possible that children are given toy guns, soldiers, and tanks to
play with?
    Children's toys today are too expressed. The absence of the
anecdotal makes the imagination work. The child can complete
the game, as a painter or poet leaves something unsaid in the

work so that there is room left for the audience to complete it, to join in the creative process. Toy-makers now leave nothing to the imagination, and violent toys should be banned altogether because they stimulate violence.

Q. But doesn't a very developed imagination also have a tendency to day-dream which you say is an obstacle to seeing the facts?

JK. In imaginative play, the child goes beyond the physical form, the obvious. It is essential to be able to go beyond the phenomenal. Seeing the facts is another education.

Q. How much of education belongs to the parents and how much to the schools?

JK. It mostly belongs to the parents. When the parents live in freedom and beauty they are the best teachers. But most of our so-called education is based on competition and violence. And television is a great generator of violence. It stimulates violent reactions in us. Merely sitting in front of the screen disturbs our subtle organism. Violence on television is widely responsible for a general acceptance of violence, since most of the time the violence expressed is considered heroic. We cannot eliminate television, but it should be used for culture, education, learning languages, etc. The news is depressing. It takes us away from a real sense of what life is.

Q. There are many who argue that we are, by nature, aggressive and that television does not really exacerbate that so much. They say the news, and even violent films, portray reality, life on the planet, and help understanding of a global situation.

JK. But television is used primarily to stimulate the bored. Of course, there are many bored souls who enjoy talking about war. It is mostly a male activity, but are we to live with our instinct leading us or shall we be led by the more noble human characteristics?

Individuals are conditioned by languages, endocrine glands, food, beliefs, traditions, superstitions, habits, education, training, ideas and so on. Certain of the biological conditioning we cannot change, but we can become more conscious of it in a bipolar approach. By "bipolar," I mean seeing it and seeing how it acts on, affects, us. However, acquired conditioning can be changed. The idea of being an independent entity which believes it can act of its own choice and so-called free will, is one of the conditionings that can be changed. All the rules of society are based on this idea of being an independent entity.

Q. You have said that society needs rules of behaviour until it is ripe to behave itself—or words to that effect. In our day there is so much confusion about how much freedom one should have or give. Parents are often at a loss as to how to guide their children, afraid to inhibit them. How much guidance should parents give?

JK. There must be authority without being authoritarian. This authority appears when the ego is absent and does not colour thinking. Today, behaviour is a fashion. The child must discover the value of beauty. When a parent gives advice to the child, it must be with the background, the conviction, that one day he will act in the right way. A child must learn what is right and what is wrong, what is functional and not functional. There must be a codified morality, but very subtle.

Q. The word functional could be interpreted in endless ways. In some countries certain behaviour is acceptable which would be completely unacceptable elsewhere. Is appropriate behaviour always relative or is there an absolute, a universally appropriate behaviour?

JK. What is functional behaviour is relative in its appearance, changing according to the situation, but the ground from which the action comes is not relative. By functional, I mean economic in gesture, in energy. The action is undertaken in the most intelligent way.

Our way of punishing must disappear. We were not chosen to punish. We have a right to defend ourselves, but not to condemn. Do we really know why someone acts as they do? Every effort must be made to find out. We are all responsible for the society we live in.

Q. You have said that codified morality is immoral. Would you explain that more?

JK. Codified morality is abstract. All that is codified is abstract because it has nothing to do with the moment itself, with the facts of the moment. It is a superimposed code. When you are free from a code, you are attentive, vigilant and appropriate to the situation. You are in the universal ground of all right action. It calls on your intelligence and creativity.

Codified morality has value for the child until a certain age, until he can see the whole impact of his actions. One must teach the child not to crush the spider because it is a living being.

Q. What do you think of the argument that perhaps it is difficult for a child to really respect animals if he knows they are irreverently killed for food?

JK. But we should not eat animals. Of course, if the child eats a duck or a fish you cannot give him a real reason to respect, love, understand and observe all living beings. But nature cannot teach this higher morality. It comes from heaven. All that is instinctive comes from nature. Because a crocodile eats another animal does not mean that humans should also. It is not appropriate to the human being. It destroys the subtle harmony of the living earth. So we must give codified morality with the view to attaining a level of inner morality.

Q. What about wearing leather from a cow? Children ask about this as well. I have found it easier for a child to understand the eating of an animal as part of the natural flow of existence than the killing of an animal to make pretty shoes.

JK. If one is vegetarian for moral reasons only, it is absolutely logical not to use any animal products at all. But food is for the subtle body also, and it is clear that eating meat does not allow for a lucid mind.

Q. For a child-like mind, cutting down a tree is not very different from killing an animal.

JK. In a society based on quality, not quantity, trees would not be cut down indiscriminately nor would animals be killed in vast numbers. It is a question of sensitivity, of offering. Who knows but the tree may offer itself to help a beautiful human being.

Q. Is this "inner morality" what is called "having a conscience?"

JK. Perhaps.

Q. At what age is it developed?

JK. At around fourteen there is a certain discrimination.

Q. So you don't think ten-year-olds are responsible for their actions?

JK. Yes, I think they have a basic knowledge of right and wrong at seven or eight.

Q. Is there not a discrepancy here in your answers?

JK. At eight they know what is right and wrong. At fourteen

they become more conscious, and at twenty-one fully so.

Q. Based on your age groups, could one say that at around 8 a child knows the difference between right and wrong, but this concept of right and wrong is still very influenced by his *immediate* surroundings, father, mother, friends. By about fourteen, she is beginning to become aware of a larger area of right and wrong beyond immediate influences—the beginning of true independence of conscience. And by, perhaps, twenty-one this independence from immediate conditioning is complete—in healthy development. So in a child under fourteen there is no truly independent knowing of right or wrong.

JK. I agree absolutely, but these numbers are abstract because each person has a different biological age. At any age there should not be simply punishment.

Q. What about large-scale organized crime?

JK. It should be publicly condemned.

Q. Again, there is a certain sector of society which believes that to ban anything, whether it be pornography, violence or sex in film, is a violation of the individual's right to freedom.

JK. But for democracy one must be ripe morally and functionally. People are not ripe. One must have the intelligence to use the freedom. You cannot give total freedom to a child until he is ripe to use it. The user of freedom must be responsible for it.

Q. As long as society is not mature, how much freedom does one allow? Or does one give total freedom and learn the long, hard way through mistakes?

JK. Yes, we must have freedom of speech, but when the leaders and intelligentsia see that it is misused there should be an education, an education in beauty.

Q. Again, is not the nude beautiful to one and pornography to another?

JK. Yes, but one must know the difference between fashion and beauty which has nothing to do with space and time. It is the difference between joy and pleasure. When society is educated, none of these issues will pose a problem.

Q. How can society be educated?

JK. There are educated people but they are often ignored. Most of our resources should be for education—not for defence. The non-violent countries should come together and show a new way of living.

Q. Philosophy, advaita included, has been criticized as naive, utopian, unrealistic, impractical. How can emphasizing the ultimate good help everyday concerns on the practical level?

JK. There is no practical or ultimate level. There is only one level. We must understand the principle, then apply it to all our activities. Then we can see whether we have really understood or not. All that is, comes from fractional seeing. The beautiful, noble, good comes from global seeing.

Q. Do you believe that there will be a utopia one day?

JK. Yes! One must have the conviction and the conviction helps make it an actuality. Non-conviction is an unhealthy state of mind, because, in the end, all is accomplished.

Q. Do you mean that the one who is pessimistic is living in time and memory and the one who believes in a utopia sees it at every moment?

JK. Yes, because in reality there *is* fulfilment at every moment. When you live knowingly in your beauty, consciousness, there is no lack. When you live in the mind, in thinking, there is always lack.

Q. So, even if we believe the planet as a biosphere is doomed, we can still be fulfilled.

JK. Exactly. Because Life can never be destroyed. It is the highest principle. It binds all opposites together.

Q. And if one lives from this highest principle it may not be too late to have a utopia?

JK. Utopia is not time-bound.

Q. So to think of a utopia evolving is not useful...

JK. It is living with the mind. But I am convinced that one day the world will be different because we go naturally towards the positive.

Q. Many would say the contrary is true—except for a few individuals.

JK. Advaita is not for the few, it is a universal truth. It belongs to all. The feeling of this truth will create a new society. A new principle must enter behaviour and education.

Sadhana

Jean Klein: During the whole day do not refer to your "I" while thinking and acting, and keep this absence of reference to the I-image in your relations with others.

The Song on Human Action
The Treasure of Dohas
from
The King's Dohas

I bow down to noble Manjusri.
I bow down to Him who has conquered the finite.

I

As calm water lashed by wind
Turns into waves and rollers,
So the king thinks of Saraha
In many ways, although one man.

2

To a fool who squints
One lamp is as two;
Where seen and seer are not two, ah! the mind
Works on the thingness of them both.

3

Though the house-lamps have been lit,
The blind live on in the dark.
Though spontaneity is all-encompassing and close,
To the deluded it remains always far away.

4

Though there may be many rivers, they are one in the sea,
Though there may be many lies, one truth will conquer all.
When one sun appears, the dark
However deep will vanish.

5

As a cloud that rises from the sea
Absorbing rain the earth embraces,
So, like the sky, the sea remains
Without increasing or decreasing.

6

So from spontaneity that's unique,
Replete with the Buddha's perfections,
Are all sentient beings born and in it come
To rest. But it is neither concrete nor abstract.

7

They walk other paths and so forsake true bliss,
Seeking the delights that stimulants produce.
The honey in their mouths and to them so near
Will vanish if at once they do not drink it.

8

Beasts do not understand the world
To be a sorry place. Not so the wise
Who the heavenly nectar drink
While beasts hunger for the sensual.

9

To a fly that likes the smell of putrid
Meat the fragrance of sandalwood is foul.
Beings who discard Nirvana
Covet coarse Samsara's realm.

10

An ox's footprints filled with water
Will soon dry up; so with a mind that's firm
But full of qualities that are not perfect;
These imperfections will in time dry up.

11

Like salt sea water that turns
Sweet when drunk up by the clouds,
So a firm mind that works for others turns
The poison of sense-objects into nectar.

12

If ineffable, never is one unsatisfied,
If unimaginable, it must be bliss itself.
Though from a cloud one fears the thunderclap,
The crops ripen when from it pours the rain.

13

It is in the beginning, in the middle, and
The end; yet end and beginning are nowhere else.
All those with minds deluded by interpretative thoughts are in
Two minds and so discuss nothingness and compassion as two
  things.

14

Bees know that in flowers
Honey can be found.
That Samsara and Nirvana are not two
How will the deluded ever understand?

15

When the deluded in a mirror look
They see a face, not a reflection.
So the mind that has truth denied
Relies on that which is not true.

16

Though the fragrance of a flower cannot be touched,
'Tis all pervasive and at once perceptible.
So by unpatterned being-in-itself
Recognize the round of mystic circles.

17

When still water by the wind is stirred,
It takes the shape and texture of a rock.
When the deluded are disturbed by interpretative thoughts,
That which is as yet unpatterned turns very hard and solid.

18

Mind immaculate in its very being can never be
Polluted by Samsara's or Nirvana's impurities.
A precious jewel deep in mud
Will not shine, though it has lustre.

19

Knowledge shines not in the dark, but when the darkness
Is illumined, suffering disappears [at once].
Shoots grow from the seed
And leaves from the shoots.

20

He who thinks of the mind in terms of one
Or many casts away the light and enters the world.
Into a [raging] fire he walks with open eyes—
Who could be more deserving of compassion?

21

For the delights of kissing the deluded crave
Declaring it to be the ultimately real—
Like a man who leaves his house and standing at the door
Asks for reports of sensual delights.

22

The stirring of biotic forces in the house of nothingness
Has given artificial rise to pleasures in so many ways.
Such yogis from affliction faint for they have fallen
From celestial space, inveigled into vice.

23

As a Brahmin, who with rice and butter
Makes a burnt offering in blazing fire
Creating a vessel for nectar from celestial space,
Takes this through wishful thinking as the ultimate.

24

Some people who have kindled the inner heat and raised it to
the fontanelle
Stroke the uvula with the tongue in a sort of coition and
confuse
That which fetters with what gives release,
In pride will call themselves yogis.

25

As higher awareness they teach what they experience
Within. What fetters them they will call liberation.
A glass trinket colored green to them is an emerald;
Deluded, they know not a gem from what they think it should be.

26

They take copper to be gold. Bound by discursive thought
They think these thoughts to be ultimate reality.
They long for the pleasures experienced in dreams. They call
The perishable body-mind eternal bliss supreme.

27

By the symbol EV AM [they think] self-clearness is achieved,
By the different situations that demand four seals
They call what they have fancied spontaneity,
But this is looking at reflections in a mirror.

28

As under delusion's power a herd of deer will rush
For the water in a mirage which is not recognized,

So also the deluded quench not their thirst, are bound by chains
And find pleasure in them, saying that all is ultimately real.

29

Non-memory is convention's truth
And mind which has become no-mind.
This is fulfilment, this the highest good.
Friends, of this highest good become aware.

30

In nonmemory is mind absorbed; just this
Is emotionality perfect and pure.
It is unpolluted by the good or bad of worldliness
Like a lotus unaffected by the mud from which it grows.

31

Yet with certainty must all things be viewed as if they were a
    magic spell.
If without distinction you can accept or reject Samsara
Or Nirvana, steadfast is your mind, free from the shroud of
    darkness.
In you will be self-being, beyond thought and self-originated.

32

This world of appearance has from its radiant beginning
Never come to be; unpatterned it has discarded patterning.
As such it is continuous and unique meditation;
It is nonmentation, stainless contemplation, and nonmind.

33

Mind, intellect, and the formed contents of that mind are It,
So too are the world and all that seems from It to differ,
All things that can be sensed and the perceiver,
Also dullness, aversion, desire, and enlightenment.

34

Like a lamp that shines in the darkness of spiritual
Unknowing, It removes obscurations of a mind
As far as the fragmentations of intellect obtain.
Who can imagine the self-being of desirelessness?

35

There's nothing to be negated, nothing to be
Affirmed or grasped; for It can never be conceived.
By the fragmentations of the intellect are the deluded
Fettered; undivided and pure remains spontaneity.

36

If you question ultimacy with the postulates of the many and
the one,
Oneness is not given, for by transcending knowledge are
sentient beings freed.
The radiant is potency latent in the intellect, and this
Is shown to be meditation; unswerving mind is our true
essence.

37

Once in the realm that's full of joy
The seeing mind becomes enriched
And thereby for this and that most useful; even when it runs
After objects it is not alienated from itself.

38

The buds of joy and pleasure
And the leaves of glory grow.
If nothing flows out anywhere
The bliss unspeakable will fruit.

39

What has been done and where and what in itself it will become
Is nothing: yet thereby it has been useful for this and that.
Whether passionate or not
The pattern is nothingness.

40

If I am like a pig that covets worldly mire
You must tell me what fault lies in a stainless mind.
By what does not affect one
How can one now be fettered?

translated by Herbert V. Guenther

Your Question

Q. When I first met you it made a tremendous impact on me, but after coming back to hear and see you very often, there is a growing anxiety in me that maybe I have missed the moment. My coming to see you is now more from affection and a need for a "dose of Jean Klein" than the urgent call it was in the beginning. I realize that time is running out for me and I am not yet liberated even after so many years of self-inquiry. I feel a bit stuck in one place. Can you comment?

Jean Klein: The first impression that you have when you meet the teacher is without any reference and the teacher meets you without any reference. One can say it is "the great meeting" where there is no preconception, no memory. There's a moment in this unique meeting when there is no expectation and no thought. It is a moment when the teacher gives you no hold for something and you are open to nothingness. In this moment, where your personality is absent, all the qualifications, hopes and expectations you had are destroyed. The presence of the teacher is empty of all qualification and stimulates your own emptiness, your own absence. In this absence is presence of what you fundamentally are.

You may not be aware of this moment, but you are unknowingly a witness to it, and it comes up later. Be one with these echoes, solicitations, which are the perfume of your unconditioned presence. Keep alive the first impression, like a painter who must leave his canvas but when he returns to it, remembers again, lives again, the impact of the vision given to him.

If you emphasize the personal aspect in the first meeting, you miss the principle which brought you to this most important meeting of your life. That is why one must be mature to meet the guru. Maturity is openness, availability. The teacher doesn't give you anything. He or she only makes possible what you are already. The teacher emphasizes not your personality, but the ultimate in you and this lights up, awakens, your own ultimate being, your own real nature.

Each time that you meet your teacher, let the same feeling come up that was present at your first meeting. Then you will avoid repetition and in openness you will grow in your establishment.

Awareness Through Body Sensing

Q. Dr. Klein, earlier this week you directed our meditation together and you talked about the breath and the exhalation of the breath. Could you say more about the breath and meditation?

Jean Klein: Inhalation and exhalation are more or less superimpositions on what is constant. So the silence, the interval after exhalation, is not an absence of activity, but an absence of function. It is presence. In the beginning, our awareness focuses on the act of inhalation and exhalation. But there comes a moment that we become indifferent to inhaling and exhaling. It is now that the body takes itself in charge concerning the breathing, and we emphasize the silence, the interval between the two activities. That is a spiritual way of using breath control and breath itself, but breath control can also be used to direct, to orchestrate, the energy in us. I prefer the first way of dealing with the breathing.

When there is reaction in a certain part of the body, you should sense it. In sensing it, the reaction, the resistance, is absorbed by the sensation. In other words, the localization is dispersed in the sensing. We can start by sensing the whole posture and the area around the contraction, or we can face the fraction first. In the latter case, we sense the contracted object part of the body and gradually the accent is released from the object until there is a sudden shift and the accent is now on awareness. Experience will tell you which is the correct way to face tension. We should sense every reaction. It is a tuning as you tune a cello or a piano. You must take your body for a harp.

This procedure in the postures can also be transposed onto the level of the mind. You become aware that you live constantly in anticipation, in end-gaining. In the body exercises we live really in the now, from moment to moment, fraction to fraction. At each moment the goal is attained.

Q. Could you say something about visualization? I find it difficult to visualize my body spreading. I can think it, but I can't visualize it.

JK. It is very often the visual image of the body which hinders you from visualizing it. So it is better to close your eyes. Just visualize emptiness in a certain part of your body, for example, the knee which is very often contracted; see empty space. Then see how this visualization acts on the physical part. You feel immediately a separation in the lower part of your legs, and an expanding. So, with the help of your representation, you can bring your knee, your leg, or other parts of your body, to a certain position which is anatomically possible on the condition that you keep the sensation. But you must practise.

Q. Can one practise yoga too much?

JK. When you love the piano you play it and do not feel it a chore, a "practice." If you are solicited to do the movements, do not refuse. But never let it become a habit. You will know it is a habit if you feel something missing in your day when you have not "practised."

Q. In doing the postures I find myself very often basking in the relaxed body or in a body sensation that is light and feels delicious.

JK. That is an achievement. One must see that the goal is not the body. The goal is the owner of the body. Ask yourself, "Where is the perceiver?" The good body feeling is only a fraction of this art of yoga.

Every object has a mission to bring us back to its homeground. The object has only two missions: one mission is to reveal the ultimate, and the second is to glorify the ultimate in many ways.

Q. What is it in us that allows for the unfolding?

JK. When the subject is fixed on the object, the body is in a state of tension. In the unfolding of the object, the body comes to a great letting go. It is only in deep relaxation that the object can dissolve in the subject. We must be completely available to all the possibilities of the object, free from choice, selection, interpretation, and so on. We must not grasp it but receive it with all our body sensitivity. When we do not direct the object, it unfolds in our multidimensional attention.

Q. Is being available a passive or active relaxed state?

JK. It is open, actively relaxed. In passive relaxation you are open to objects. In active relaxation you are open to the self.

Q. So in exploring a perception, should one be first passively receptive?

JK. Yes, let the object come to you. Then there is a kind of switchover where you go from passive to active availability, and finally this dissolves and what remains is only consciousness.

Note: This article is excerpted from the book *Beyond Knowledge* by Jean Klein.

LISTENING

Volume 9
1994

The Day of Listening: July 2, 1994 303
Jean Klein

Sonnet 318
William Shakespeare

Your Question: *I feel that I have come to an
impasse* 319
Jean Klein

The Approach on the Body Level: *Listening to
the body* 321
Jean Klein

The Day of Listening
Santa Barbara, July 2, 1994

Jein Klein: Today is not the same day as other days. It is a new day. Don't superimpose yesterday onto today. Live in non-conclusion. This calls for listening. There is not a listener, there is simply listening, listening to both the inner and outer world without comparison, judgment, and so on. We are invited.

(long silence)

It asks for a new way of looking, free from the person that we think ourself to be. It is a bi-polar seeing, being open to our own world and the outer world, aware of the facts and, at the same time, aware of how the seeing acts on us, frees us from the person. This open seeing is an act of thanking, thanking for being allowed to thank, for being free to thank, for being allowed to be.

We may feel it as an offering. It is something tremendous that we thank that we are allowed to be. In this moment we are free, free from what we are not. We can only see what we are not. What we are, we can never see. It is the seer itself.

Thanking where there is nothing to thank makes us free, because in the act of thanking there is nobody who thanks and nobody to thank. Now, let us talk about something beautiful—

friendship, human relations, music, painting, architecture, love. What else is there to talk about?

Q. You said we can never see what we are, but is it possible to see what we are not?

JK. Yes.

Q. In seeing what we are not, there is a feeling of not being that, of that being an appearance only.

JK. Yes. You are freed from identifying with what you are not. When you see what you are not, you are what you are. But what you are cannot be seen. You can only be it.

Q. I am trying to understand your word, "thank." There's a sense of joy and beauty in it. But I don't understand thank, because who is there to thank, what to thank?

JK. There is nobody to thank. There is only the beauty of thanking. You can only be it, be the thanking, the unconditioned being. First you feel that you are allowed to be, then you are the thanking. Nobody is left to thank. It is just thanking for the love of thanking. Thanking for the love of thanking, it sounds a bit like Heidegger, no? *(laughs)*

Q. Can you talk about intuition?

JK. When you really feel certain that you are not the body, senses and mind, there is a total giving up. This giving up is the moment when you are really free from what you are not. It appears to you like an intuition; it is instantaneous. In this moment you feel yourself free, free from your body, senses and mind.

Q. There's no mooring anywhere.

JK. Thanking where there is nothing that thanks and nobody to thank is for me the highest feeling of beauty.

(long silence)

What you really are, you can never find objectively, you can never find positively. You cannot. When you find it positively, you objectify it. It is only at the end, when we are being completely free, that we can say, "I am." Otherwise, we make an object of it. What we are fundamentally, is the highest subjectivity. What we are can never be contacted in an affirmative way.

It is very interesting when you give yourself up in the evening to sleep, and you lay aside all qualifications. There is a difference when you say, "I am" and when you say, "I am not." In "I am" there is still the possibility that you are making it positive. It is very subtle. When you give yourself to sleep, and you say, "I am," it is not the same feeling as the real "I AM." But there comes a moment which you cannot provoke, when the inner desire comes to find yourself, your inner substance, in "I am not." In this "I am not," there is a total dissolving, and, at the same time, you are completely free.

When you say, "I am not," you cannot say, "I am" anymore. It just comes up spontaneously as a consequence. The highest level of being is, "I am not." There is no more possibility of making it positive. To know that I am not needs capacity, absolute maturity.

Q. So one must have a capacity of absolute maturity.

JK. Yes. You feel, without feeling it, that there is no longer any return.

Q. I don't quite follow that.

JK. That's very good.

(laughter all round)

Q. This knowledge, this knowing that I am not, does not belong to the mind, does it? It belongs to the globality. Is that a way to say it?

JK. Yes. But when you say, "I am not," behind the "I am not" there lurks an "I am". So you must come to the double absence. It is only in the last "I am not" that the "I am" takes presence.

Q. A sage who realizes "I am" after he dies, after the body dies, is he eternally awake in a certain way, or is it similar to anybody else whose body dies?

JK. Of course I give you the answer free from speculation. When there is the separation between the body and the "I am," you go in the "I am."

Q. So there's a certain awakefulness in the "I am" that's always there.

JK. Absolutely. Your seed is there. There is a seed.

Q. So that's why it's important for a person to clearly understand this, while they have a body. Besides making their life happier on earth, if they realize what they are not, there's also a reason after death why it's important.

JK. What you will realize in this period, is that the body, senses and mind are expressions, expressions of the Ultimate.

Q. Is it important for a person to die in a certain way, in an open way, in a peaceful way?

JK. Absolutely.

Q. So at the time one dies, one finds oneself in openness.

JK. The person is no longer bound to time, one is in the timeless.

Q. Once a sage finds himself in the timeless, then he's in the timeless... eternally, forever.

JK. Yes.

Q. Awake in the timeless, forever. So this is why it's important for consciousness to wake up and start knowing itself, while it has a body.

Q. *(Another questioner)* I'm not sure I understand any of this. It seems to me that consciousness is, and body, mind, senses are just superimpositions.

JK. Yes.

Q. They bring the whole idea of time and space. So if you plainly see what you are not, the issues of what will happen or what used to be have no relevance. These only belong to the body-mind. But you never change. There is really no time in which to change.

JK. There's no beginning, no becoming. Absolutely.

Q. But for the sage, there's something... the seed is a little more awake. The seed is a little more active, or less passive.

JK. No. Active and passive have nothing to do with it.

Q. But it's not the same for a sage and an ordinary person after death, is it?

JK. When you go from the "I am" to the body, senses and mind, and remain free—I am neither this nor that—there is no more question of "I am" or "I am not". It goes. Life takes it. There is only life. When you have given up body, senses and mind, the "I AM" is so tremendous.

Q. And that tremendousness lasts eternally, in a certain way.

JK. Yes. You can no longer ignore what you are.

Q. Even if you don't have a body.

JK. What you are has nothing to do with the body.

Q. One other question that belongs to the mind. When an ordinary person dies, does any of their mind structure continue on in any way, or is it completely reintegrated into the everything?

JK. Dissolved. Yes. Completely dissolved.

Q. So it's not that something continues on from lifetime to lifetime.

JK. No.

Q. It goes like rain. It comes down and goes into the ocean, and some other new rain comes down.

JK. I cannot give you the precise answer, because I don't know it. In any case, it has no relevance to our subject here. It is anecdotal, more a question from curiosity than the deep desire to know.

Q. It doesn't apply to our subject, I realize that. But may I ask one other question? Many people have described their transition to living in consciousness as very violent and difficult. I've read accounts of people who've gone through it, and it doesn't seem like anything one would want to go through. Many people had a very difficult time with very strong eliminations and things like that. Is that the case for everybody?

JK. I don't feel it so. They are mostly pathological cases.

Q. For you, was it a violent thing?

JK. No. Absolutely not. Full of tenderness. Full of tenderness.

Q. Did it go on for a year, or was it one moment?

JK. The awakening is in one moment, but we are always living beyond time.

Q. It seems that the only difference between the realized and the unrealized is that the process of dying is different. But after death there is no difference. Is that true?

JK. Let us see first the terms realized and unrealized. The moment somebody is realized, he is free from the realizing. A realized person knows that there is nothing to realize. An independent entity doesn't exist. They are free from the realizing. Give it up, and see how the understanding acts on you. You will be free.

(long silence)

Ask the question for yourself, "Who is there to realize?" You will never find a "who."

Q. Does the psychological mind come to a standstill?

JK. It is completely stopped. It stops immediately, and there is understanding. It is only this ultimate understanding which makes everything else understandable.

Q. So curiosity about death and dying is meaningless.

JK. Absolutely.

Q. Sometimes at night when I have a nightmare, a terrible dream that is just unbearable, the instant I wake up, I am so full of thankfulness, because I realize it was just a nightmare, it wasn't happening at all.

JK. Yes. It is a moment of separation.

Q. But that feeling of thankfulness is, to me, a little bit like what you're saying.

JK. Absolutely.

Q. So joyful to be alive

JK. Yes. There is a metamorphosis in this moment.

Q. When you were speaking about thanking earlier, you used the word "allow," that we were allowed to thank.

JK. Yes. Permission.

Q. Could you speak about that—what the perspective of that word is?

JK. What it means for me?

Q. Why you use that particular word.

JK. In the word "allowed" there is no residue of volition, personal volition. There is a giving up of all volition in being allowed to be. There is nobody to ask, to allow.

Q. And no one to merit.

JK. Exactly.

Q. So that is why the word... it does feel like that, whenever the mind stops and there is a shift, that one has been allowed. And yet, that isn't true.

JK. It is a beautiful word.

Q. It is, but it has legal connotations and connotations of merit, and it's dualistic in a certain way. I know you don't mean it that way, but it feels that way.

JK. I don't feel it in that way. Allowing to be means, for me, that there is absolutely no qualification. Allowing to be is total freedom. It is something beautiful, no? Allowing. Don't you feel it?

Q. Gratitude.

JK. Yes, it is beautiful. There is sacredness in it, holiness. It arises spontaneously after understanding. There is a moment when there is nothing more to be understood; the understanding has been completely integrated.

Q. When one feels startled, does this come out of spontaneity, or more from biological fear?

JK. Psychological fear, perhaps. I don't see that it's biological fear.

Q. It's defensive.

JK. Yes. I think it is psychological fear. It's the ego-mind. Psychological fear is the ego-mind.

Q. Biologically, though, when you are startled, this is a defensive reaction that is useful and adaptive. So I see that it can be psychological, but a biological reaction tends to be very spontaneous. If you watch an animal, they are continually startled.

JK. Yes. But all this becomes clear with deep understanding. It must become being understanding, where all that belongs to intellectual understanding is completely absorbed.

Q. You said the opening happens in a moment, without preparation, without bringing your mind to it. And yet you say there has to be a maturity. Having maturity implies a progression of sorts, a building up of something, a coming to something. I don't quite see how these two fit together. Or does one simply have or not have maturity?

JK. You cannot exclude the understanding. It is a total understanding. In this understanding you are out of time. It is instantaneous, abrupt. You feel that you are taken in charge. But you must be attentive to the fact that you are taken in charge. There is nobody taking you in charge, yet you feel yourself free as if there is someone taking you in charge.

Q. Is the attentiveness the maturity?

JK. Yes. Being taken in charge is in this moment much stronger. You know that you are being taken in charge, but you don't know it objectively any more. You are taken by yourself, I would say. But there is no more self.

Q. In terms of this capacity, can one come to know that one has the capacity for this type of maturity?

JK. In maturity you are no longer in the state of "I can" or "I cannot."

Q. When you say maturity, do you mean *sattva*, purity, a quiet mind?

JK. It is beyond *sattva*. You feel that you are totally in security, that you are totally taken in charge.

Q. Is the *sattvic* state necessary?

JK. The *sattvic* stage belongs to an entity. What you are is not an entity.

Q. But so does maturity.

JK. Maturity belongs to an entity, too.

Q. Would you say that maturity is sattva plus understanding?

JK. In maturity, the idea of sattva no longer comes into your mind. You feel you are taken. There is nobody to be taken. It is important, when the moment arrives, that you feel yourself completely taken in charge, that the entity which usually takes charge has completely vanished. You haven't the slightest idea of being somebody. Keep this empty feeling. It has nothing to do with memory.

Q. What's the role of the teacher in this maturing, this waiting without waiting?

JK. The teacher first shows you that you are not body, senses and mind. You are not, because there is a knower. When you see for yourself that you are not body, senses and mind, see how it acts on you, what it produces in you.

There will come a glimpse, that you say to yourself, "I am." Very often there comes a kind of blank state. It's good to say, "I am not body, senses and mind." But it can bring you to a blank state. But then you come to a moment when you see really what you are not, there comes a tremendous power in you, a tremendous energy which is no longer used to emphasize what you are not, or what you are. You are really in the "I am not." When you are completely in the "I am not," then you are.

Q. This energy that is felt, is its origin that energy which was held by the notion of the person, and is now released?

JK. There is no more time. There is only energy, one energy. You live always disposed to be. Your individual energy dissolves in the total energy. Properly speaking, there is no more independent entity.

Q. I gather from what you're saying that the body, senses and mind continue, but there's no further identification with them as being who I am. They continue as a part of the total manifestation. The manifestation goes on, but there's no identification.

JK. Yes. The only chance, if you can speak of a chance, is after death. It is very dangerous to speak of time—of thirty days, of three days, or five days. The traditionalists like this, but it's dangerous. In thirty days you may have the chance, or in five days. These are only cakes for little children.

Q. The days, the time, belong to the entity, to the imaginary person. It is its way of functioning. But it all takes place in timelessness, which never changes. It's not an issue.

JK. There's an absolute dissolving. You can only go to a certain distance, to a certain moment. But I tell you, it is the last moment. There are no other moments. Other things are more or less logical deduction, not truth.

Q. In your books there's a sense, in reading them, that you communicate availability, openness, to us.

JK. Yes.

Q. Simply that. You make yourself available to the openness so that if anything can come, we will be taken.

JK. Yes.

Q. And you were taken. That is the sense you describe.

JK. Yes.

Q. Very beautiful.

Q. So maturity is saying, "Yes," to the invitation.

JK. Absolutely. Look forward to it already!

Q. Look forward?

JK. Say, "Yes!"

Q. Aha! *(laughter)*

Q. *(Another questioner)* So maturity is when the entity sees that he or she says, "No," all the myriad ways that the entity refuses the invitation.

JK. But when the invitation is refused, it means it has no envelope.

Q. No envelope?

JK. Yes. Otherwise, you could not refuse it. You would not refuse it.

Q. It seems to me that I have absolutely no choice whatsoever when a moment will come, and I feel this intense beauty or peace. I feel as if I have no choice, inasmuch as I cannot do anything to promote this. And I feel I've been questing or inquiring for a long time—maybe twenty years now—and still I have no choice. I don't have a choice, in listening to you, whether I'm going to understand a single word. There are moments when there is real understanding.

JK. As long as there is the person, as long as you exist as a personal entity, there is never freedom or choice.

Q. It is this that I find very difficult to live with.

JK. There is no free will. There is no free will or destiny. But this is the highest understanding that you can have, that there is no free will or destiny. These belong to a personal entity. Without the person where is free will? Where is destiny? In understanding this, it makes you free. No?

Q. All these things belong to appearances. You said before, "I am not that." What's the difference in all this? We can't do anything. But always in front is the chance to see what I am not. That's always there. It becomes the guru, the real guru. The chance to see what I am not. I've been looking for so many years through all these tricks—maybe forty years—but I was never interested in knowing what I am not. I was always wanting to become something more.

(silence)

Q. In the last few weeks you have mentioned this double negative several times to me. I keep turning it around, "What is this double negative?" So, I'm seeing now this subtracting the mind, subtracting the body, subtracting the senses, until you come down to zero. And this is just a way of speaking, but when you subtract two negatives, you have a positive, but when you subtract zero from zero, it's like you've moved over into some completely new territory.

JK. It's positive in that moment.

Q. It's positive, but it's not a positive zero.

JK. No. Choicelessness is positive. It must be. It must come to a double choicelessness.

Q. That's what I'm turning around right now, that double choicelessness.

JK. You will see it in the light. Can we remain in silence.

(Long silence)

No localization in the forehead.

The optic nerve frees you behind.

(Silence ...)

Sin of self-love possesseth all mine eye
And all my soul and all my every part;
And for this sin there is no remedy,
It is so grounded inward in my heart.
Methinks no face so gracious as is mine,
No shape so true, no truth of such account;
And for myself mine own worth do define,
As I all other in all worths surmount.
But when my glass shows me myself indeed,
Beated and chopp'd with tann'd antiquity,
Mine own self-love quite contrary I read;
Self so self-loving were iniquity.
'Tis thee, myself,—that for myself I praise,
Painting my age with beauty of thy days.

Sonnet 62
William Shakespeare

Your Question

Q. It seems that I have come to an impasse. On the one hand I feel I know your teaching quite well and understand it to the best of my capacity. On the other hand, nothing moves. There have been no life-churning insights, no lasting shifts in the way I function. I feel stuck. Can you help me?

Jean Klein: Be still. Stop trying. You are still convinced there is someone who can achieve something. This conviction is a deeply rooted conditioning. Nothing can come from the mind. Your impasse is an opportunity.

The seeker is the sought and the sought is the seeker. As soon as this becomes a true insight there is a transfer of energy from the object part (what is looked for) to the subject (the looker, or rather, the looking).

It is an instantaneous understanding where all our grasping, becoming and striving comes to an end. It is a moment in our brain and in the rest of our body. It is the same insight as the sudden understanding that all that you can see, do, find, is an object in space and time. In seeing this, what you are shines forth in its timelessness. You find yourself free from any reference. It is your objectless immensity.

It is a feeling of being totally open to all, but open to nothing specific, a feeling of complete availability. Then you are open to what you are, which is openness itself. You find yourself in a state of fervent welcoming without any idea of what you welcome. The mind no longer has role to play because it has seen its limits, or been forced to its limits as can happen after a crisis in one's life. In welcoming without welcoming anything, all the energy that was once turned outwards now comes back to you, back to its source. There is an implosion, a switch-over, where welcoming itself becomes alive, full of energy. It welcomes its own welcoming. You see that you are the welcoming.

Knowledge, accumulated knowing, never purifies the person. It is sterile. It has no dynamism, no power. Only this higher principle of understanding brings transmutation on the phenomenal level. This understanding takes place in the absence of all striving to become. Striving not to become is still striving. To give up may be difficult. That is why we say here, welcome, be open to your openness, which is your real nature.

The Approach on the Body Level

Jean Klein: Our body is a beautiful musical instrument, like a Stradivarius, but, it must be tuned. We are the tuner. To tune this instrument that is so sensitive, so secret, calls for a complete metamorphosis of oneself, and this can only happen when we are one with our instrument, with our body. We must be very sensitive to tune our bodies. We must find just the right tone for tuning, because the tone is not only vibration, it is more than vibration.

One tone contains all the tones. One chord attunes all the other chords. We need to have a bipolar listening, listening inside, attuning to the inside and to the outside. We must listen to what happens inside, in our body, and to what also comes from the so-called outside. Strictly speaking, there is no outside and inside.

This beautiful instrument has to be sensed. It is in sensing that we come to the right tuning. It calls for a very high art of listening. All our muscle structure should be maintained in tune in inaction and also in action. It is a bipolar listening. We must become able to listen. Hearing these fine vibrations comes first in meditation. There is a very important moment when you listen inside, when you listen to the listening itself. When you are aware in listening, there is no listener and nothing is listened to. There is only listening. *(long pause)*

It is tremendous to discover oneself in listening. But first there is listening to an object, then comes listening to ourself. When listening is Silence, our musical instrument, our body, is completely penetrated by this objectless listening. Then there is something born that is beyond the human being.

You are not body, senses and mind. Really live in the absence of what you are not and this reality will be the background of life. Live in the absence of yourself. In the absence of yourself there is presence. We should take every opportunity to listen to ourselves without directing, without changing, or looking for something new. When we listen to ourselves and sustain the listening, there's transformation, there's a kind of metamorphosis.

This directionless listening is fixed neither in the forehead, nor in the heart, nor in the abdominal region. Listening is absolutely objectless. It is really a bird that flies everywhere. See when it lands. The moment you become aware that you fix it, in that awareness an emptiness will appear and this becomes openness. Don't put the bird in a cage. Open all the doors.

Be aware in the morning that before the body wakes up there's another kind of waking up. Then you feel the body waking up in this already awakeness. See how the body appears to you in this moment. You will feel how the old conditioned body tries to come back, the old thoughts, feelings, habits and so on. Go to the tactile sensation. It may first appear in the hands. Evoke this tactility, and you will feel a letting go. Sense it. It is enough.

Become aware of the shoulders and also of the forehead. You should let go completely in your bed. Put all the weight of your body, head, shoulders, shoulder blades, hands, and the legs, on the bed, on the ground, until all the parts are heavy. Have the impression that the energy comes from the earth and it comes to the human body and the body is inter-penetrated by this energy. It is something beautiful. You will become aware that your tensions are defences which are reactions. Let it become so tangible for you in the morning that you keep this knowing as the background throughout the day. It is a kind of inner touching. You feel much more alive. It is only possible to go beyond the contraction of your body by sensing your body, by being aware.

When there comes this expansion of the body, you become free from the forehead, and you feel your self localized behind, in your old brain. Don't strain to achieve it, it belongs to you, it makes you free from the body, it makes you free from space, from direction. I would say, you're beyond space.

You must become free from the meditator. This is a very deep saying. Make it your own. There is no meditator, there is only meditation. The mind can be still without trying to be still. It is only in your absence that there is stillness, presence. In the absence that you are not, there is presence. But it is not an objective presence, this presence. It is a double absence. And when you have it, don't move away from it. At the slightest motion you go away from it.

Abandon all residue in the forehead. Only then can knowledge become being the knowing. Knowledge takes place in the forehead, in front of you. Being knowledge is localized nowhere. But temporarily it is localized as if behind you. This feeling of going behind is very important because it takes you away from the factory of thoughts in the forehead. When you are localized behind you at the base of the skull, you cannot think. Even the impulse to think dies down. No formulation can occur when you are localized behind. But eventually even this subtle localization dissolves and you find yourself nowhere, living in nowhere.

Keep the flavour of our meeting alive.

LISTENING

Volume 10
1995

Art and Artistic.. 327
Jean Klein

Sadhana: *From your silence comes creativity* 346

The man that hath no music 347
William Shakespeare

Bhartrhari 348
Harold G. Coward

Wonder: Poems by William Wordsworth................... 350

The Theory of Beauty 351
Ananda K. Coomaraswamy

From *Timaeus*.. 366
Plato

Music and the Body 367
Jean Klein

Your Question: *Seeing from behind?* 371
Jean Klein

Art and Artistic

Q. When one is totally committed to seeking one's real nature, earnest as you say, can one at the same time be a committed artist?

Jean Klein: When you are a real truth-seeker you are not interested in anything else. You are only still, and asking what is truth and what it is not. You see that truth, your real nature, is the ultimate negativity, the end of all positivity, the negation of all that is objective and, therefore, knowable. To be an artist, to discover artistry, is time-bound. To be a truth-seeker is instantaneous. Looking for truth is looking for space.

Q. When you have found your real nature can you then become an artist, writer, musician?

JK. Absolutely, but your art is completely different. It is an offering. There is no one to offer. It is thanking.

Q. Where does the stimulus to produce come from?

JK. The need to manifest inner beauty in time and space.

Q. Because we generally believe that art is an expression of ourselves, our feelings, thoughts, emotions, ideas.

JK. This is artistic production, not art. There is good and bad artistic production, but art per se points to our real nature. In true art, that is, art which comes from truth, there is no self-expression.

Q. Do you agree then with Wagner when, agreeing with Schopenhauer's philosophy, he said, "What music expresses, is eternal, infinite and ideal; it does not express the passion, love, or longing of such-and-such an individual on such-andsuch an occasion, but passion, love, or longing in itself, and this it presents in that unlimited variety of motivations, which is the exclusive and particular characteristic of music, foreign and inexpressible to any other language."

JK. Yes. But it is more than that. All that is perceived through any of the senses is a vibration. Music comes from the vibration of all that is objective, not only inner states, but also outer forms. We see a landscape and hear its vibration. We feel the vibration of the blue sky or the stormy sky. The scent of a flower has a vibration.

Q. By vibration, do you mean how it acts on our body?

JK. All that is manifested has vibration, is composed of vibration, and our cells hear this vibration. The creator, the composer, becomes aware of this action in himself and uses it. The creation comes back to the creator; the source as an object comes back to the perceiver.

Q. What about experimenting with new forms, new media, new words, and so on?

JK. There is no experimenting, because that comes from the mind and keeps you in the mind. The only impetus is to express the light and you push to find it. You come out of the known into the unknown and remain in this unknown until a certain vision appears.

Q. The vision can only come out of complete emptiness?

JK. Absolutely. It is a special quality of being, of hearing, of relaxing, of giving up. You have the inner position that allows you to be taken by the vision. You do not produce creativity. It comes to you. You do not try to be original. That is mind stuff. When you try to be original your production remains intellectual.

Q. How can one know the art that comes from the enlightened mind and that which does not?

JK. You cannot know it. You can only feel it. You feel it and it makes you free, free from all that you are not.

Q. Can someone who is not enlightened produce art that makes you feel free?

JK. Accidentally, yes. They touch their freedom without knowing it. When you have once touched your freedom, it will solicit you again.

Q. Does the creation of art arise out of a compensation, however subtle?

JK. Yes, in a certain way. It is a compensation for being unable to know what you are. You express adoration through words, form or sounds. All art is adoration. When you don't feel it as this, it is a compensation.

Q. Can you say that when you have once felt truly inspired, you know that it is in you and it can appear again?

JK. Exactly. Like when you go in the dark to a town you visited once long ago and you feel your way around, then suddenly feel you are on the right path that will take you where you want to go.

Q. I don't quite see why an enlightened being, who is fully content with just being, would still feel the inner desire to express this in music, art, writing. Is this not the case in history where few sages are also artists?

JK. I agree. But it is inherent in a human being to transmit the inner non-experience to his neighbour. How it is done depends on his gifts. However, I have met beautiful beings who have not appreciated beauty in art or music or literature.

Q. You mean sages? Can one be a sage and not admire beauty, not appreciate beauty?

JK. Yes. It may not produce an echo in one.

Q. Well, I really can't understand how that is possible. Surely beauty recognizes beauty?

JK. Some people are unable to transpose it.

Q. Is it because the *sagesse* of the sage is not integrated in his body?

JK. Yes, this is one of the reasons. Some bodies and minds have a deeper conditioning than others. Where the body-mind is very sattvic the awakening finds no obstacle.

Q. Is the work of Gaugin or Van Gogh art or artistic?

JK. Really speaking it is still artistic. In the artistic work, one emphasizes the expression, the relation between colour and form. In art, the inner feeling is emphasized. This inner feeling directly stimulates an inner feeling in the onlooker.

Q. And this inner feeling has no representation in emotion, ideas, sensation, and so on.

JK. No, it is pure feeling without object which is a spiritual experience.

Q. When one looks at, or participates in, a good artistic work, what does it give you?

JK. It brings you a feeling of harmony because of the harmony of the composition.

Q. And isn't this a spiritual experience?

JK. Not exactly. In a spiritual experience the production is no longer in your mind. There is only a feeling of beauty which has no concrete representation. Goethe said real art makes *zeit und raum vergessen.* Artistic work is an enchantment of the senses. It elevates the senses like looking at a beautiful sunset—but in a beautiful sunset you can forget the I, the me!

Q. Then it is all a question of whether the art stimulates one to lose oneself in the senses or whether one is taken completely beyond all feeling.

JK. Art reveals the highest in you, and you see it from the highest in you.

Q. When one is lost in sensorial experience, one can forget oneself. Most human activity is oriented toward forgetting oneself in sensorial experience. If one forgets oneself this way, how is this different from the forgetting in art? Or, put another way, what is the difference between forgetting oneself in our experience and forgetting oneself in a non-experience?

JK. The first keeps you in the senses.

Q. You are lost in the experience. You are not beyond the experience.

JK. Exactly. We don't need to transpose real art, it transposes us. We are brought to a new dimension.

Q. Knowingly brought or unknowingly?

JK. Unknowingly. It points directly to us. It frees us from space and time.

Q. Is music a language?

JK. Yes, language that must free us from language.

Q. What is language?

JK. It is to objectify something, a sentiment, sensation, thought, emotion.

Q. Why do we have the need to objectify?

JK. To make it understood.

Q. For ourselves or others?

JK. Both. We objectify it to explore it ourselves and to communicate it.

Q. Where does the desire to communicate come from?

JK. From love.

Q. An anthropologist would say "from our instinctive social behaviour/nature."

JK. Perhaps.

Q. Isn't the language of music culture-bound like all languages?

JK. The expression depends on the knowledge and tools at the artist's disposal, but the impetus for creation comes from the vibration of all that is.

Q. So, as you said earlier, our cells are imprinted with the vibration of all around us. Does the palette of tones in music come from our human responses to these vibrations, excitement, speed, crescendo, diminuendo, calm, conflict and resolving, growing and stopping, flowing and standing still?

JK. I am sure of it. The urge to make music comes from the inner desire to offer, to thank, to communicate, to be one with. It comes from beauty itself, our real nature, which is love, silence.

In a work of art the creator and participant are in complete unison. There is great joy in oneness. Music has, of all the arts, the greatest power to unite.

Q. When we paint a landscape, what are we painting? In other words, what makes art?

JK. Reproduction is never original. Generally, people look at the image, but the painter must be free from the image. When you see the landscape from your wholeness and paint from your wholeness, it is art. First you feel it, then you see it. You feel the harmony in the landscape, objects in relation to one another. You feel the light, colour, volume.

Q. So you don't paint what you see, but what you feel?

JK. Yes, the first and most important element is the feeling.

Q. In a more abstract landscape you emphasize the feeling aspect and in a more reproductive painting you bring in what is visible. Is it the talent of the artist to juggle these two, feeling and seeing?

JK. Yes. The feeling is percept. The artist first lives completely in the percept. Seeing is concept. An experienced artist lives in the percept for a long time before allowing just the necessary amount of concept to actualize the percept in the work of art. The percept keeps the work new, young. The concept can destroy it.

Van Gogh emphasized life, movement. He felt through movement, energy. Gaugin emphasized volume and form and colour. Monet emphasized the vibration of the multiplicity of colours and light. Braque, colour and volume. Cezanne colour, and so on.

Q. Is what is aesthetic always ethically acceptable or can art shock our ethical values?

JK. Art is not for shocking. It is for revealing beauty to us.

Q. But sometimes great art has shocked society. For example, nudity was not always acceptable in art. Surely the truth must shock conventional ethics at times?

JK. It shocks the conventional ethic, but not the aesthetic.

Q. You have said that when we act according to a higher principle, our acting is spontaneously aesthetic, ethical and functional. What does this mean exactly if art can shock ethics but not aesthetics?

JK. What is ethical and aesthetic is universally true, beyond time and space.

Q. So we are not talking about the ethics of fashion or law, but an ethic that comes from the spontaneous transposition of a higher principle to the sphere of communication.

JK. Exactly, a communion that elevates feeling and thinking.

Q. So art can shock the bourgeoisie?

JK. Yes, but this shock is only acceptable if it brings a meta-morphosis to a profoundly higher understanding. To do this it must always be aesthetic.

Q. So the shock may only be on the level of relative ethics. The aesthetic, the beauty, is never relative.

JK. Absolutely.

Q. Is any subject worthy of art, even violence?

JK. Yes, if it is not vulgar. Violence must reveal nobility, valour, beauty.

Q. What is vulgarity?

JK. That which emphasizes the object part and so ridicules beauty.

Q. So whatever is over expressed is vulgar?

JK. Yes, mostly! There is great beauty in economy of expression because beauty is not objectifiable.

Q. It can only be hinted at?

JK. Exactly. Which is why art production must always leave room for the observer to complete it with his own feeling. The one only stimulates the beauty in the other.

Q. It does not dictate it. Can one become what one really is solely through following one's love of beauty to its end?

JK. It brings you to the right direction. But if you remain in the beauty object, art, music, poetry, you cannot come to beauty without objects which is our real nature. One should explore beauty, never finding an answer. In reality, we can only ask. In asking we are open, free, because the answer can never be expressed. It is always in waiting. It is in emptiness between two forms, the silence between two sounds. One should live with the highest negativity.

Q. Can it be said that certain music or works of art have an ill effect on us?

JK. Of course, when it is not music or art. All our organism is affected by vibration of sound and light. Real art is not an offence to our organism. Music and painting can have a therapeutic effect but most so-called popular music is simply noise. Music is composed of three elements: harmony, melody and rhythm. Béla Bartòk is one of the finest composers. He works with the three elements without recourse to reference and familiar pattern. Music is the supreme harmoniser.

Q. You have said that in much contemporary poetry there is no music. What do you mean?

JK. The meaning is emphasized in much poetry today. It is often too intellectual, not enough is felt. Thinking, reasoning is emphasized too much.

Q. Do you feel today's poetry is often over-expressed?

JK. Yes. Not enough is left hidden, suggested, less obvious.

Q. Much poetry is born from the "one thousand voices of dissent."

JK. Yes, it has become political. It doesn't point to the ultimate. It's a lack of real imagination. It's stuck on the social, realistic level.

Q. There is the counter argument that if poetry goes too far towards the realm of the aesthetic, the beautiful, it is not real poetry because it is an escape from life, and poetry is about life as it is now, history in the making.

JK. In love today, there is no dimension. Living has become stuck in objects. Poetry should elevate us from our daily existence, take us beyond conflict. A real poet has the capacity to transpose any circumstance in daily life to a level of freedom.

Q. Are you saying the poem should point to the ultimate freedom, or can it point to many freedoms: social, psychological, physical and so on?

JK. In my view, the greatest poetry points to ultimate freedom, freedom from the "me." But there are many freedoms that can be written about.

Q. Surely, for a poet, there are as many freedoms as there are conflicts!

JK. Yes.

Q. Today there is a great emphasis on reading poetry aloud. The music and rhythm of the poem often depends on the spoken reading rather than being intrinsic to the written poem. Often only the creator of the poem can read the poem aloud, bring it alive. What do you think of poetry that is dependent on performance? Does it die with the poet? Can poetry be great and yet not be universally available? Or is this movement simply a breaking away from the medium of writing, a return to the oral tradition, and even a reflection of the trend away from books?

JK. That's an interesting question that calls for a long discussion. Perhaps we should continue it another day.

Q. You have also said that art must give one a bad night. What do you mean?

JK. You, both as the artist and the audience, must feel enormously concerned with it. Then it becomes alive in you. You must live with it day and night.

Q. The argument that beauty is subjective or in the eye of the beholder can be interpreted afresh in the light of non-dualism. Would you comment?

JK. Beauty is not subjective because there is, in reality, no subject. When the eye of the beholder is free from the subject, from duality, then it sees its own beauty in the object.

Q. In all objects?

JK. Beauty appeals to your whole being. What is not beautiful acts on your whole organism in an inharmonious way.

Q. Is there such a thing as ugliness?

JK. I do not say ugly. I say: not harmonious, not ethical, not practical. Ugly is an ugly word. But one can use it, of course.

Q. If I put the question another way, is it better to surround oneself with certain sounds, colours, objects than others?

JK. Certainly, there are tones and colours which elevate us, which affect our action, thinking and feeling. We must become familiar with bipolar observation in daily life: seeing what is and how these facts act on us mentally and physically. Then we become sensitive to what stimulates beauty and harmony in us.

Shakespeare said in *The Merchant of Venice*, "The man that hath no music in himself … Let no such man be trusted." Because such a person is blind to his deepest responses and does not feel the gift of thanking.

Q. How would you describe the response to a great work of art?

JK. It touches our original nature. There is first wonder or astonishment because there is no reference to what you know. When you are exhausted by the beauty you come back. You don't say thanks but there is thanking.

Q. What is an aesthetic experience? Does it occur during the wonder? Is it wonder or does it come afterward?

JK. After the wonder you spontaneously ask what in the work brought you to the wonder. Aesthetic experience takes place in the mind. It refers to something, to form, colour, sound and so on.

Q. Can wonder happen in front of a work of nature or human hand?

JK. Yes, it can happen at any moment, maybe when looking into the eyes of a child or the beloved.

Q. Can an aesthetic experience also take place in the presence of nature?

JK. Absolutely. But the aesthetic experience cannot bring one to universal love. When you are in wonder you look through the eye of God.

Q. What is the difference between wonder and the mystical experience?

JK. It is exactly the same experience, coloured perhaps differently according to conditioning and affectivity.

Q. You've said that a mystical experience is still in subject-object relationship, yet wonder is not.

JK. It would be more accurate to say that most, but not all, not the purest, mystical experience remains in subject-object relation.

Q. Is there a difference between your use of the words wonder and admiring?

JK. In wonder you are absorbed completely, in admiring the admired is in you.

Q. You mean that in wonder you are lost in the object, and in admiring the object is lost in you?

JK. Exactly.

Q. They are both non-dual states?

JK. Yes. The object is one with consciousness, in both instances, but in wonder the object is emphasized and in admiration the subject is emphasized.

Q. I want to ask you about the process of the creative impulse. You said that the artist must live with the percept for some time to become imbued with it. What do you mean by percept here? Is it the first vision? How activated is it on the level of the senses?

JK. The percept always appears to the senses. So the artist lives with this new sensation until he is impregnated. It takes time. It's a kind of meditation.

Q. So it's not just a vision in the mind?

JK. No, all your muscles, blood, bones are penetrated.

Q. Does this percept, sensual vision, appear suddenly or gradually?

JK. The first glimpse, first impact, is instantaneous.

Q. Is the solution, how to put it in space and time, gradual or instantaneous? For example, when Van Gogh stood in the orchard and was struck by the vibration, energy, movement and light of the apple trees or poplars, did he know, in that moment, how to paint them or even that he would paint them?

JK. No. He didn't, in that moment, refer to anything.

Q. So he lived for some time with the impact, and felt and thought about how to actualize the impact.

JK. Yes, because the impact is movement, a vibration. It causes itself to grow in him.

Q. Does this impact happen to everyone?

JK. No, but there are many who may feel it, but are not disposed, talented or built up as an artist is, to feel the need to actualize it. An artist explores and questions the impact on himself, on his senses. Then he uses his particular talent to express it in writing, painting, sculpture.

Q. Or music? Does the musician find his inspiration in the same way, from an impact on the senses, or is there another source?

JK. The composer listens to the impact on his emotions and subtle feelings. The senses play a role, but their role is quickly transposed to the level of mind and feeling. He or she may see a landscape and see the silence of time in the landscape, the absence of time. He hears the harmony of the atmosphere, of what his senses absorb and later comes the rhythm, maybe a largo or adagio in this case, and melody. The composer of music does not dwell on the sensual level but transposes it to the tonal level.

Q. For Bach, weren't many compositions born from a feeling of adoration?

JK. Yes, and thanking, which he transposed into tones, harmony, rhythm and melody.

Q. What did Stravinsky mean when he said that he was only "the vessel through which Le Sacré [du Printemps] passed? I heard and wrote what I heard." Is it the seeing of a whole structure combining harmony, rhythm and melody, or is it more of a condensed vision on which the composer elaborates?

JK. The latter. It is really a gift from Grace when it appears at once. Stravinsky meant there was nothing personal in his music. It is the universal which plays with the wind, which gives the tempi modifications, the different vibrations of all the tempis. Life is lived in different tempi. Life is manifested in vibration.

Q. In the beginning was the word, "... and the word was vak." So the initial perception in music is sound?

JK. Yes, the musician lives with sound modification.

Q. Does the composer experiment or does it, as Stravinsky says, always come through him?

JK. It is very fortunate when it comes all at once, as a whole composition. Usually there is some playing and hearing. Music is a higher manifestation than philosophy or science, said Beethoven. It creates a higher emotion, a more profound feeling of truth.

Q. Although the senses may be less emphasized when composing music than in other art forms, when listening to music all of the senses are affected, perhaps more strongly than in any other art form.

JK. It is true. Because hearing is the most powerful of the senses.   *SMELL*

Q. The truth is heard not seen. Sruti is heard, heard with one's whole being.

JK. Yes. There is no comparison. Hearing is less veiled from its essence than other sense perceptions. In the other senses, parasites come in.

Q. Why is that?

JK. It is so.

Q. Could it be because everything we are, all that is, is vibration, vibration too subtle to feel with the gross tactile sense so that it is only "heard"? So hearing is the closest to our real nature.

JK. Exactly. A very good explanation.

Q. And when the truth is heard, it literally resonates as true in our whole organism?

JK. Of course. Otherwise it would not be the truth. Even our cells recognize the truth and truth brings a re-orchestration.

Q. What is the difference between writing in music and writing in words?

JK. It depends only on whether you have a musical or word dictionary. Both can only be composed in silence. Writing sounds based on sounds is not music, nor is thought constructed out of thought, poetry. Both must come from the silence, the unknown.

Q. Otherwise you produce only clichés?

JK. Absolutely.

Q. Might a philosopher or truth-seeker explore the impact the object makes on him philosophically and spiritually rather than sensorialy, how it fits into his geometrical expression of the truth—to use your phrase?

JK. Precisely.

Q. Can one come to the truth through the senses?

JK. I would say no.

Q. Then I would ask about the experience of verticality that one can experience by initially exploring the sensation in the postures, for example. This feeling of verticality is identical with oneness, the present, the point of the heart where time and space, the vertical and horizontal meet, and cancel each other. Is this not a glimpse of truth brought from the senses?

JK. Not from exploring the senses per se as an artist does. The artist stays with the object, the perception and its side effects in the body. The artist explores every aspect of the object. The truth-seeker, on the other hand, emphasizes the subject. He lets the object return to the subject, dissolve in the subject.

Q. So an artist in a certain way grasps the object and a truth-seeker releases it?

JK. Yes, the truth-seeker never emphasizes the object, but the seeing, the hearing. The seen is brought back to the seeing, the heard to the hearing.

Q. I have heard you say that melancholia is often—if not always—the disposition of a truth-seeker. Is this so and why?

JK. Yes, because truth has not yet come to him. But this melancholy is not depression.

Q. It is the same with an artist?

JK. Yes, absolutely. Before the unfolding, is desire mixed with melancholy.

Q. The melancholy of unfulfillment.... You once told someone who was writing a play that the vision for this kind of writing should come to one in a flash, as an entire story, so that one knows what is going to happen before starting to write. Yet, from my own experience writing a book, and from what I've read about how other writers create, they may start with only an idea or a few characters and then, one might say, the book writes itself. Could you comment on this?

JK. It is like our discussion of music and art. If one is lucky or graced enough to have the whole play in its entirety handed to one, then that is wonderful. But there must, in any case, be the essence, the seed, whether it comes from a single character or an idea. You refer to this essence throughout the whole creative process. If you lose it, you lose the thread, the creative dynamism. To come to this essence at all times, the mind must, in a certain way, be still, free from invading and obtrusive thoughts. You must give the essence the opportunity to unfold.

We all have often had the experience of not being able to "remember" or find the right word to describe something, and we keep coming back to find it. Coming back to what? To a feeling, an essence of where it might be. It is very interesting to observe the mechanics in us of what happens when we are trying to remember something.

Q. Don't we search without searching because the harder we try, the more it recedes? And, often, when we forget about it, it comes to us.

JK. Precisely. You can transpose this experience in life. Don't push to formulate and conclude what is not ready to show itself. But live with the unformulated taste.

Sadhana

Jean Klein: See how your body and mind are in constant activity all day. You need only half a minute to be aware of it. Sense your body without there being a senser. Give up what is felt, and abide there.

From your Silence comes creativity. Nothing new comes from thinking.

Come ho! and wake Diana with a hymn:
With sweetest touches pierce your mistress' ear,
And draw her home with music.
>Jes. *I am never merry when I hear sweet music.*
>Lor. *The reason is, your spirits are attentive:*
For do but note a wild and wanton herd,
Or race of youthful and unhandled colts,
Fetching mad bounds, bellowing and neighing loud,
Which is the hot condition of their blood;
If they but hear perchance a trumpet sound,
Or any air of music touch their ears,
You shall perceive them make a mutual stand,
Their savage eyes turn'd to a modest gaze
By the sweet power of music: therefore the poet
Did feign that Orpheus drew trees, stones, and floods;
Since nought so stockish, hard, and full of rage,
But music for the time doth change his nature.
The man that hath no music in himself,
Nor is not mov'd with concord of sweet sounds,
Is fit for treasons, stratagems, and spoils;
The motions of his spirit are dull as night,
And his affections dark as Erebus;
Let no such man be trusted. Mark the music.

The Merchant of Venice; Act V, Scene 1
by Willliam Shakespeare

Bhartrhari
Harold G. Coward

In the *Rg Veda* several hymns are devoted to inspired speech *(vak)* and the same trends are continued in the Brahmanas and the Upanisads (*Rg Veda* 10.10.114.8). Speech is described as the creation of the gods (*Ibid*. 10.10.125.3). It permeates all creation (*Ibid*. 10.10.114.8) But the Brahmanical religious tradition, with which Bhartrhari lived, went even further in identifying speech or language with the Divine. The *Rg Veda* states that there are as many words as there are manifestations of Brahman. Even in the more recent Hindu Scriptures, the Aranyakas and Upanisads, there is a continued equating of speech and Brahman. "The whole of Speech is Brahman." (Brihadaranyak Unpanisad 4.1.2)

In this respect there seem to be close parallels between the Brahmanical view that the Veda and Brahman are one, and the viewpoint expressed in Christian Scripture at the beginning of the Gospel according to Saint John. "In the beginning was the Word, and the Word was with God, and the Word was God." Both the Christian and the Brahmanical viewpoints seem to agree that speech and the Divine coexist. But there are significant differences that must be carefully noted. Whereas the Christian Scripture conceives of an absolute beginning of order when God speaks and through his speaking creates, the Brahmanical view, shared by Bhartrhari, believed in a cyclic view of creation with no absolute beginning. There may be beginning points for each cycle of creation, but there is no first cycle. The whole of the cosmos has constantly been going on through cycles of creation-dissolution, creation-dissolution… beginninglessly. At the dissolution of each cycle a seed or trace (*samskara*) is left behind out of which the next cycle arises. It is an agricultural image of seed-flower-seed…

The significant thing to note in relation to Bhartrhari is that Brahmanical religion describes the nature of the seed, from which each cycle of creation bursts forth, as "Divine Word."

Various symbols are used to indicate the divine nature of speech and its evolution to form each cycle of creation. Professor Murti puts it well when he says, "The Brahmanical tradition stemming from the Veda takes language as of divine origin *(Daivi Vak)*, as Spirit descending and embodying itself in phenomena, assuming various guises and disclosing its real nature to the sensitive soul." The "sensitive soul," in Brahmanical religion was the seer or rsi ---who has purged himself of ignorance rendering his consciousness transparent to the Divine Word. The *rsi* was not the individual composer of the Vedic hymn, but rather the seer *(drasta)* of an eternal impersonal truth. As Aurobindo puts it[1] the language of the Veda is a "rhythm not composed by the intellect but heard, a divine Word that came vibrating out of the Infinite to the inner audience of the man who had previously made himself fit for the impersonal knowledge." The *rsi's* initial vision is said to be of the Veda as one, as a whole, the entirety of Brahman. This represented in the *Mandukya Upanisad* by the *mantra* AUM, which includes within itself the three levels of ordinary consciousness-waking, dreaming, and deep sleep-yet also reaches out beyond to the transcendent where the sound itself comes to an end. Brahman, which is said to be speech, is also said to be AUM.

[1] Aurobindo Ghose, *On the Veda*, Pondicherry; Sri Aurobindo Ashram Press, 1956, p. 6.

WONDER

The Rainbow

My heart leaps up when I behold
A rainbow in the sky:
So was it when my life began;
So is it now I am a man;
So be it when I shall grow old,
*   Or let me die!*
The Child is father of the Man;
And I could wish my days to be
Bound each to each by natural piety.

It is A Beauteous Evening

It is a beauteous evening, calm and free,
The holy time is quiet as a Nun
Breathless with adoration; the broad sun
Is sinking down in its tranquillity;
The gentleness of heaven broods o'er the Sea:
Listen! the mighty Being is awake,
And doth with his eternal motion make
A sound like thunder—everlastingly.
Dear Child! dear Girl! that walkest with me here,
If thou appear untouched by solemn thought,
Thy nature is not therefore less divine:
Thou liest in Abraham's bosom all the year;
And worship'st at the Temple's inner shrine,
God being with thee when we know it not.

by **William Wordsworth**

Theory of Beauty
from The Dance of Shiva
Ananda K. Coomaraswamy

Aesthetic emotion—rasa—is said to result in the spectator—rasika—though it is not effectively *caused*, through the operation of determinants *(vibhava)*, consequences *(anubhava)*, moods *(bhava)* and involuntary emotions *(sattvabhava)*[1]...

...In order that a work may be able to evoke rasa one of the permanent moods must form a master-motif to which all other expressions of emotion are subordinate.[2] That is to say, the first essential of a rasavant work is unity—

As a king to his subjects, as a guru to his disciples,
Even so the master-motif is lord of all other motifs.[3]

If, on the contrary, a transient emotion is made the motif of the whole work, this "extended development of a transient emotion tends to the absence of rasa," [4] or as we should now say, the work becomes sentimental. Pretty art which emphasizes passing feelings and personal emotion is neither beautiful nor true: it tells us of meeting again in heaven, it confuses time and eternity, loveliness and beauty, partiality and love...

...the *Dasharupa* declares plainly that Beauty is absolutely independent of the sympathetic—"Delightful or disgusting, exalted or lowly, cruel or kindly, obscure or refined, (actual) or imaginary, there is no subject that cannot evoke rasa in man."

Of course, a work of art may and often does afford us at the same time pleasure in a sensuous or moral way, but this sort of pleasure is derived directly from its material qualities, such as tone or texture, assonance, etc., or the ethical peculiarity of its theme, and not from its aesthetic qualities: the aesthetic experience is independent of this, and may even, as Dhanamjaya says, be derived in spite of sensuous or moral displeasure.

Incidentally we may observe that the *fear* of art which prevails amongst Puritans arises partly from the failure to recognize that aesthetic experience does not depend on pleasure or pain at all: and when this is not the immediate difficulty, then from the distrust of any experience which is "beyond good and evil" and so devoid of a definitely *moral* purpose.

The tasting of rasa—the vision of beauty—is enjoyed, says Vishvanatha, "only by those who are competent thereto": and he quotes Dharmadatta to the effect that "those devoid of imagination, in the theatre, are but as the wood-work, the walls, and the stones." It is a matter of common experience that it is possible for a man to devote a whole life-time to the study of art, without having once experienced aesthetic emotion: "historical research", as Croce expresses it, "directed to illumine a work of art by placing us in a position to judge it, does not alone suffice to bring it to birth in our spirit," for "pictures, poetry, and every work of art produce no effect save on souls prepared to receive them." Vishvanatha comments very pertinently on this fact when he says that "even some of the most eager students of poetry are seen not to have a right perception of rasa." The capacity and genius necessary for appreciation are partly native ("ancient") and partly cultivated ("contemporary"): but cultivation alone is useless, and if the poet is born, so too is the rasika, and criticism is akin to genius.

Indian theory is very clear that instruction is not the purpose of art. On this point Dhanamjaya is sufficiently sarcastic:

"As for any simple man of little intelligence," he writes, "who says that from dramas, which distill joy, the gain is knowledge only, as in the case of history and the like (mere statement, narrative, or illustration)—homage to him, for he has averted his face from what is delightful." [5]

The spectator's appreciation of beauty depends on the effort of his own imagination, "just as in the case of children playing with clay elephants." Thus, technical elaboration (realism) in art is not by itself the cause of rasa: as remarked by Rabindranath Tagore "in our country, those of the audience who are appreciative, are content to perfect the song in their own mind by the force of their own feeling." This is not very different from what is said by Shukracharya with reference to images: "the defects of images are constantly destroyed by the power of the virtue of the worshipper who has his heart always set on God." If this attitude seems to us dangerously uncritical, that is to say dangerous to art, or rather to accomplishment, let us remember that it prevailed everywhere in all periods of great creative activity: and that the decline of art has always followed the decline of love and faith.

Tolerance of an imperfect work of art may arise in two ways: the one *uncritical*, powerfully swayed by the sympathetic, and too easily satisfied with a very inadequate correspondence between content theme, and the other *creative*, very little swayed by considerations of charm, and able by force of true imagination to complete the correspondence of content and form which is not achieved or not preserved in the original. Uncritical tolerance is content with prettiness or edification, and recoils from beauty that is "difficult": creative tolerance is indifferent to prettiness or edification, and is able from a mere suggestion, such as an awkward "primitive" or a broken fragment, to create or recreate a perfect experience.

Also, "the permanent motif becomes rasa through the rasika's own capacity for being delighted—not from the character of the hero to be imitated, nor because the work aims at the production of aesthetic emotion." How many works which have "aimed at the production of aesthetic emotion," that is to say, which were intended to be beautiful, have failed of their purpose.

The degrees of excellence in poetry are discussed in the *Kavya Prakasha* and the *Sahitya Darpana*. The best is where there is a deeper significance than that of the literal sense. In minor poetry the sense overpowers the suggestion. In inferior poetry, significantly described as "variegated" or "romantic" (*chitra*), the only artistic quality consists in the ornamentation of the literal sense, which conveys no suggestion beyond its face meaning. Thus narrative and descriptive verse take a low place, just as portraiture does in plastic art: and, indeed, the *Sahitya Darpana* excludes the last kind of poetry altogether. It is to be observed that the kind of suggestion meant is something more than implication or *double entendre*: in the first case we have to do with mere abbreviation, comparable with the use of the words *et cetera*, in the second we have a mere play on words. What is understood to be suggested is one of the nine rasas.

It is worth noting that we have here a departure from, and, I think, an improvement on Croce's definition *"expression is art."* A mere statement, however completely expressive, such as: "The man walks," or $(a+b)^2 = a^2+2ab+b^2$, is not art. Poetry is indeed a kind of sentence:[9] but what kind of sentence? A sentence ensouled by rasa,[10] i.e., in which one of the nine permanent moods is implied or suggested: and the savouring of the corresponding flavour, through empathy, by those possessing the necessary sensibility is the condition of beauty or *rasasvadana*.

What then are *rasa* and *rasasvadana*, beauty and aesthetic emotion? The nature of this experience is discussed by Vishvanatha in the *Sahitya Darpana*:[11] "It is pure, indivisible, self-manifested, compounded equally of joy and consciousness, free of admixture with any other perception, the very twin brother of mystic experience (*Brahmasvadana sahodarah*), and the very life of it is supersensuous *(lokottara)* wonder."[12] Further, "It is enjoyed by those who are competent thereto, in identity, just as the form of God is itself the joy with which it is recognized."

For that very reason it cannot be an object of knowledge, its perception being indivisible from its very existence. Apart from perception it does not exist. It is not on that account to be regarded as eternal in time or as interrupted: it is timeless. It is again, supersensuous, hyper-physical *(alaukika)*, and the only proof of its reality is to be found in experience.

Religion and art are thus names for one and the same experience—an intuition of reality and of identity. This is not, of course, exclusively a Hindu view: it has been expounded by many others, such as the Neo-platonists, Hsieh Ho, Goethe, Blake, Schopenhauer and Schiller. Nor is it refuted by Croce. It has been recently restated as follows:

"In those moments of exaltation that art can give, it is easy to believe that we have been possessed by an emotion that comes from the world of reality. Those who take this view will have to say that there is in all things the stuff out of which art is made—reality. The peculiarity of the artist would seem to be that he possesses the power of surely and frequently seizing reality (generally behind pure form), and the power of expressing his sense of it, in pure form always!" [13]

Here pure form means form not clogged with unaesthetic matter such as associations.

It will be seen that this view is monistic: the doctrine of the universal presence of reality is that of the immanence of the Absolute. It is inconsistent with a view of the world as absolute *maya*, or utterly unreal, but it implies that through the false world of everyday experience may be seen by those of penetrating vision (artists, lovers and philosophers) glimpses of the real substrate. This world is the formless as we perceive it, the unknowable as we know it.

Precisely as love is reality experienced by the lover, and truth is reality as experienced by the philosopher, so beauty is reality as experienced by the artist: and these are three phases of the Absolute. But it is only through the objective work of art that the artist is able to communicate his experience, and for this purpose any theme proper to himself will serve, since the Absolute is manifested equally in the little and the great, animate and inanimate, good and evil.

We have seen that the world of Beauty, like the Absolute, cannot be known objectively. Can we then reach this world by rejecting objects, by a deliberate purification of art from all associations? We have already seen, however, that the mere intention to create beauty is not sufficient: there must exist an object of devotion. Without a point of departure there can be no flight and no attainment: here also "one does not attain to perfection by mere renunciation."[14] We can no more achieve Beauty than we can find Release by turning our backs on the world: we cannot find our way by a mere denial of things, but only in learning to see those things as they really are, infinite or beautiful. The artist reveals this beauty wherever the mind attaches itself: and the mind attaches itself, not directly to the Absolute, but to objects of choice.

Thus we return to the earth. If we supposed we should find the object of search elsewhere, we were mistaken. The two worlds, of spirit and matter, Purusha and Prakriti, are one: and this is as clear to the artist as it is to the lover or the philosopher. Those Philistines to whom it is not so apparent, we should speak of as materialists or as nihilists—exclusive monists, to whom the report of the senses is either all in all, or nothing at all. The theory of rasa set forth according to Vishvanatha and other aestheticians, belongs to totalistic monism; it marches with the Vedanta. In a country like India, where thought is typically consistent with itself, this is no more than we had a right to expect.

The State of Beauty

It is very generally held that natural objects such as human beings, animals or landscapes, and artificial objects such as factories, textiles or works of intentional art, can be classified as beautiful or ugly. And yet no general principle of classification has ever been found: and that which seems to be beautiful to one is described as ugly by another. In the words of Plato: "Everyone chooses his love out of the objects of beauty according to his own taste."

To take, for example, the human type: every race, and to some extent every individual, has an unique ideal. Nor can we hope for a final agreement: We cannot expect the European to prefer the Mongolian features, nor the Mongolian the European. Of course, it is very easy for each to maintain the absolute value of his own taste and to speak of other types as ugly; just as the hero of chivalry maintains by force of arms that his own beloved is far more beautiful than any other. In like manner the various sects maintain the absolute value of their own ethics. But it is clear that such claims are nothing more than statements of prejudice for who is to decide which racial ideal or which morality is "best"? It is a little too easy to decide that our own is best; we are at the most entitled to believe it the best for us. This relativity is nowhere better suggested than in the classic saying attributed to Majnun, when it was pointed out to him that the world at large regarded his Laila as far from beautiful. "To see the beauty of Laila," he said, "requires the eyes of Majnun."

It is the same with works of art. Different artists are inspired by different objects: what is attractive and stimulating to one is depressing and unattractive to another, and the choice also varies from race to race and epoch and epoch. As to the appreciation of such works, it is the same; for men in general admire only such works as by education or temperament they are predisposed to admire. To enter into the spirit of an unfamiliar art demands a greater effort than most are willing to make. The classic scholar starts convinced that the art of Greece has never been equalled or surpassed, and never will be; there are many who think, like Michelangelo, that because Italian painting is good, therefore good painting is Italian. There are many who never yet felt the beauty of Egyptian sculpture or Chinese or Indian painting or music: that they have also the hardihood to deny their beauty, however, proves nothing.

It is also possible to forget that certain works are beautiful: the eighteenth century had thus forgotten the beauty of Gothic sculpture and primitive Italian painting, and the memory of their beauty was only restored by great effort in the course of the nineteenth. There may also exist natural objects or works of art which humanity only very slowly learns to regard as in any way beautiful; the western aesthetic appreciation of desert and mountain scenery, for example, is no older than the nineteenth century; and it is notorious that artists of the highest rank are often not understood till long after their death. So that the more we consider the variety of human election, the more we must admit the relativity of taste.

And yet there remain philosophers firmly convinced that an absolute Beauty (*rasa*) exists, just as others maintain the conceptions of absolute Goodness and absolute Truth. The lovers of God identify these absolutes with Him (or It) and maintain that He can only be known as perfect Beauty, Love and Truth. It is also widely held that the true critic (*rasika*) is able to decide which works of art are beautiful (*rasavant*) and which are not; or in simpler words, to distinguish works of genuine art from those that have no claim to be so described. At the same time we must admit the relativity of taste, and the fact that all gods (devas and Ishvaras) are modelled after the likeness of men.

It remains, then, to resolve the seeming contradictions. This is only to be accomplished by the use of more exact terminology. So far have I spoken of "beauty" without defining my meaning, and have used one word to express a multiplicity of ideas. But we do not mean the same thing when we speak of a beautiful girl and a beautiful poem; it will be still more obvious that we mean two different things, if we speak of beautiful weather and a beautiful picture. In point of fact, the conception of beauty and the adjective "beautiful" belong exclusively to aesthetic, and should only be used in aesthetic judgment. We seldom make any such judgments when we speak of natural objects as beautiful; we generally mean that such objects as we call beautiful are congenial to us, practically or ethically. Too often we pretend to judge a work of art in the same way, calling it beautiful if it represents some form or activity of which we heartily approve, or if it attracts us by the tenderness or gaiety of its colour, the sweetness of its sounds or the charm of its movement. But when we thus pass judgment on the dance in accordance with our sympathetic attitude towards the dancer's charm or skill, or the meaning of the dance, we ought not to use the language of pure aesthetic. Only when we judge a work of art aesthetically may we speak of the presence or absence of beauty, we may call the work rasavant or otherwise; but when we judge it from the standpoint of activity, practical or ethical, we ought to use a corresponding terminology, calling the picture, song or actor "lovely," that is to say lovable, or otherwise, the action "noble," the colour "brilliant," the gesture "graceful," or otherwise, and so forth. And it will be seen that in doing this we are not really judging the work of art as such, but only the material and the separate parts of which it is made, the activities they represent, or the feelings they express.

Of course, when we come to choose such works of art to live with, there is no reason why we should not allow the sympathetic and ethical considerations to influence our judgment. Why should the ascetic invite annoyance by hanging in his cell some representation of the nude, or the general select a lullaby to be performed upon the eve of battle? When every ascetic and every soldier has become an artist there will be no more need for works of art: in the meanwhile ethical selection of some kind is allowable and necessary. But in this selection we must clearly understand what we are doing, if we would avoid an infinity of error, culminating in that type of sentimentality which regards the useful, the stimulating and the moral elements in works of art as essential. We ought not to forget that he who plays the villain of the piece may be a greater artist than he who plays the hero. For beauty—in the profound words of Millet—does not arise from the subject of a work of art, but from the necessity that has been felt of representing that subject.

We should only speak of a work of art as good or bad with reference to its aesthetic quality; only the subject and the material of the work are entangled in relativity. In other words, to say that a work of art is more or less beautiful, or *rasavant*, is to define the extent to which it is a work of art, rather than a mere illustration. However important the element of sympathetic magic in such a work may be, however important its practical applications, it is not in these that its beauty consists.

What, then, is Beauty, what is *rasa*, what is it that entitles us to speak of divers works as beautiful or *rasavant*? What is this sole quality which the most dissimilar works of art possess in common? Let us recall the history of a work of art. There is (1) an aesthetic intuition on the part of the original artist,—the poet or creator; then (2) the internal expression of this intuition—the true creation or vision of beauty, (3) the indication of this by external signs (language) for the purpose of communication—the technical activity; and finally, (4) the resulting stimulation of the critic or *rasika* to reproduction of the original intuition, or of some approximation to it.

The source of the original intuition may, as we have seen, be any aspect of life whatsoever. To one creator the scales of a fish suggest a rhythmical design, another is moved by certain landscapes, a third elects to speak of hovels, a fourth to sing of palaces, a fifth may express the idea that all things are enlinked, enlaced and enamoured in terms of the General Dance, or he may express the same idea equally vividly by saying that "not a sparrow falls to the ground without our Father's knowledge." Every artist discovers beauty, and every critic finds it again when he tastes of the same experience through the medium of the external signs. But where is this beauty? We have seen that it cannot be said to exist in certain things and not in others. It may then be claimed that beauty exists everywhere; and this I do not deny, though I prefer the clearer statement that it may be discovered anywhere. If it could be said to exist everywhere in a material and intrinsic sense, we could pursue it with our cameras and scales, after the fashion of the experimental psychologists: but if we do so, we should only achieve a certain acquaintance with average taste—we should not discover a means of distinguishing forms that are beautiful from forms that are ugly. Beauty can never thus be measured, for it does not exist apart from the artist himself, and the *rasika* who enters into his experience.

> All architecture is what you do to it when you look upon it.
> Did you think it was in the white or grey stone? or the lines of
>   the arches and cornices?
> All music is what awakes in you when you are reminded of it
>   by the instruments,
> It is not the violins and the cornets… nor the score of the

baritone singer.
It is nearer and further than they. [15]

When every sympathetic consideration has been excluded, however, there still remains a pragmatic value in the classification of works of art as beautiful or ugly. But what precisely do we mean by these designations as applied to objects? In the works called beautiful we recognize a correspondence of theme and expression, content and form: while in those called ugly we find the content and form at variance. In time and space, however, the correspondence never amounts to an identity: it is our own activity, in the presence of the work of art, which completes the ideal relation, and it is in this sense that beauty is what we "do to" a work of art rather than a quality present in the object. With reference to the object, then, "more" or "less" beautiful will imply a greater or less correspondence between content and form, and this is all that we can say of the object as such: or in other words, art is good that is good of its kind. In the stricter sense of completed internal aesthetic activity, however, beauty is absolute and cannot have degrees.

The vision of beauty is spontaneous, in just the same sense as the inward light of the lover (*bhakta*). It is a state of grace that cannot be achieved by deliberate effort; though perhaps we can remove hindrances to its manifestation, for there are many witnesses that the secret of all art is to be found in self-forgetfulness. And we know that this state of grace is not achieved in the pursuit of pleasure; the hedonists have their reward, but they are in bondage to loveliness, while the artist is free in beauty.

It is further to be observed that when we speak seriously of works of art as beautiful, meaning that they are truly works of art, valued as such apart from subject, association, or technical charm, we still speak elliptically. We mean that the external signs—poems, pictures, dances and so forth—are effective reminders. We may say that they possess significant form. But this can only mean that they possess that kind of form which reminds us of beauty, and awakens in us aesthetic emotion. The nearest explanation of significant form should be *such form as exhibits the inner relations of things*; or, after Hsieh Ho, "which reveals the rhythm of the spirit in the gestures of living things." All such works as possess significant form are linguistic; and, if we remember this, we shall not fall into the error of those who advocate the use of language for language's sake, nor shall we confuse the significant forms, or their logical meaning or moral value, with the beauty of which they remind us.

Let us insist, however, that the concept of beauty has originated with the philosopher, not with the artist: *he* has been ever concerned with saying clearly what had to be said. In all ages of creation the artist has been in love with his particular subject—when it is not so, we see that his work is not 'felt'—he has never set out to achieve the Beautiful, in the strict aesthetic sense, and to have this aim is to invite disaster, as one who should seek to fly without wings.

It is not to the artist that one should say the subject is immaterial: that is for the Philosopher to say to the philistine who dislikes a work of art for no other reason than that he dislikes it.

The true critic *(rasika)* perceives the beauty of which the artist has exhibited the signs. It is not necessary that the critic should appreciate the artist's meaning—every work of art is a *kamadhenu*, yielding many meanings—for he knows without reasoning whether or not the work is beautiful, before the mind begins to question what it is "about." Hindu writers say that the capacity to feel beauty (to taste *rasa*) cannot be acquired by study, but is the reward of merit gained in a past life; for many good men and would-be historians of art have never perceived it. The poet is born, not made; but so also is the *rasika*, whose genius differs in degree, not in kind, from that of the original artist. In western phraseology we should express this by saying that experience can only be bought by experience; opinions must be earned. We gain and feel nothing merely when we take it on authority that any particular works are beautiful. It is far better to be honest, and to admit that perhaps we cannot see their beauty. A day may come when we shall be better prepared.

The critic, as soon as he becomes an exponent, has to prove his case; and he cannot do this by any process of argument, but only by creating a new work of art, the criticism. His audience, catching the gleam through him—but still the same gleam, for there is only one—has then the opportunity to approach the original work a second time, more reverently.

When I say that works of art are reminders, and the activity of the critic is one of reproduction, I suggest that the vision of even the original artist may be rather a discovery than a creation. If beauty awaits discovery everywhere, that is to say that it waits upon our recollection (in the sufi sense and in Wordsworth's): in aesthetic contemplation, as in love and knowledge, we momentarily recover the unity of our being released from individuality.

There are no degrees of beauty; the most complex and the simplest expression remind us of one and the same state. The sonata cannot be more beautiful than the simplest lyric, nor the painting than the drawing, merely because of their greater elaboration. Civilized art is not more beautiful than savage art, merely because of its possibly more attractive *ethos*. A mathematical analogy is found if we consider large and small circles; these differ only in their content, not in their circularity. In the same way, there cannot be any continuous progress in art. Immediately a given intuition has attained to perfectly clear expression, it remains only to multiply and repeat this expression. This repetition may be desirable for many reasons, but it almost invariably involves a gradual decadence, because we soon begin to take the experience for granted. The vitality of a tradition persists only so long as it is fed by intensity of imagination. What we mean by creative art, however, has no necessary connection with novelty of subject, though that is not excluded. Creative art is art that reveals beauty where we should have otherwise overlooked it, or more clearly than we have yet perceived. Beauty is sometimes overlooked just because certain expressions have become what we call "hackneyed"; then the creative artist dealing with the same subject restores our memory. The artist is challenged to reveal the beauty of all experiences, new and old.

Many have rightly insisted that the beauty of a work of art is independent of its subject, and truly, the humility of art, which finds its inspiration everywhere, is identical with the humility of Love, which regards alike a dog and a Brahman—and of Science, to which the lowest form is as significant as the highest. And this is possible because it is one and the same undivided all. "If a beauteous form we view, 'Tis His reflection shining through."

It will now be seen in what sense we are justified in speaking of Absolute Beauty, and in identifying this beauty with God. We do not imply by this that God (who is without parts) has a lovely form which can be the object of knowledge; but that in so far as we see and feel beauty, we see and are one with Him. That God is the first artist does not mean that He created forms, which might not have been lovely had the hand of the potter slipped: but that every natural object is an immediate realization of His being. This creative activity is comparable with aesthetic expression in its non-volitional character; no element of choice enters into that world of imagination and eternity, but there is always perfect identity of intuition-expression, soul and body. The human artist who discovers beauty here or there is the ideal guru of Kabir, who "reveals the Supreme Spirit wherever the mind attaches itself."

NOTES

1. Dhanamjaya, *Dasarupa*, iv, 1.
2. Ibid., iv, 46.
3. Bharata, *Natya Sastra*, 7, 8.
4. *Dasarupa*, iv, 45.
5. *Ibid.*, 1, 6.
6. *Ibid.*, 1V, 50.
7. *Jiban-smriti*, pp. 134-5.
8. *Dasarupa*, iv, 47. 9. Ibid., iv, 46.
10. *Vakyam rasatmakam vacakam—Sahitya Darpana*, 3.
11. vv. 33, 51, 53, 54.
12. Wonder is defined as a kind of expanding of the mind in "admiration".
13. Clive Bell, *Art*, p. 54.
14. Bhagavad Gita, III, 14
15. Walt Whitman

All audible musical sound is given us for the sake of harmony,
which has motions akin to the orbits in our soul, and which, as
anyone who makes intelligent use of the arts knows, is not to be
used, as is commonly thought, to give irrational pleasure, but as a
heaven-sent ally in reducing to order and harmony any disharmony
in the revolutions within us. Rhythm, again, was given us from the
same heavenly source to help us in the same way; for most of us lack
measure and grace.

from ***Timaeus***
by Plato

Music and the Body

Q. How can I best listen to music?

Jean Klein: Beethoven wrote to one of his admirers that music is a higher manifestation than knowledge or philosophy. We must give all our intelligence and hearing capacity to listening. It is only a muscle structure that is in complete relaxation that can receive the vibration produced by sounds. You must be in total receiving without memory, judgment or anticipation. Prepare yourself before listening to music so that you don't hear with only the ears but with your whole body.

Generally the ears, like the eyes, are in grasping, looking for the familiar and for security. This grasping position hinders our pure listening and predisposes us, prejudices our listening in favour of the known and familiar. But sounds absorbed from a position of openness brings us to a new sensation of spaciousness and expansion.

Take music seriously. Vibration affects every cell of our bodies. Do not use "background music" to fill up silence and space. You must be one with the listening, following music earnestly. It is a kind of language which must not be reduced to gossip. Only when you listen to music in openness can you really know what is good music and what is not. Real music comes from harmony and stimulates our own harmony. In listening in this profound way we are freed from hearing just noise. Even the most sublime music is noise if heard in a wrong way.

Q. Is it possible that for someone very versed in music there may be some anticipation of harmony or...

JK. Someone skilled in music can know all the wonders and complexities of the art. Most people are in anticipation, finishing the phrase from memory. A musicologist has the capacity to compose the music as he hears it. He must guard against too active a participation. He must not conduct the music, but let the music conduct him.

You hear the sound production and you hear the echo which these sounds leave in your whole being. A musicologist may hear only the skeleton but not the music of his own body. He doesn't hear the music so much as hear what he knows. The greatest musicians and conductors listen in not-knowing. Like a great painter, all their talent and faculty is passive-active. Not interfering but ready for creativity. The ordinary listener tends to look for the melody. That is not music or listening. That is listening to gossip. He must free himself from this tendency to look for security in melody. That is why some modern musicians have broken away from melodic structure and emphasize the simultaneous hearing of harmony, rhythm and melody.

Q. You said we should not live with background music...

JK. Background music doesn't exist. There is only background noise.

Q. Very few people are comfortable with silence. Why is that?

JK. Because they superimpose an absence of noise. They don't hear the silence, feel the silence. Because they are not knowingly the silence, they must find a hold in noise.

Q. This way of escaping from silence is a modern epidemic.

JK. Yes, a disease which feeds itself with itself.

Q. You mean we escape to noise because we are nervous and it makes us more nervous?

JK. Yes, modern man is constantly in action, looking for activity and compensation. It comes from insecurity because we have created obligation.

Q. Can music be used in the background in healing? For example, the largo in Vivaldi's Four Seasons is proved to reduce brain activity, to bring one to the delta state.

JK. When it is not music but sound production. We know that certain sounds free us from tension. As a flower needs a seer, so music needs a hearer. As long as there is not a conscious passive-active relation between the hearer and the music, it is not music. One should never have sound in the background of other activity. When you use sounds for healing specifically it takes full participation from the patient.

Q. Surely certain background sounds, if you like, can have a calming effect on the body.

JK. Only if you give your attention to it, otherwise it is noise, an escape from silence.

Q. So the masseuse who uses a soft background sound during a massage is not helping by creating a relaxing ambiance? And what about all the so-called New Age music used in many situations?

JK. It's not music. The masseuse is one with the body of the client. In this oneness there is no room for distraction. I see no need at all for background sound. If you do not hear the river or the bird there is no river or bird.

Q. Are you saying that sound vibration cannot have a positive effect on the body-mind unless the hearer gives his or her attention to it?

JK. Absolutely.

Q. But you also say that background sound vibration, noise, can have a negative effect. I don't understand why, when we are not listening, vibration can only affect us negatively and not positively. If certain sounds stimulate harmony in certain organs doesn't this happen on the level of physics, not psychology? Couldn't the sound heal the organ even when the patient is sleeping?

JK. I agree, the organs can be affected in a soothing way, but to come to a real integration or a real healing, our presence is necessary.

Q. So background sound is not necessarily negative during healing?

JK. I agree, but the great healer is our presence. One should be open to a total hearing where there is no conclusion. It is the music which concludes in you without reference to any structure. Music has more than a therapeutic effect. It has a profound spiritual value. It frees the hearer from the heard.

Q. Is there a physiological change in the aesthetic experience or in wonder?

JK. Yes, in both. There is a feeling of freedom. The experience is confirmed on the level of the body. There is always a feeling of affection, not affectivity, but love.

Your Question
Excerpt from Dialogue at
Joshua Tree, May 25, 1995

Q. What do you mean by seeing from behind?

Jean Klein: You feel yourself behind and look from behind, hear from behind. It gives you a new quality. First you must know how to see yourself from behind, and then you will know yourself in front.

Q. Does feeling from behind take you out of the forebrain?

JK. Yes. You don't feel yourself located in the object. You have the sensation of expansion behind you. You are not identified with the object. You have the feeling that the perceiver is behind you, that you are no longer stuck to the object. Body, senses and mind are all objects, objects that need a perceiver to be known. A perceiver can never be known, only what is perceived can be known.

When you knowingly say, "I am not the body, senses and mind, because these do not exist on their own, they need consciousness to be known," you become integrated; it gives you enormous distance. Then you perceive and live with the surroundings free from psychological involvement. You see facts as they are, free from bad and good. This is whole seeing, global seeing. You know when you are psychologically involved in daily life. But here there is no interpretation, there is only seeing facts as they are. It is important to see how this way of living, this way of seeing, this way of touching, acts on you, how you feel. Then you have a functional relation with your surroundings, also aesthetic and ethical. You see the truth, you see the beauty, you see the functional. Our seeing mainly refers to the ego. You do not see the situation in its *verité*. When you are appropriate to the situation, then you observe what is aesthetic, ethical and functional. It belongs to you, but this doesn't mean it is appropriated to your ego. You are taken by the seeing. One can say it is not you who see it, it is the seeing who sees it.

Q. The seeing tells you how to act appropriately.

JK. Yes.

Q. You don't have to think it up.

JK. Yes.

Q. Is that what you mean by choiceless living?

JK. Yes. It is free from tension. It is functional being. In this functional being, all that is aesthetic and ethical appears very clear to us.

Bibliography

Chandidas
   Love Songs of Chandidas the Rebel Poet-Priest of Bengal
   Deben Bhattacharya (trans)
   New York: Grove Press, 1970

Coomaraswamy, Ananda K.
   The Dance of Shiva: Fourteen Indian Essays.
   New York: Farrar Straus Giroux, 1957

Coward, Harold G.
   Bhartrhari
   Boston: Twayne Publishers, 1976.

Eckhart, Meister
   Selected Writings
   Oliver Davies (Introduction, trans)
   London: Penguin, 1995

Eliot, T. S.
   The Four Quartets
   London: Faber and Faber, 2001

Ellis, Normandi (trans)
   Awakening Osiris: A New Translation of the Egyptian Book of the Dead
   Grand Rapids, MI: Phanes Press, 1988

Guenther, Herbert V (trans)
   The Royal Song of Saraha
   Seattle and London: University of Washington Press, 1969

Hill, Stephen (ed.)
   Visions of Europe
   London: Gerald Duckworth and Co., 1993

Ibn 'Arabi, Muhyiddin
   The Universal Tree and the Four Birds
   Angela Jaffray (trans)
   Oxford, Anqa Publishing, 2006

Lao Tsu
   Tao Te Ching
   Gia-fu Feng (trans), Jane English (trans)
   New York: Alfred A. Knopf, 1972

Plato
   The Symposium.
   London, Penguin, 1999

   Timaeus and Critias
   Desmond Lee (Introduction, trans)
   London: Penguin, 1972

Rumi, Jalal ad-Din
   Rumi: Poet and Mystic (1207-1273)
   Reynold A. Nicholson (Introduction), A. J. Arberry (Preface)
   London, George Allen and Unwin Ltd., 1964

Saraswathi, Swami Sri Ramanananda
   Tripura Rahasya: The Secret of the Supreme Goddess
   Bloomington: World Wisdom, 2003

Seng-T'San
   Hsin-Hsin Ming
   Gyoskusei Jikihara (trans), Richard B. Clark (trans)
   New York: White Pine Press, 2001

Shakespeare, William
   The Sonnets
   Stephen Orgel (ed), John Hollander (Introduction)
   London: Penguin, 2001

Tagore, Rabindranath
   Songs of Kabir
   New York, Dover Publications, 2004

   Gitanjali
   London, Macmillan and Co. Ltd., 1914

Blossoms in Silence
A Unique Book by Jean Klein

Blossoms in Silence is a limited edition book of Jean Klein's sayings, designed and produced under Jean Klein's close supervision in 1994. A book to be treasured not only for its beauty but also as a continuing source of inspiration. The format includes the following special features:

- abstract black and white drawings
- text printed with hand-set type on handmade paper
- hard cover with hand-sewn, hand-bound contents
- approximately 60 pages, 7" high by 9" wide
- each copy numbered and signed by Jean Klein, up to a total of 200 copies

You can only understand what you are not.
What you are, you can only be.
When understanding dissolves in being,
there is sudden awakening.

Jean Klein

A limited number of copies of *Blossoms in Silence* are still available, please apply to: marysd@rain.org or contact the Jean Klein Foundation at: jkftmp@aol.com

Printed in the United States
208512BV00001B/46/P